PURE BEEF

AN ESSENTIAL GUIDE TO ARTISAN MEAT
WITH RECIPES FOR EVERY CUT

LYNNE CURRY

EPBM

ECHO POINT BOOKS & MEDIA, LLC
BRATTLEBORO, VERMONT

Published by Echo Point Books & Media
Brattleboro, Vermont
www.EchoPointBooks.com

Pure Beef
ISBN: 978-1-63561-504-3 (casebound)

Cover image by Lisovskaya Natalia /shutterstock

Interior design by Joshua McDonnell
Typefaces: Avenir, Berkeley, Calibri, Garth, Weiss, Whitney

Cover design by Alicia Brown

The following companies donated equipment and beef during
the creation of this cookbook:
    Country Natural Beef: www.countrynaturalbeef.com
    Cutco Cutlery: www.cutco.com
    Le Creuset: www.lecreuset.com
    Mishima Ranch Wagyu: www.mishimaranch.com
    Organic Prairie: www.organicprairie.com
    Painted Hills: www.paintedhillsnaturalbeef.com
    Sous-Vide Supreme: www.sousvidesupreme.com

For

VICTORIA FLYNN

Contents

Acknowledgments

I have wanted to write a cookbook for a long time. Recently, I realized that I needed those years of preparation to connect with all of the exceptional people who would one day help me create it.

The first is my husband, Benjamin. He didn't question my decision to write a book with two children under the age of four, and then made it all possible. Benjamin diverted our little girls so that I could have dominion over the kitchen, ate innumerable recipe test suppers, and put his own writing aspirations on hold so that I could pursue mine.

Judy Amster became my mentor after I phoned her for an article on cookbook collectors in 1999. I never wrote the article, but Judy has traveled the long road with me, listened to every kvetch and kvel, and advised me on recipes from her vast culinary knowledge base. She understands better than anyone else what this means to me.

Cory Carman and I became friends when our oldest children were babies. I picked her brain about raising grassfed beef and she picked mine about cooking it, a conversation that continues to this day. She has tutored me on sustainable ranching practices, global warming research, and cattle breeding while inspiring recipes with her questions. Cory encouraged me to leave nothing out and then led me to the experts who informed me about the range of topics covered in this book.

I am especially grateful to author and Portland State University professor Madeleine Pullman, researcher Lauren Gwin of Niche Beef Processor Assistance Network, and meat scientist Bob Dickson of Dayton Natural Meats for their time and interest in my project. Dan Probert of Country Natural Beef, K'lynn Kennedy of Painted Hills, and Shane Lindsay of Mishima Wagyu also answered rounds of questions about beef production. After I trespassed into his Boardman, Oregon feedlot to have a quick look around, John Wilson of Beef Northwest forgave me and then became my best source on feedlots. John Harrington educated me about third-party certification while Ann Colonna gave me a crash course in sensory science for creating the beef taste test.

Butchers Kevin Silveira of Valley Meat, Tracy Smaciarz of Heritage Meats, Dannie Cummings of Sheridan Meats, Tray Satterfield of Eat Oregon First, and Camas Davis of the Portland Meat Collective all improved my understanding of the butcher's craft. Joseph O. McCormack from the Wallowa Band Nez Perce Trail Interpretive Center, Inc. and rangeland ecologist Mike Hale helped me to nail down errant facts. Any errors or omissions that stand are mine.

I cannot recompense Lindsay Gott for her role as recipe researcher, tester, and kitchen soul mate. Her standards for excellence exceed even my own, and everything that she touched became better. Kristen Rainey conducted initial research into nutritional claims about grassfed beef. When it came time for writing, Michelle Wildgen navigated me through an overabundance of words to come out on the other side with the story I hoped to tell. My dear friend Jane Slade reviewed my manuscript at the eleventh hour and offered her insights as an inquisitive home cook, editor, and health-oriented eater. All of the following have been great sources of support and love: my mastermind group of Becky Nunn, Chris Fagan, Maren Van Nostrand, and Susan Wright-Geiger; my writing posse of Susan Badger-Jones and Lois Barry; my parents, Frank and Elaine Sampson, who have never doubted my instincts; and my children, Molly and Cecelia.

Recipe testing in my kitchen with Adele Nash and Kit Phelps was a highlight of this project and both gave their talents generously. Linda Faus, who has tested every recipe I've written for the *Oregonian* also helped to get these recipes off the ground and offered technical support on slow cookers. I want to thank all the home recipe reviewers who invested their own hard-earned money and precious time to give these recipes a whirl: Audrey Aiken, Beth and Chris Alderson, Matthew Amster-Burton, Leslie Ashburn, Sarah Bahn, Barbara Balmer, Katherine Deumling, Erin Donovan, Elizabeth Enslin, Ambler FitzSimons, Edwin Gott, Bridget Hammond, Ryan Hartman, Patricia Heatherwood, Theresa Iserman, Charlotte Johnson, Heather Jones, Cathy Kennedy, Lisa Kosglow, Yvonne Litaker, James Lombardo, Marya Nowakowski, Dayl Paytel, Janet Pulsifer, Jerry Qualle, Pam Royes, Marcy Strazer, Rose Szapszwewicz, Kendra Wehmeyer, Marsha Wirtel, Polly Wood, and Suzanne Wright.

Sarah Jane Freymann, an agent with tremendous patience and fortitude, worked tirelessly to find this book a home. That Geoffrey Stone of Running Press took a chance on an unknown author is my great fortune.

Designer Josh McDonnell led the team that photographed the recipes on location in my kitchen and at Carman Ranch. I'm so grateful to photographer David Reamer, Galvin Collins, and Caroline Ford who styled all the food to make it as stunning as the scenery.

There is no better place to write a book about beef—especially grassfed beef—than eastern Oregon. Many local ranchers shared their experience (and their good meat) so that mine would broaden, and they include: Sara Miller and Mike Hale of Bunchgrass Beef, Liza Jane and Craig Nichols of 6 Ranch, Todd and Angie Nash of Marr Flatt Cattle Company, Joanie and Doug Fluit of Fluit Family Farms, Jill and Vicki McClaran, and Janie Tippet. They represent the many small-scale and family ranchers throughout this country who work tirelessly to feed us while caretaking our lands.

INTRODUCTION

HOW A FORMER VEGETARIAN CAME TO WRITE A BEEF COOKBOOK AND WHY IT HAD TO BE WRITTEN

On a clear September afternoon, I mingled with a crowd dressed in skirts and khakis in an open pasture beneath snow-rimmed mountains. While a John Deere tractor paced the rolling fields behind the brown ranch house, people sipped cocktails of vodka distilled from local rye and waiters passed deviled eggs, Romano bean bruschetta, and beef heart kabobs. The aromas of oil and meat drifted from a camp stove where a chef was bent cooking. Nearby, the herd of cattle shouldered the fence like spectators. Beyond them stood rows of long white tables—the dining room that awaited us for a farm-to-table dinner.

An iron dinner bell clanged. Wearing jeans and a navy T-shirt, Erika Polmar, Plate & Pitchfork's founder, jumped up on a hay bale. We clustered around her like horses at a watering trough as she welcomed us, her ninety guests. For eight years, she'd organized on-farm dinners in the Portland area. This one on the Carman Ranch in the Wallowa Valley of northeastern Oregon was the first on a cattle ranch, and at 350 miles from the metropolitan area, the furthest afield. After a talk and a tour, we would all sit down to a five-course celebration of grassfed beef—a wine-paired, whole-animal menu of steak tartare, glazed short ribs, and grilled strip loin, accompanied with late-summer vegetables.

Rancher Cory Carman took her turn up on the bale to narrate her family's ninety-seven-year history with registered Angus and Hereford cattle. More than a few must have been surprised to see that our host was a doe-eyed, thirty-one-year-old tall drink of water. I watched the rapt faces in the crowd as she told them how it hadn't been her plan to come back to the ranch. After Stanford and public policy work in Washington, D.C., she returned one summer, met Dave Flynn, and stayed. Within four years, this fourth-generation rancher and her husband had converted the family business into a certified grassfed beef operation. They'd reintroduced heritage pigs and free-range chickens, and recreated the model sustainable family farm for the twenty-first century.

I recognized a handful of locals in the group, primarily friends and neighboring ranchers. Everyone else had invested in a twelve-hour round-trip drive to one of the most remote and beautiful places in the Pacific Northwest. The Wallowa Valley's grasslands have supported cattle since the 1840s when the Nez Perce Indians ran herds before the homesteaders took over everything. Throughout the years that beef has fallen in and out of favor, the people in this corner of Oregon have continued their cattle drives and spring branding parties, weaning the calves and venturing out in winter storms to feed the waiting herd. Recently, many of them, like Cory and Dave, have broken from family tradition to raise their beef cattle solely on good grass.

I lucked into living in this rural place where raising livestock and chickens, canning and gardening, foraging and butchering have never gone out of fashion. Now, standing in the warm autumn sun with perfect strangers, I suddenly grasped how precious these practices were to people who didn't have it all in their own backyard. I sensed their deep satisfaction at seeing the contented cows, walking through the musky pastures, and listening to these young ranchers' story. Their commitment and curiosity overjoyed me, and I hung back along the fence watching the stream of people flow through the field toward the waiting tables. In the golden light, I saw it all anew.

This collection of people represented all the others who crave a closer connection to the source of their food and the people who produce it. Over the past ten years, I've observed the changes within this small agricultural community where change comes so slowly that some here still ranch on horseback out of cellphone range. The artisan beef movement is momentous to these ranchers, the cattle, the lands. And we, the eaters, are the greatest beneficiaries.

I love grassfed beef for its resounding flavors. It starts out faintly sweet, like the clover stem I chewed as a kid while lying on the lawn in the summertime, then blooms with earthy and savory nuances. Even raw, its cherry-colored flesh and butter-colored fat stand apart from conventional beef. It looks and cooks, tastes and chews, like no other beef I've had before.

After spending years learning to cook each and every precious cut, I wrote *Pure Beef* for all those who love beef and others who are venturing

back to meat. Intended as a complete guide to artisan beef, it offers everyone the benefits of a leisurely, informative, and delicious ranch-to-table experience—with more than 125 recipes that highlight a new approach to cooking and eating meat.

You'd expect the writer of a beef book to be a devout carnivore. Yet it is both strange and natural that I came to write this book: strange, because for nearly twenty years, I didn't touch beef, and natural, because for almost ten years, I've stocked a large chest freezer full of it.

At sixteen, I declared myself a vegetarian. For the next ten years, I called myself a vegetarian, but in today's terms, "pescatarian" is much more accurate, since I ate fresh seafood on occasion. At times, "flexitarian" would also apply: during my junior year in France, I somehow didn't equate country pâté with meat. Its salty pork and warm-spice richness spread on a crackling baguette tantalized me too much not to try it.

Then, shortly after my wedding, meat found me. My husband, Benjamin, and I had quit our jobs to travel throughout Mexico and Central America, and for months I navigated around the meats proffered at market food stalls and in-home eateries. I lived on avocados, tortillas, and mangoes, until one crisp and sunny day in March, when I found myself in a stone room in the coffee-growing mountains of Guatemala.

The ninety-year-old mother of our host family spoke only Mayan, but smiled beatifically at us. She hovered by the low-burning stove while Benjamin and I sat at a bare wooden table, swatting flies and smiling back at her. The firebox clicked open and she withdrew two brown strips from the coals. With a few light strokes of her mocha-colored hands, she brushed off the ash and offered the beef to each of us. It looked like a plump piece of jerky, but was warm and supple. I glanced at Benjamin, and he looked back at me, but I already knew that I could not refuse her.

I hardly remember chewing. I was instantly mesmerized by the alluring flavors in my mouth. Like no other meat I'd ever tasted, it was lean but tender and sweet, and with lingering flavors, like vintage red wine and soft-ripened cheese. It was my first bite of grassfed beef.

Several years later, we moved from Seattle to the mountains of eastern Oregon near where Benjamin had grown up on a wheat farm. Back then, this valley was far removed from the urban artisanal food scene. I sacrificed farmer's markets, fresh seafood, and my beloved job at a four-star restaurant in exchange for an artist community with unlimited backcountry hiking and skiing in the wilderness. For months, I lamented the café's weak coffee, the processed restaurant food, and the grocery store that closed at 9 p.m. sharp.

Soon, however, I learned the ropes of rural life. Word of mouth led me to locate pastured eggs and raw milk, to hear about someone's over-active tomato crop, or wild huckleberries, morels, or horseradish root. I invested in messy, marathon canning sessions with friends. Generous fishermen bestowed trout and steelhead, and when the fishing season slowed in the late fall, local talk turned to hunting bird, deer, and elk. I bartered with a ski guide for a piece of his elk and learned from a woman hunter how to cook the steak fast in butter in a hot cast-iron skillet. I felt like that traveler

again, reconsidering my long-held conceptions that meat was heavy and stultifying. *This* meat felt healthful and energizing.

One fall day, about six months after I'd moved to Oregon, I got a phone call from an engineer who raised sheep asking if we'd like any lamb. On his property just below the snow-tipped peaks, I picked out a well-muscled seven-month-old male—shockingly unlike the storybook lambs I'd imagined—that stood apart from the flock, and a few months later packed the meat in the freezer.

Word got around. Hobby farmers phoned, season by season, to sell us their free-range chickens, pigs, goats, and turkeys. The price tag often came with an offer to help slaughter them, and I got a taste of the true labors and the life-and-death realities of raising animals for food. Because they had been well cared for all their lives and because the killing was swift, I never felt conflicted about eating them. So, when the call came from Sara Miller to buy a share of beef, it seemed only reasonable to scale up from small animals to large. Hundreds of miles from the coast, in a place where the snow hugs the ground from November to April, meat turned out to be my best option—more reasonable than farm-raised salmon or processed soybeans from the supermarket (or, for me, veganism).

That year, I ordered a one-quarter share of one of Sara and her husband Mike Hale's five head of Longhorn steers. I placed my order while the steer still lived out on the lands, agreeing to share the meat among three other families—a practice that's now referred to as cow-pooling.

The steer was killed by a mobile butcher on the ranch where it was raised, then transported to a custom butcher shop, where it was processed according to my cutting order into roasts and one-pound packages of steaks, stew meat, and ground beef. That November, as I stacked eighty-seven pounds of freezing, bone-hard cuts into my basement chest freezer, I was stunned by what comprised a cow: hefty, bone-in chuck roasts, arm roasts, and boneless rump roasts, plus enough ground beef to keep our local fast-food restaurant in burgers for a month. There were fat-ribboned short ribs, marrow-filled soup bones, and steaks labeled "round" and "cubed," whatever that meant. T-bones and loin steaks were few, and I tracked down only one measly package no bigger than my palm labeled "tenderloin."

When I wanted to cook beef, I pulled out whatever shrink-wrapped piece I grasped before my fingers got frostbitten. Once the meat defrosted, I could see what I'd be working with: for lean steaks, from T-bones to top round, I applied what I'd learned about cooking ultra-lean game meat such as that elk. For the rest, I relied on old-time community cookbooks and Asian recipes—both so versatile and frugal with the lesser cuts I had in spades—and my own experimentation.

By spring, I'd pot roasted, stewed, and slow-roasted my way through a more expansive cooking repertoire. When the snows finally melted off our back deck in April, I grilled hamburgers for the first time ever. Like home ownership, grilling that meat was my rite of passage into adulthood.

And what hamburgers they were, more substantial in texture and bolder in flavor than I thought possible. When friends raved about them, we proudly announced the beef was grass-fed. At the time, I had no idea what this really entailed—the depth of knowledge, the level of skill, or the strength of commitment required

from ranchers who use nothing but grass to grow muscle good enough to eat. I was just glad for local food raised with care and respect by folks in our own community.

It's been nine years since that first quarter cow. We get our beef every year from Sara and Mike, who have expanded their herd to fifty head. That check is a big check to write, but I remind myself that the cost per pound averages out to be about the same as extra-lean ground beef from the store. Each cut is worth no more and no less than another, so we value the chuck as much, if not more, than the T-bones. It is also the best beef money can buy, sustaining my family throughout the year and complementing seasonal vegetables and fruits, whole grains, local milk and cheese, plus occasional wild fruits and mushrooms. In stir-fries and pot pies, pasta sauces and casseroles, steak and roast dinners, beef is an ingredient in the whole meal, never the star of the show.

Like me, a lot of people are rediscovering beef, drawn in by the nutritional benefits of grass-fed beef and the giant steps in animal welfare. Thanks to rising demands for better beef, there are more options on the market than ever before. We can choose from natural, organic, and grass-fed beef, along with the standard commodity beef that's always been there. These new choices raise more questions than ever: If I'm going to eat beef, what type should I eat, and where should I buy it? How should I cook it? How much should I eat?

To understand how beef is made and sold, I spent one year following the food chain from the rangelands in Oregon to regional meat processors and retailers. My head still reels with the complexities of food policy and health, the economies of large- and small-scale production, and the ethics and natural systems at play. The most exciting thing I learned is how some systems are changing.

Inquisitive meat eaters who want to know what the cattle consumed and how they were handled from birth to their final breath are shifting the way beef is produced in this country: consultants are teaching gentle handling techniques to veteran ranch hands, feedlots are giving cattle access to pasture, and processing plants are adopting Temple Grandin's humane slaughtering concepts. The meat counter is now filled with information on labels, third-party certification stamps, and rating charts for animal welfare standards encompassing everything from weaning age to transport. The artisan beef movement is revolutionizing an entire industry and we cannot underestimate the force of our buying choices in a sensitive pennies-on-the-dollar market. It's already affected the way many of us think about meat and its place in our lives.

Pure Beef contains two sections: the content in part 1 addresses all of the issues today's beef consumers want to know, and the recipes in part 2 organize all of the beef cuts into a framework for cooking.

Part 1 is a narrative rooted in one of the places in America where great beef is being produced, Oregon's Wallowa Valley, where I live. I write about the ranchers I know to share on-the-ground information that everyday beef buyers and meat eaters want to understand fully. These ranchers are some of the leaders inspiring exciting changes throughout the country while confronting head-first the challenges, opportunities, and flaws in our food system. Some topics may seem unsavory for a cookbook, but I address them all because nowadays the whys and whats and hows are all intertwined with good cooking and eating.

Part 2 focuses on what I have found to be the best ways to handle grassfed beef. Amidst the glowing health reports about grassfed beef, there's been little accurate information about how to treat it and how to cook it well. What is widely circulated has never jibed with my experience or with the techniques that have worked for me year in and year out.

What's more, few cookbooks have devoted much attention to the cuts I've used—the lesser cuts I value most, and those common in orders for half and quarter cow shares. Over the years, friends have called me to ask what to do with left-over round steaks or the short ribs stockpiled in their freezer. Local ranchers have consulted with me to advise their beef customers (cow-poolers like me) how to cook every cut in their annual order. I've taught cooking classes and given cooking demonstrations at the farmers market to give people confidence when handling this "new" beef.

The recipe chapters that form part 2 are a culmination of all that I've learned with the help of butchers, chefs, meat scientists, researchers, and the local cooks of Wallowa County. This collection organizes all the beef cuts into chapters that match them to best cooking methods, from braises and stir-fries to grilled meats and roasts. The recipes highlight techniques and temperatures to explore the wide range of options. And, if you're new to cooking with grassfed beef, there's plenty of guidance built into the recipes to achieve your own success.

I'm not out to convince you to convert to grassfed beef. If you love grain-finished beef, this book will inform you and steer you toward the best meat that truly *is* as good as it looks. Eating should be nothing less than delicious pleasure. Ultimately, when we go into the kitchen, after all of the hard decisions are made, this is our focus—and it is the heart of this book and every recipe in it.

About one month before I sent this manuscript to my publisher, I went to the local copy shop to print a draft. When I walked in, I recognized the cropped silver hair and long drape of chocolate-colored robe of our resident Buddhist monk. Her back was to me, and when she turned, her eyes widened in greeting behind her bifocals. "What have you been up to?" she said.

I paused uncomfortably, knowing she was a vegetarian, and then said, "I'm working on a beef cookbook."

"How wonderful!" she said, beaming. "You know, so many people want to eat meat. How great that you'll be able to share with them the best ways to do it."

She lay her palm on the freshly printed pages still hot from the machine and spoke enthusiastically about non-judgment, mindfulness, and gratitude for the life energy that nourishes us. In a few sentences, this devout vegetarian illuminated everything that I had wanted to incorporate into this book.

"And for goodness sakes, enjoyment," she added. "Just enjoy it!"

Her message harkened back to the September dinner on the ranch. At my table of eight that night, we served ourselves family style from platters as the sun dropped over the mountain's broad back. We savored each bite, pulled on sweaters, and talked like old friends. When the first stars appeared, so did the main course. I remembered forking a slice of grilled beef loin and a tangle of green beans onto my plate. As I chewed, essences of mushroom and minerals rounded out into complex and concentrated tastes that hummed in my mouth until I took the next bite.

That experience is one I recapture whenever I step into the kitchen to cook with the best-quality ingredients I know. It's all in my hands—and with this book, in yours, too.

THE BEEF CASE

HOW GRASS BECOMES BEEF

One evening in late July, I was jogging down a gravel road that parallels the old railway. The air was cooling rapidly as the sun slipped toward the lip of the mountain range. Everything looked trimmed in gold leaf—the grasses going to seed, the Ponderosa pines, and the white rail fence bordering a small pasture. Until I was upon him, I didn't notice the horned Hereford bull standing abreast the barbed wire fence. He was so close to the road, his yard-long horns might have struck me if he had turned his head. They curved outward into fine tips, like skewers. I sidestepped to give him berth and my pulse rate quickened. What delicate genetic wiring kept this formidable half-ton creature from plowing right through the fence lines? But he only followed me with his pink-rimmed eyes, chewing steadily, as I jogged past.

Considering I don't live on a ranch, I've had more contact with cattle than seems reasonable. Roughly twenty-five thousand cows, more than three times the number of people, populate the place I now call home. I've witnessed a calf being born on a February morning as I drove by, the steam rising from the warmth as the calf plopped onto the snow-splattered ground. Late winter is the traditional calving season, timed for the calves to be weaned by fall, and babies curled on the hay feed in the fields are an everyday sight. Grazing cattle are the icons of the rural landscape, so ordinary that we hardly notice them. Only when I nearly collided with that bull did I stop and consider the miracle that they perform for us every day of their lives.

Cattle and Grass

For beef cattle, eating is their one and only job, and they are perfectly engineered to do what we cannot: digest fibrous plants. In apparent leisure, they forage diverse grasses, legumes, and other plants as if they're composing the perfect mesclun salad mix. Using their binocular vision, cattle constantly scan the landscape on a mission for their next grazing spot. They sample with their tongues, then curl them around the tastiest and most nutritious bites to yank off the tender tips. Unlike sheep and goats, their ruminant cousins, cattle have no front teeth or prehensile lips, only a bony upper plate, lower teeth, and broad molars for chewing. While they stand contemplatively chewing their cud, an astounding biochemical process ensues within their gut. Their digestion extracts abundant nutrients locked up in plants that are essential to human life.

Even if, like Fletcherites, we chewed every bite one hundred times or puréed grass into smoothies, we could never digest that stringy cellulose into usable energy. The enzymes in our feeble single stomach are just not up to the task. It takes a rumen, the largest of these bovines' four stomachs, and its colonies of bacteria to ferment the fibers and manufacture the pure protein that feeds them. A food chain unto themselves, these beasts have the capability to transmute chlorophyll produced by the sun's energy into muscle loaded with flavorful compounds. With human intervention, those muscles become our meat.

Healthy Meat?

Before it was associated with heart attacks—and ages before mad cow disease, E. coli, environmental degradation, and global warming—beef was a wholesome, nourishing, and desirable food source. Generous in fats, its protein was rich in heme iron, a type more readily absorbed into the bloodstream than plant-based iron. How sensible, then, that for tens of thousands of years, humankind diverted precious energy stores into getting more of it. An amenable herbivore, the giant auroch, evolved alongside humankind until both depended on one another. The cattle cohabitated with their breeders and offered a generous and reliable meat supply to grow each generation stronger, healthier, and longer living.

Suddenly, in the 1970s, beef fell out of favor in the United States. High in fat and cholesterol, it was the prime suspect for atrociously high rates of heart disease. When the twin risks of diabetes and cancer were linked to eating beef, a steak seemed as hazardous as smoking. For thirty long years, beef hasn't been able to shake its disgraced reputation, and today, eating a juicy hamburger is still a guilty pleasure.

Along came grassfed beef with its apparently sterling health report: less overall fat, saturated fat, and calories, and more omega-3s, CLAs, and vitamins A and E. In a stunning reversal of everything we'd been told about beef, it seemed possible that this "new" beef might actually be *good* for you.

Beef Nutrition

What gets lost in the newsflashes about grassfed beef is that *all* beef is a power-packed source of amino acids, vitamins (A, B6, B12, D, and E), and minerals (iron, zinc, selenium, phosphorus, niacin, and riboflavin), and it always has been. Any beef you buy today contains a third less fat than it did before the low-fat revolution. With the plunge in beef sales, the industry reacted quickly and decisively to change breeding and feeding practices to produce leaner beef. In total fat and saturated fat counts, a three-ounce portion of most retail beef cuts is on par with the same amount of chicken (on a range between a boneless breast and thigh).

On top of the meat industry's fat overhaul, nutritionists have revised their initial understanding of the impact of fats and cholesterol in the diet. Good fats, those that stimulate the immune system and may even prevent heart disease, cancer, and diabetes, co-exist in beef with the bad artery-clogging fat. Half of the saturated fat in beef is monounsaturated, the type that can lower cholesterol and reduce blood pressure. One-third is stearic acid, shown to have no net effect on blood cholesterol levels. The most recent nutritional guidelines green light four to seven ounces of lean beef per day—a portion that concerns many health advocates as excessive in a country where annual beef consumption averages just under sixty pounds for every American.

Antibiotics and Hormones

Much of the health concern about beef stems from the feedlot practices developed to maintain cattle in confinement while maximizing their growth. To prevent bloat, acidosis, and liver infections, confined cattle receive daily doses of additives that improve digestion and are injected with slow-release pellets of synthetic estrogen that can add up to forty extra pounds. The Federal Drug Administration (FDA) and The National Cattlemen's Association contend that the residues in the meat from these animals are not a risk to human health. Still, much of the public's hearts and minds have turned against these practices. Of particular alarm are the public health dangers of antibiotic resistant bacteria in muscle meats carrying superbacteria such as Staph (*staphylococcus aureus*) and in waterways from toxic runoff linked to feedlot manure lagoons.

If keeping cattle on grass is better for our own health and the public's, it's hard to fathom how much it benefits the animals themselves. My own awareness grows each time I'm in close contact with the ruminants who feed us and the people who raise them on grass.

The Grassfed and Grain-Fed Difference

Beef cattle are born on one of the country's 750,000 privately owned ranches where they spend the first stage of their lives living in pastures and nibbling the fresh grasses. After weaning at about six months, some calves remain on their home ranches to graze and, in winter, to be fed hay, which is dried and stored grasses. Consuming only plants their whole lives, these cattle are raised to maturity and slaughtered between one thousand to twelve hundred pounds anywhere from sixteen to thirty-six months old. This beef is "grassfed."

All the rest, about 95 percent of the annual calf crop, are trucked from the ranch (sometimes via a stocker producer for additional weight gain on grass) to feedlots concentrated in the Midwest, Great Plains, Southwest, and the Pacific Northwest. Confined to pens, the cattle consume daily rations of mash—a blend of cereal grains that can include corn, barley, sorghum, or wheat (plus ionophores to help them digest the feed, protein supplements that can include chicken meal, by-products from food processors, and roughage in the form of wet ground corn stalks called silage). The cattle reach a slaughtering weight of 1,200 to 1,400 pounds between sixteen and twenty-four months of age. This beef is "grain-fed."

The move to the feedlot is a radical rift in the cows' lifestyle and diet. Research studies show that their rumens react immediately, dropping in pH, which reduces bacterial synthesis. The grain-based feed gradually changes the nutritional composition within their muscles, the same ones we ultimately eat.

Animal breed, sex, and age all play a role in any beef's nutritional makeup, but scientists and nutritionists agree that what affects it most is what the cow ate—especially during the final three to six months of its life, the stage called finishing. In side-by-side comparisons of grain-fed and grass-fed beef samples, there are striking differences in their nutritional profiles, most notably in the levels of essential saturated fatty acids and antioxidants. Some of these contrasts you can actually see and others you can taste.

FATS

Nearly all of the research comparing grain-fed to grassfed beef hinges on fats, what scientists call lipids. You can see it in the thick white edge of fat around the muscles and the strands of fat within the muscles called intramuscular fat, or marbling. Beef from animals that never ate anything but grass is consistently lower in overall fat and saturated fat. While cholesterol levels are constant no matter the feeding regimen, grassfed beef has a better balance of those fatty acids, such as stearic acid, that do not raise cholesterol.

The point of feeding cows grain is to pack on the pounds. No wonder they're fattier. It's logical that an animal that strolled around all day eating plants would be leaner than one that stood in a pen and was fed the equivalent of a fast-food diet. (One rancher put it to me this way: "Would you rather eat an athlete or a couch potato?")

Things get more complicated when we delve into a class of nutrients called beneficial fatty acids. The subjects of intense nutritional study, certain polyunsaturated fatty acids (omega-3s) show promise of protecting us from heart attacks, cancer, and immune disorders. Surprisingly, many of these life-enhancing fatty acids start out, in one form or another, in grass.

Outside of fish, the best sources for omega-3-type fatty acids are flaxseed, walnuts, canola, wheat germ, tofu, and grass. Grasses are loaded with certain omega-3s produced in their chloroplasts (ALA and EPA/DHA). Cattle fed only plants synthesize more of these fatty acids into their fat and flesh through the bacterial activity in their rumens. The lower pH in the rumen of grain-fed cattle inhibits this synthesis. While grassfed beef doesn't carry nearly the omega-3s of flaxseed or fish, it has two to four times more than meat from grain-fed animals. Is it enough to matter—or in scientific terms, to have a biological effect?

Researchers are striving to determine whether the levels of these good, unsaturated fats in grassfed beef bring any benefit to human health. A consensus seems to be emerging among nutritionists worldwide that it's the ratio of omega-6s to omega-3s that matters most and the lower the better. In all cattle, omega-6 is fairly constant, but the higher concentrations of omega-3s in grassfed cattle shift the ratio to more healthful 2:1 and lower (on par with wild game meats), compared to the feedlot beef ratios averaging 7:1 and as high as 14:1. The omega-3 level is one of the reasons why grassfed beef has a more intense taste than grain-fed beef that people describe as "gamey." (Meanwhile, trials to increase omega-3 levels in feedlot beef with supplements like fish oil have failed because the beef has a distinctive and off-putting fishy flavor.)

CLA, or conjugated linoleic acid, also enthralls the nutritional community because of its potential cancer-preventing, heart disease-reducing, and supportive immune system properties. Unfortunately, all of the current CLA research to date is based solely on animal studies, and inter-national health experts haven't agreed on a daily intake for it to have a biological effect. What they do agree on is that we don't ingest enough of this fatty acid. Since grass is the lone source, consuming more foods from the pastured ruminants who produce CLA (both dairy and meat) is the surest way to get more.

Finally, grassfed beef supplies more antioxidants, including vitamin A and E and glutathione (GT) that protect cells against cancer-causing free radicals. Compared to grain-finished beef, the butter-colored fat of grassfed beef contains seven times as much carotene, a compound that produces vitamin A, which keeps the lining of the eyes, mucous membranes, lungs, intestines, and the skin healthy while producing more white blood cells. Immunity-enhancing vitamin E is also three times as high in grassfed beef than in grain-fed beef.

Although it looks strange to many, this yellowish fat, which becomes more so with an animal's maturity and time on grass, is a sign of healthfulness in beef. From study to study, what becomes convincingly clear is that the nutritional quality of the fat begins to wane the moment cattle leave the grasslands for the feedlot.

Back to Pasture

During a chilly downpour in May, my family went to Carman Ranch to help our friends Cory Carman, Dave Flynn, and their three pre-school-aged kids gather cattle. Since November the herd had dwelled in a pasture awaiting a daily hay delivery from Dave. After a long, snowy spring the grasses were shamrock green, and they looked good enough to eat.

Turning cattle back onto the grass is an annual event at many family ranches. The only difference is that none of the Carman Ranch cattle would ever go to a feedlot. No calves would suffer the stresses of separation and transport or the change in diet and climate.

In the corrals, I stood amidst the mother cows who shifted aimlessly around me, sniffed the air, and bellowed for their calves. They were so close I felt the warmth from their hides and smelled their damp earth-and-dung scent. I felt small next to their wide flanks, and a trill of anxiety coursed through me that I'd get crushed against the wooden fence slats. But they edged away without seeming to take any notice, more at ease than I was with our longstanding interdependence.

Husbanding large livestock is serious labor any way you go about it. I watched as Dave led the cows through a green metal chute. He looked delighted to be out in the rain, replacing green ear tags and giving immunizations. He was powerful yet gentle while handling these giants who depend entirely on his care. Like all ranchers, his relationship to them transcends profits and loss statements, with no vacation or sick days included. From my perspective, the responsibility is awesome.

Many romanticize the return to pasture-based ranching methods, but raising beef demands far more than just letting cattle graze on their own as nature intended. It calls for deep understanding of the natural grass cycles and the soil's minerality and water absorption qualities. Ranchers like Dave and Cory who practice intensive rotational grazing use a system of lightweight movable fencing to create smaller, temporary paddocks that prevent overgrazing while restimulating plant growth and regenerating the soils.

Throughout the spring and summer, Dave would restring the fence lines into fresh pasture every few days. By moving them frequently, the cattle would nip only the tips of the plants once, ideally, fertilize them, and crush some of them, returning carbon into the soils. For her part, Cory would continue annual experiments on her family's lands to maximize plant restoration, weed control, and carbon sequestration (along with marketing and selling their beef in Portland). By managing their lands in this fashion, they are some of the many ranchers taking an active role in creating a future that is healthier in every respect.

We drove our rigs to a nearby pasture to gather the yearlings—one-year-old steers that would become next season's beef. They waited in a cluster by the gate as if they knew something good was in the offing. Dave rode the four-wheeler, calling out commands to his Border collie who darted after those that stopped to feast on the waist-high grasses along the ditch. Another friend drove the hay truck—loaded with all five of our kids—to lure the cattle down the quarter mile of quiet country road. There, the cattle would rejoin their herd at the home ranch where they were born.

As the cows turned up the driveway, the rain relented and the sun warmed the damp, sweet grasses that stood lush and ready. We guided the herd, but once inside the fence lines, all took off in a trot toward the pasture. We gathered to watch as mothers, calves, juvenile heifers, and steers began to eat, four hundred necks bent to the grasses.

Next to me, Dave was soaked through his stained tan work coat and his smiling cheeks were splattered with mud. "This is a great day," he said.

▨▨▨ **COW 101** ▨▨▨

We call them all cows, but, technically speaking, "cow" is an adult female *bos taurus* that has birthed a calf. Mother cows are impregnated each year by a bull or by artificial insemination and nine months later give birth, ideally all on their own. Any one-year-old, male or female, is a yearling. Young males are typically castrated at birth to become steers, since bulls are of limited use and need to be kept separated from the herd. Only one bull is required for about twenty-five to forty cows (depending on the age and terrain) during the breeding season. Females less than two years old are heifers (*heffers*); they become cows only after their first calf. Some heifers are bred and become replacement mother cows, the foundation of the herd, but most are sold along with the steers to supply the beef market.

2 WHAT'S THE BEEF?

One afternoon, I opened my door to a thick-shouldered Latino man in a white polo and baseball cap that read "Yummy Meats." By way of greeting, he asked, "Where do you buy your beef?" On the street sat his white Yummy Meats minivan with the sliding side door wide open and a broad chest freezer inside. "Um," I stalled, not wanting to tell him that I bought my beef from one of the dozens of local ranchers in the valley—like everyone else I knew. He had only the slimmest chance of making a sale in this town.

"This is better than what you can get at Costco," the salesman said. He slapped his boxes down on my wooden front porch and whipped one open so I could feast my eyes on six rib-eyes. "It's all-natural," he added. I was curious enough to lean forward for a peek. What did "natural" really mean? Could I tell just by looking?

Each steak was odorless, boneless, and blood-less, frozen in its own plastic cryovac packaging: picture-perfect red steaks ringed with pristine fat and smooth muscles mottled with marbling. "There are no hormones, and we don't use any dyes," he said. I'd heard about hamburger meat washed with ammonia, but I hadn't even considered that dye might be a beef additive.

More boxes flew open. Rosy New York steaks and filet mignons clinked against one another like rocks in a stream. I asked where the meat came from. Gazing at the jumble of meat on my porch, he murmured that the meat was from somewhere near Olympia. He was so earnest, and I felt bad that he'd have to take his cargo back, wherever it had come from.

No matter where we buy it—the supermarket, the farmers' market, the Internet, or even a custom butcher shop—making a beef purchase today is no simple prospect. We have to make a snap decision, forced to believe quality claims and buy on trust. With all of the options for natural, organic, and grassfed beef bearing marketing claims of every kind, who can keep it all straight?

Only twenty-five years ago, nearly all beef came from the same giant stream, running from feedlots to beef processors to retailers stamped "USDA inspected." Today, labels from "pasture-raised" and "natural" to the USDA Organic seal adorn beef packages like the patches on my old Girl Scout sash. All of these categories are an effort to help us distinguish among the variety of newer beef product lines. Like the Yummy Meats salesman, labels can't tell the whole story.

Commodity Beef

This generic beef is what you find at most supermarkets, shrink-wrapped and ready to cook. It comes from the main beef supply chain, a highly centralized and industrialized meat processing and distribution system that has made beef affordable and accessible. Different breeds from ranches across the country are pooled into the commodity feedlot system designed to create a standardized, reliable product. The only information about the beef available to the consumer is the quality grade based on marbling, typically either choice or select (the tiny percentage of prime, the highest grade, goes to restaurants), along with the new nutrition label. It's safe to assume this beef is from cattle that spent four to six months in confinement and were treated with growth-promoting hormones and antibiotics.

Four corporations dominate the beef processing industry, but it's impossible to track any beef back to its source after it enters the commodity market. This lack of traceability, especially with ground beef, which can be a mix from hundreds of different animals, has become a major concern and the cause for repeated beef recalls due to E. coli 0157:H7 infection and other food safety issues.

It's worth noting that kosher and halal meat also comes from the commodity pool. It is slaughtered according to the orthodoxies of each religious order in a certified plant and processed separately from other meat, but that's the only difference.

Natural

According to USDA regulations, the natural label applies to any meat that can be described as "minimally processed" and is free from preservatives and artificial ingredients. All labels and label claims have to be reviewed and approved by the USDA based on an affidavit signed by the beef producer. In general, natural brands are grain-finished to conform to the characteristic flavors and textures most consumers prefer. Some natural labels include additional claims about subjects of concern, notably prohibiting the use of growth hormones and non-therapeutic antibiotics.

Problems with the natural label stem from the fact that the definition refers only to the meat, not what the animal ingested during its lifetime. Coupled with the fact that this term has been applied beyond its legal definition makes many industry experts and consumers skeptical about its meaningfulness. However, it's important to single out those natural brands backed by third-party certifications for their claims, such as an all-vegetarian diet and humane animal handling (Certified Beef, page 27). Read labels carefully (and between the lines) to distinguish among the producers in this marketing category. They range from industry giants and alliances of independent ranchers that contract with feedlots to local producers who supplement their cattle's natural grazing habits with grain-based finishing feeds.

Organic

Under the organic law, in effect since 2002, all feed must be certified organic, whether it is predominantly grain or exclusively grass, and contain no animal by-products. (Before the outbreak of mad cow disease, or bovine spongiform encephalopathy, meat-processing wastes were blended into rations; chicken feathers are still a common feedlot ingredient.) The USDA Organic label on a package of beef certifies that the beef is free from growth hormones and antibiotics and that the animals are given seasonal access to pasture. Unlike a natural beef label, the organic seal assures consumers that every entity that handled the beef—from the farm to the processing plant—was certified organic by an independent third-party certifier (Certified Beef, page 27).

Grassfed

In the strictest sense, grassfed beef comes from cattle that consumed only mother's milk and forage, including grasses, legumes, and grass hay, and lived exclusively on pasture. However, this category is the most variable of them all. Grass can make up the cattles' entire diet, or a large portion of it; beware of labels that read "pasture-raised" and "range-raised." When in doubt, contact the rancher or look for third-party certification to authenticate a grassfed claim.

Producers of grassfed beef range from companies such as Panorama, the largest organic grassfed beef supplier in the U.S. whose member ranchers produce seven thousand head of cattle each year, to hobby farmers with five head to sell.

Grassfed production does not flow through the standard production stream from feedlot to processing plant as commodity and most natural and organic brands do. Access to slaughtering facilities is one of the major barriers to production for small-scale producers and a significant expense. Grassfed beef is a seasonal product with most cattle slaughtered during the growing season between June and November, and the meat is typically sold frozen.

American Wagyu

Wagyu refers to a black breed of Japanese cow renowned for its extreme marbling and shocking prices. In the U.S., what's usually sold is a crossbreed of Wagyu bull with Black Angus cow, also called Kobe-style after the province in Japan where these cattle originated. They grow immense, weighing 1,600 pounds at slaughter, a third heavier than standard beef. Their extreme fattiness is not due to beer or massages (all myths), but is the result of genetics. Maturity factors in, too, since Wagyu are raised to a minimum of twenty-five months of age—more time to deposit the marbling, or intramuscular fat, that's made them famous.

American Wagyu are typically raised on specialized mixed-grain feed high in roughage and the meat contains less saturated fat per ounce than commodity beef. Rarer still is grassfed Wagyu, now available online, which offers the health benefits of 100 percent pasture-raised meat along with the supreme tenderness of this luxury beef.

CERTIFIED BEEF

The principle behind third-party certification is to offer assurances to consumers to help them make purchasing decisions in line with their values. This became necessary to prevent beef brands from making unverified marketing claims like "natural" and "pasture-raised." A seal from an independent party has become one way to guarantee the authenticity of any claim for natural, grassfed, organic, or humane animal treatment. All third-party certification programs involve voluntary on-farm inspections (at a cost to the producer) to certify that their livestock operation practices are in accordance with their marketing and labels.

The USDA Organic seal, for example, verifies that the beef was produced in compliance with the federal National Organic Program regulations (Organic, page 26). Non-profit organizations also oversee certification programs directed toward particular issues. For example, an Animal Welfare Approved (AWA) or Certified Humane seal certifies that the animals were treated humanely, while a seal from the American Grassfed Association validates that the beef is 100 percent grassfed. Food Alliance certification encompasses animal welfare and sustainability criteria, including social justice and environmental stewardship into its standards, setting a high bar for the beef production system (Sources, page 271).

Artisan Beef Markets

The natural, organic, and grassfed beef market is tiny, comprising less than 3 percent of the national industry. But after decades of declining beef consumption, the artisan beef movement is stimulating so much growth that supply cannot match the demand. The range of choices that consumers see at the supermarket is also creating new opportunities for ranchers large and small.

In the past, commodity beef was a rancher's only option. Most ranches were cow-calf operations, which means that each year, they produced a crop of calves, which they sold at auction (sometimes live but often via video and now Web) based on the commodity price of the day or preset futures market pricing, the same speculative enterprise that determines the values of corn, rice, soybeans, and other commodities. In other words, the ranchers took whatever they got and hoped it covered their operating loans from the previous year.

The new option for small-scale ranchers today is to diversify among all the available markets—commodity, natural, and grassfed. One cattleman following this path is Todd Nash, who founded Marr Flat Cattle Company in 2002.

On an unseasonably warm day in late January, I jumped into his flatbed truck as he led his three hundred-odd mother cows to the highway on the way to their winter birthing grounds. All of these cows were pregnant and they moved at parade pace. For the past nine months, these Angus crossbreeds had lived far from civilization in open wild country so remote that packs of wolves had been preying upon them. Like many ranchers,

Todd depends on permits to run his cattle seasonally on public lands. But there's relentless public pressure to revoke grazing rights and let the lands go back to nature. Beef producers like him and even biologists wonder what will happen to the grasslands when there's nobody there to manage them and control invasive weeds, or enough ruminants—deer, elk, and cattle—to keep them vital.

Grazing on the same grasslands that fattened the Nez Perce tribe's cattle nearly two centuries ago, the Marr Flat cattle are self-reliant, rugged, and healthy. Now, they were headed to a town pasture to give birth—the same pasture by the highway where each year I watched them produce the year's calf crop. Todd had been riding these public lands on horseback fifteen miles a day, gathering cows from the rocky ridges of the steep canyon country. He looked pleased to be sitting comfortably on the truck's bench seat and nibbling on a hamburger ("probably an old dairy cow," he quipped) and fries. He explained how Marr Flat had been shifting its operation toward the natural and grassfed markets, and that he sold to two natural programs, Painted Hills and Country Natural Beef.

Country Natural Beef is one of the oldest and most successful cooperatives in the country. It began in 1986 with fourteen Oregon families who decided to take the rope into their own hands. Instead of being at the mercy of the live animal auction prices, they would own their animals from beginning to end, contracting with a feedlot and processing plant, and taking their meat to stores themselves. There they could tell customers in person how the animals were raised with compassion in low-stress conditions without hormones or antibiotics.

Now over one hundred ranching families strong, Country Natural Beef's third-party certification offers the same assurances to the customers who buy it at Whole Foods and Burgerville, a Portland-area fast-food chain. Country Natural Beef partners meet standards that encompass animal feed and care, worker safety and fairness, water quality, and wildlife habitat impacts. Plus, the cooperative ensures traceability—the ability to track every beef carcass back to the ranch where the animal was raised.

But Todd admitted that it depressed him to see his animals in the feedlot, a surprising comment from the president of the local Stock Growers Association. He stopped the truck to let the cows catch up and said, "On these ranches where they're raised is a pretty good life." In the past year, he'd kicked off his own grassfed beef program, direct-marketing Marr Flat Cattle grassfed. He sold about fifty head grassfed and was encouraged by people's response to it. "They say, 'Wow, you're doing it right from start to finish.'"

He planned on keeping more of his cattle for grassfed. "To have really good grassfed you have to have good grass," he said. "But it's harder to control because the meat tastes of what they ate." It also means making the time and effort to reach out directly to a customer base, a real challenge for many independent ranchers.

The following April, provided the grasses were ready, the Marr Flat cows and all their calves would trail the thirty-one miles back to his permitted land to graze. After another season on the range, some of those calves would go to a commodity feedlot and flow into the conventional beef pool without any special label attached. Others designated to become branded natural beef sold for a markup at grocery stores would spend ninety days in a feedlot receiving hormone- and antibiotic-free rations. And Todd would reserve some of the calves on the ranch where they'd graze freely on the native grasses until they were eighteen months old and ready to be sold as grassfed beef in half and quarter shares directly to friends, neighbors, and other customers.

How remarkable that all of that beef started out the same, I said to him. Where they spent the last phase of their lives and what they ate turned them into completely different meat.

"It's all in the finishing," he said.

Cattle Breeds, From Heritage to Specialty

The first American beef cattle were Longhorns, small-framed cattle descended from the Spanish imports to the New World. Hearty, adaptable, and quick footed, they were ideal for the long-distance cattle drives from the Texas pastures to the Kansas feedlots of the 1850s. Once the railroads took over and centralized the beef industry in the Midwest, endurance wasn't a trait worth preserving. Instead, Longhorns were crossbred with stout, short-horned English and Continental breeds to produce what we recognize as beef cattle today. Industrialization demanded large-framed livestock that gained weight quickly in the feedlots to make marbled meat—Angus, most notably. The beef cattle were selected for consistency and reliability, like Red Delicious apples and iceberg lettuce.

For cattle ranchers, the genetic line of their animals is a major preoccupation. One of the most important traits is the cattle's adaptability to the climate, since some breeds are better suited to cold and dry conditions, while others fare better in moist, temperate environments. They spend precious time and money attending bull sales and studying data about each animal in order to influence the characteristics of their herd. Since their livelihood depends on good fertility, ranchers select mother cows that birth easily, bond with their offspring readily, and produce milk plentifully. A hardy mother cow calves for more than a dozen years. Ranchers also consider the ability to gain weight steadily on native pastures and resistance to common conditions like eye cancer and parasites. Cattle with calm dispositions are easier to handle and can be more productive, so temperament is also a factor in the complex breeding decisions ranchers make every year.

While crossbreeds are most common, some beef producers are marketing heritage purebreeds such as Galloway, Highland, and Devon. Miniature breeds are also becoming popular and are a good choice for those with limited storage as well as a preference for very small cuts. Rare, and in some cases endangered, cattle are suited to certain climates where they are raised exclusively on grass. Buying purebred beef supports biodiversity and sustainable agriculture, but many different cattle breeds, in the right hands, can become exceptional grassfed beef (Sources, page 270).

DAIRY BEEF

All cattle breeds are capable of producing milk and putting on muscle for meat. But some types of cattle are much better at one than the other, a discovery made in Europe about five centuries ago. Through selective breeding, the Dutch, British, and Spanish created two specialized types of cattle, the beeves and the milkers, genetic lines that exist to this day.

There are more than one hundred cattle breeds, but Angus crossbreeds flow through most feedlots because they are fast growing and adaptable with a good frame size, producing a high yield of marbled meat. Holstein and Jersey cows bred to maximize their natural milk-producing gifts populate the dairies. Once they've passed their milking prime, at four or five years old, some of these dairy cows, called cull cows, become meat. (Incidentally, this is the age that beef cattle were slaughtered in the late nineteenth century.) Beef from cull cows makes up 17 percent of all beef sold, though you won't see it labeled. Meat from mature animals is known to be more flavorful (though less tender, which is why it's all ground). It's still treated like a secret in the meat industry, but when I learned this tidbit, it struck me as to how cattle serve us in so many ways—from the fatty acids in tires to the gelling products in toothpaste to the glue for matchsticks—whether we realize it or not.

Where to Find High-Quality Beef

The artisan beef movement is making all types of beef more widely available. Each of these sources provides a range of benefits. (See Sources, page 270, for directories of local beef producers and other educational resources.)

BUTCHER SHOPS

With the surge in interest in artisan beef, more boutique butcher shops have opened and have reemerged in grocery stores in larger cities. In their lighted cases, you can see a range of beef types and brands that can include natural, organic, and grassfed. Freed from the supermarket's shrink-wrapped packaging, the meat cuts display variations in muscle color and composition, and you'll be able to ask questions about the brands on display. An inquisitive and well-informed butcher will know all the details about what the cows ate, where they came from, and how they lived. Buying retail cuts individually, however, is the most expensive way to go.

MEAT BUYING CLUBS

Within communities, people are banding together to buy their beef from a local rancher. This avenue supports the rancher while offering bulk cost savings to buyers. It also brings the benefits of a direct relationship between the customer and the beef producer so that you can learn everything you want to know about what the cattle ate, how they lived, and where they were slaughtered and processed. While you won't be able to hand-select every cut, there's flexibility depending on the specifics of membership and opportunities to split orders with other families—an essential for those without extra freezer space for storing a cargo of beef. You'll find this option through word of mouth or existing Community Supported Agriculture (CSA) networks in your area.

INTERNET ORDERS

For those without ready access to high-quality butcher shops, farmer's markets, or CSAs, artisan beef brands are widely available via the Internet. Nearly every rancher direct marketing his or her beef has a website, and many offer a range of packages that vary by weight and cut for online purchase. Bulk ordering saves money in the long run, though you'll incur shipping costs. Before placing an order, get recommendations from other trustworthy sites or acquaintances and look for third-party certifications to verify marketing claims.

COW-POOLING

The most economical option for buying artisan beef is the old-fashioned way—buying a half or quarter share directly from a rancher. Once called locker meat, this was the way neighbors in communities like mine divvied up an animal among two to four families. Now called cow-pooling, it still works the same way. During the grazing season, you order directly from the beef producer in your region then fill out a cutting order form provided by the meat processor (one more good reason to become familiar with the Pure Beef Cut Guide, pages 42-43). In the late summer or fall, you receive the meat cut, packaged, and frozen for a year's worth of eating.

Buying beef in bulk is a strange idea to some, but consider that it wasn't long ago that paying farmers for a whole season's worth of produce delivered weekly was the same. Cow-pools operate much like CSAs and offer similar benefits of price

How to Choose Your Beef

breaks and a relationship with your food producer.

Compared to the price point for retail cuts, cow-pooling brings a major discount. The cost typically averages five to seven dollars per pound for everything from rib-eyes to stew meat. The downside is that you have to shell out several hundred dollars in advance and need to have the storage space for the frozen beef cuts. (A three-cubic-foot freezer, the size of a standard upright refrigerator, will fit a quarter share—about ninety pounds of meat—though not much else. You can split a quarter with a friend for an eighth, or as many do, invest in a small, energy-efficient chest freezer.)

Cow-pooling brings you in direct contact with a rancher and is mutually beneficial. The rancher sells all the beef cuts at once, which is one of their greatest challenges in the retail world where only the most popular cuts sell fast. You have the opportunity to learn everything you want to know about the animal's life, or to visit the ranch to see for yourself. Around here, it's becoming common for ranchers to host annual appreciation picnics for their beef customers, complete with campfires and a cookout. Being served a hamburger from the person who provides your food is the ultimate farm-to-table experience.

If you want to find out which type or brand of beef you love best, do a taste test. You can question your own assumptions about what you do and don't like, recognizing that most people prefer familiar foods.

I've participated in several beef taste tests, some formal, some not, comparing grain-fed to grassfed, dry-aged versus wet-aged, and fresh versus frozen. It's a real challenge to discern among the host of flavors in your mouth, though it gets easier with practice. I've also found that varying amounts of salt and char from a fiery grill can interfere with the ability to fully sense the meat itself.

By now, I've tried beef from many local and regional producers. Remarkably, each is a unique eating experience. I've learned that the meat's taste is not just a product of good breeding or the grasslands the cow grazed during its lifetime. The very best beef is the result of skillful handling from pasture to plate—how it was raised, slaughtered, butchered, aged, cut, and stored. There is exceptional beef out there—and more all the time as beef producers hone their craft. It's up to you to find your own; you are the one and only judge who matters.

A beef taste test is fun and illuminating to do with a group of friends. You need only a couple pieces of meat and a few simple guidelines. If there's a clear winner, you may decide to go in together and direct-purchase your beef from a rancher (Sources, page 270).

How to Taste Artisan Beef

Taste testing falls in the field of sensory science. It's a tightly controlled and statistical world where ordinary people give food industry experts profit-making (or -breaking) information about their products. It all boils down to what's good and what's not, which is what we all want to know.

For in-home use, a taste test is a great tool for making sound buying decisions. Should I spend more for a grassfed steak? Is organic tastier than natural? Is there a difference in ground beef brands or heritage breeds? For the most reliable results, you'll want to keep bias out of the picture and limit the variables, which involves a little sensory science.

Ann Colonna is the Sensory & Consumer Program Manager at the Food Innovation Center Experiment Station in Portland. She orchestrates dozens of taste tests for corporations each year, sampling baby food, salad dressings, and beef. She even sets them up for herself at home to make her own purchasing decisions among the array of products available. She offered me these pointers for conducting your own taste test to get results you can trust to put your money on:

- **DECIDE WHAT YOU WANT TO LEARN.** Do you want to know if you prefer grain-finished versus grassfed? Are you comparing beef breeds or brands? Focus on one attribute at a time.

- **COLLECT THE SAMPLES.** Two samples are enough, but you can test as many as you can handle before your taste buds become fatigued. (Ann recommends a limit of five at a time.) Try to make the samples as similar as possible in cut, size, thickness, etc. Most people choose steak, but I think that ground beef creates a more level playing field for all beef types. If you salt the meat, measure the salt so that the samples will be equally seasoned.

- **DESIGN A SCORING SHEET** (see the sample on the next page). It can be a simple checklist or include a complete descriptive analysis. Remember that you don't need to be like a wine connoisseur and detail all the nuances of earthy notes and wild essences. At the basic level, you just want to identify which sample you like best.

- **COOK THE SAMPLES.** Whatever you do, try to cook the samples as uniformly as possible. Also, think about how browning could influence your tasting, especially if it's uneven from sample to sample. Consider baking three- to four-ounce ground beef patties in a 450°F oven (about 10 minutes to an internal temperature of 155°F) instead of grilling or frying them. Serve them on identical plates (even color can influence your perceptions).

- **CONDUCT A "TRIANGLE TEST"** to make sure that there is a discernible difference. In this blind test, one person assigns a random letter to each of three samples, two of which are from the same sample, while the third is from a different sample. (You can switch roles and do it again, so that everyone has a chance to taste.) If people correctly identify the one piece that was unique, continue with the taste test. According to Ann, this is the most critical part, because if there is no difference—at least one you can taste—it's pointless to continue.

- **SCORE OR RATE THE SAMPLES.** Try not to be influenced by other people's reactions. Eat a piece of bread between beef bites, and taste again. Ponder and take your time. It's simple but not easy. Use your scoring sheet to rank or grade the samples and identify your favorite.

- **INTERPRET YOUR RESULTS,** and if you'd like to discuss why you like one sample more than another, use the descriptive analysis terms below, or make up your own descriptors.

BEEF TASTING SCORING SHEET

SAMPLE A

1. Consider all the characteristics (texture, flavor, and juiciness) to mark the box that best describes your overall impression:

☐ Like extremely   ☐ Neither like nor dislike   ☐ Dislike extremely

2. Rate the sample according to each characteristic:

TEXTURE

☐ Very tender   ☐ Somewhat tender   ☐ Very chewy

FLAVOR

☐ Bland   ☐ Somewhat flavorful   ☐ Very flavorful

JUICINESS

☐ Very dry   ☐ Somewhat juicy   ☐ Very juicy

3. Describe what you liked or disliked about the sample (optional, see list of Taste Descriptors on the right):

Likes: Dislikes:

....
....
....

SAMPLE B

1. Consider all the characteristics (texture, flavor, and juiciness) to mark the box that best describes your overall impression:

☐ Like extremely   ☐ Neither like nor dislike   ☐ Dislike extremely

2. Rate the sample according to each characteristic:

TEXTURE

☐ Very tender   ☐ Somewhat tender   ☐ Very chewy

FLAVOR

☐ Bland   ☐ Somewhat flavorful   ☐ Very flavorful

JUICINESS

☐ Very dry   ☐ Somewhat juicy   ☐ Very juicy

OPTIONAL:

3. Describe what you liked or disliked about the sample (see list of Taste Descriptors on the right):

Likes: Dislikes:

....
....
....

Tasting Descriptors: The Artisan Beef Institute's Carrie Oliver conducts beef tastings across the county to help people learn about the uniqueness of beef. Like wine, beef is a product of the place where it comes from, and has as much variation. Carrie developed these descriptors in 2007 with a panel of experts, which included a master sommelier, chef, rancher, and psycholinguist, and has refined it in beef tasting sessions with hundreds of beef lovers. I've reprinted here with her permission as a helping hand in identifying some of the tastes on your tongue.

DAIRY NOTES
Butter
Roquefort
Stilton
Parmesan

SWEET NOTES
Maple Syrup
Caramel

SOUR NOTES
Tangy
Acidic
Lemony
Ammonia
Acrid

SAVORY NOTES
Nutty
Roasted Walnuts
Roasted Chestnuts
Black Pepper
Bell Pepper
Herby (e.g. sage, thyme)
Spinach
Umami
Caramelized Vegetables
Baked Potato
Buttered Popcorn
Polenta
Corn

GAME NOTES
Liver
Lamb
Venison
Feral, Wild

EARTHY NOTES
Mushrooms
Porcini Mushrooms
Shitake Mushrooms
Grass
Iron
Flint
Metallic
Blood
Mineral
Must
Barnyard
Sewage

OCEAN NOTES
Fresh Ocean Breeze
Seaweed
Baked Clams
Carp
Mackerel

CHAPTER 3

HOW TO COOK LIKE A BUTCHER

O f all the steps involved in the process of transforming muscle into beef, butchering is the last step and a crucial one in determining the quality of the meat. It is surprisingly bloodless, a fact I learned at Valley Meat Services.

This custom meat processor occupies a white storefront in Wallowa, Oregon, the first town you reach after winding through the river canyon to emerge into this wide valley. The butcher shop sits one block behind Food City market, out of sight of the main highway and the tourists in RVs headed for Wallowa Lake. But hunters and all of the local ranchers depend on the services offered within by butcher Kevin Silveira.

A former log truck driver, Kevin opened his state-inspected custom meat cutting shop in 2004, the days before butchers were rock stars. He's cut all my meat—lambs, hogs, and beef— ever since. Bald and bearded, with a middleweight boxer's build, Kevin trained with a world-weary and talented meat cutter. He can singlehandedly break down a 350-pound side of beef and then piece it back together again like a 3-D jigsaw puzzle. Few of today's butchers have those skills, never mind the time or space to handle whole sides. Most are used to working with smaller animals and the beef sections called sub-primals that arrive boxed and wet-aged in bags from big meat processing plants. (New-wave butchers are trying to learn the craft from veterans like Kevin to get up to speed.)

Kevin is a jovial guy who laughs often and

heartily—especially when customers assume that their cow share will yield nothing but pure steak— but his smile can disappear in the flash of his knife from July through February, when he's slammed and in no mood for chit chat. This is why I picked late spring to spend as much time as possible observing Kevin at work.

Cattle arrive at Valley Meat already killed, skinned, eviscerated, and divided into the symmetrical halves called sides (Harvest Day, page 39). This is unlike other meat processing plants, such as Dayton Natural Meats, a small USDA-inspected facility in Oregon's Willamette Valley where the cattle arrive live and walk onto the kill floor. Stunned unconscious with a captive gun, they are hung upside down and bled. Once the head and hooves are removed, the animals are skinned, eviscerated, and split into sides. They're washed, inspected, treated with an antimicrobial, and chilled in a drip cooler for twenty-four hours to below 40°F—some of the many food safety firewalls in the process.

Kevin and his crew can cut and wrap a side of beef every thirty minutes—a total of eight whole animals within a ten-hour workday. Compared to the two thousand per day at the giant Tyson processing plant just over the Washington border, or the forty head each day at Dayton, that's peanuts. No matter the scale, the process of breaking down each side of beef into pieces that fit in a skillet calls for formidable levels of endurance, skill, cold hardiness, and a fearlessness of sharp objects.

One day at Valley Meat, a dozen sides of

grassfed beef hung dry-aging inside the shop's walk-in refrigerated meat locker. In most meat processing plants, dry aging has gone by the wayside because the necessary fourteen to twenty-eight days take up too much precious time and space and reduce yields through moisture loss. It's all a matter of taste, but many people find dry aging critical to giving the muscles their due time to dry and contract, concentrating the flavors, and letting the calpain enzymes do their tenderizing work.

As I watched Kevin's workers muscle in six sides of grain-fed beef along a system of rails and pulleys hung from the ceiling, I saw that the contrasts with the grassfed bodies were dramatic. Corn-finished at a local farm, the carcasses wore a thick coat of fat, and each side outweighed the grassfed by one hundred pounds.

Between the twelfth and thirteenth ribs is the place where USDA inspectors peek inside the rib-eye muscle to gauge yield and grade the meat on a scale of standard, select, choice, and prime. They look for the thickness of the fat around the muscle and the marbling within it. Grassfed beef hardly ever rates above select because the intramuscular fat doesn't develop from grass the way it does from high-carbohydrate feedlot diets. (These days, less beef than ever—no matter where it comes from—is making prime and choice, the two highest grades, which may call into question the preeminence of the USDA's rating scale in judging beef. It's only one measure of quality, and a shallow one at that. Sure, fat is flavor, but that grassfed is so much beefier has something to do with amino acids, turpenes, and a host of flavonoid mysteries that demand far more research.)

The cutting room was outfitted with band saws, stainless steel cutting tables, and a washing machine–sized meat grinder. It felt as cold as the meat locker and I kept my fleece on under the white coat Kevin had loaned me. Three fresh-faced apprentices stood by to trim, grind, and

wrap according to each customer's cutting order and Kevin's explicit instructions.

The carcass hung upside down from the gambrel cord, the loop of the achilles near the hock, its neck aimed at the ground. With the tip of his slender boning knife, Kevin counted the ribs upward, to find the place where he would divide the hulk of the shoulder called the chuck from the chest cavity. He lifted an electric saw off its hook on the wall and cut horizontally through the backbone, and hoisted the chuck onto his table saw. He pointed to the ruby muscles at the cut line and said, "I could get two more rib steaks off of there if I wanted to." Then flicked on the machine and sliced off the neck and the forearm, tossing the parts onto the table where his assistants boned it for the grind. Without wasting a moment, he measured off and cut three-inch-thick chuck roasts with the band saw. As quickly as I could dice an onion, he had dismantled that entire primal into cuts for packaging, ready to cook.

He was methodical and watchful as he worked, neither wasteful nor stingy. As a cook and a long-time customer, I appreciated his high standards when he removed bone chips and sinew from the trim meat slated for the grinder. "I don't put anything into the ground beef that I wouldn't want to eat myself," he said with a grin.

The art of butchery, despite its gory associations, has an element of finesse. Smooth and even, well-trimmed, manageably-sized, and correctly labeled cuts are part of what quality-conscious butchers like Kevin offer their customers. As he expertly tied a rib roast and took the time to trim a sirloin roast into a shape that would cook evenly, it seemed he had in mind the cook who would next handle this meat.

Kevin scoffed about the new trendy cuts when I asked him on other visits to show me the location of muscles marketed as flatiron, bavette, and culotte. Butchery is a trade learned the old-fashioned way, and Kevin is old-school. Those fancy, foreign names amused him. Nevertheless, he indulged me, and as he butterflied the top blade roast—the now-famous flatiron—to remove the sheath of gristle between the marbled meat, he appeared a bit interested in it himself.

The chilled room took on the faint scent of tin and a vague savoriness as he sawed, sliced, and carved his way through the rib, loin, and round. Bits of meat littered the concrete floor. Kevin paused to point out the color differences in the flesh, from the deep red of the sirloin to the blush of tenderloin. "The most-used muscle has the most amount of fla-vor," Kevin said. He mentioned how he liked to make corned beef out of bottom round roast, aka rump roast, that ultra-lean, troublesome cut, and cast off other bits of culinary know-how.

As a rule, butchers are no-nonsense, with little time on their hands for pleasantries, but ask for their opinion with genuine curiosity and they open up. From my time at Valley Meat and at other butcher shops, I appreciate how a butcher can be a cook's best resource. I've come to think of their pragmatic and penny-wise approach as cooking like a butcher, and it's formed the basis for these cooking principles I swear by:

- Cooking like a butcher is being smart about how you cook each cut. It entails applying the correct cooking methods for the right amount of time to bring out the meat's best potential, no matter if it's a T-bone steak or a cube steak.

- Cooking like a butcher is using each cut scrupu-lously, such as selecting the plentiful, cheaper round cuts—thinly sliced—for stir-fries and reserving premium steaks for the grill.

- Cooking like a butcher is knowing what you like from the direct experience of handling it, cooking it, and forming your own opinions.

- Cooking like a butcher is practicing good sanita-tion and safe meat handling practices at all times and treating the meat with care from start to finish.

- Cooking like a butcher is stepping beyond the safety of steak to try grilling a roast, making corned beef, or grinding sausage to appreciate all that beef can be.

- Cooking like a butcher is recognizing that price is not the same as value, which is what the most versatile cuts like brisket, chuck roast, and top round roast have in spades.

- Cooking like a butcher is appreciating the tastiest, underappreciated cuts, like top round and chuck-eye steak (the "poor man's Delmonico"), and eschewing the overrated tenderloin.

- Cooking like a butcher is having the skills that can make you a more versatile and confident cook, including deboning a roast to cut your own steaks, trimming your own meat, and *always* slic-ing against the grain.

- Cooking like a butcher is leaving well enough alone when it comes to a rib-eye steak or strip loin, because it's hard to improve on them.

- Cooking like a butcher means always having a sharp knife.

HARVEST DAY

One evening in Portland, Oregon, I attended a dinner celebrating Wallowa Valley cattle ranchers and organized by Slow Food, the international organization devoted to sustainable foodways. All three ranchers were women, who gave short talks to the fifty diners about to sample their grassfed beef. One rancher, 6 Ranch owner Liza Jane Nichols, dove into talking about her Corriente, purebred descendants of the first Spanish breeds introduced to the Americas. In describing the cattle's healthy, free-ranging life on her family's ranch, she mentioned the quickness with which they were killed. "Happy cow, dead cow," she said. Shocked laughter ripped through the room, and then silence for three slow heartbeats.

Killing animals is our last great taboo, wrote farmer, poet, and essayist Brian Brett. Death is the unspeakable truth of beef eating that most people don't want to think about, never mind discuss. Perhaps that is why it's called "harvesting."

Rancher Cory Carman once confided that she used to lie awake at night before every slaughtering day. After many harvests, she says, she now understands that she and the cows have a nonverbal contract. "I promise them a comfortable life," she said, "and then it ends one day." Bob Dickson who runs Dayton Natural Meats said that the slaughter is the most difficult part of the process, for his staff and the USDA inspector alike.

There is such a thing, I've learned, as a good kill: when the cattle are clueless and it's quickly done. No happy accident, a good kill is the result of calculated efforts to keep the animals calm, whether they're slaughtered in a processing facility, large or small, or on the farm. By acknowledging and even witnessing this killing—not denying or glossing over it—I have become more aware of what the meat means.

On the morning I watched an on-farm harvest, a traveling butcher arrived at the McClaran Ranch in Joseph in his enclosed trailer. One of the oldest and largest family ranches in the county, the McClarans run one thousand head on their own lands and on public land allotments. Longtime members of Country Natural Beef, the family still sells a portion of their cattle to the commodity, or generic market. But the McClaran daughters, who are in their twenties and taking over the ranch, are most interested in grassfed beef production. On this day, twelve of their grassfed animals were to be harvested, exempted from USDA inspection when purchased live as in a cow-pool (page 32). (For all other sales, ranchers must haul their animals a minimum of three hours to the nearest USDA-approved facility. The scarcity of slaughtering facilities is a hardship on them all.)

Bearded, with weary blue eyes, the slaughterer I'll call Don wore a gown-length green rubber apron. A scabbard on a chain hung low on his waist. A hero in this community, Don travels from farm to farm, harvesting pigs, sheep, goats, and cattle. He's expert and irreplaceable, but wary of any attention to his craft. His assistant that day was Kevin, my butcher from Valley Meat, who was pitching in for the day. This job is so arduous that Don was having a hard time keeping good help. One of the McClaran cowboys and I watched from a distance, talking in whispers, as Don set to work.

"C'mon girl," he said softly, leading a Black Angus heifer into the pen. The moment was tense as he took aim with his rifle and dispatched her with a single shot. She fell, and without delay, he slashed her throat with a smooth stroke of his short-bladed knife. For several uncomfortable moments, I watched the body quiver. Her hooves thrashed three times, and then she lay still.

With death behind us, everyone breathed again as Don set to work. He used that same knife, pausing to sharpen it with the steel on his chain belt, to remove the head and hooves and slit the belly. He obliged me by cutting out the cheeks, some of the parts and offal I'd come to claim. He slipped the hook at the end of a hydraulic lift through the gambrel cord loop and switched on the lift, hoisting the animal off the ground to peel off the hide. Upended, the distended four-chambered stomach fell from the abdominal cavity into Don's arms. He heaved it aside and cut out the heart and watermelon-sized liver. With an electric saw, he divided the whole into halves straight down the spine. He loaded the dressed carcass into the van for delivery to Valley Meat's locker and turned, straightened up his back, and with a solemn look on his face, walked toward the animals awaiting him in the pen.

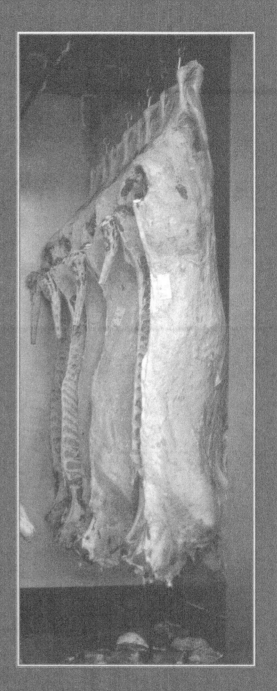

The Pure Beef Cut Guide

Consider this custom-made beef cut guide like a map. The geography of the large muscle groups, their fat rivers and bone borders will, like a good map, help you navigate in the kitchen. Putting the beef cuts in context can broaden your understanding of why certain cuts respond best to specific cooking methods. And, with time and familiarity, this giant beef cut chart will make sense to you.

Every country has its own meat cutting traditions, and it's freeing simply to note that cut charts vary; the placement of those divisions is not based on universal law. The Italians map the parts much differently than the Argentinians, as well as the French, the British, and the Japanese. Cut lines reveal how each cuisine values the various parts of the carcass and determine how those parts are cooked.

Cutting decisions are judgments, preferences, and practices that are as arbitrary as the state lines on the US map. Some of the divisions are natural, such as the seams between muscles, but most are like a border cutting across a river—necessary to create order in the natural world. There was a period of time when you'd get different cuts from a Chicago butcher than from a California butcher, based on passed-down knowledge. The concentration of the beef processing and packaging, and the publication of *The Meat Buyer's Guide* by the North American Meat Processors Association, have standardized the cut chart nationwide.

With the resurgence of beef butchery, times are changing once again. Custom butchers can make cutting decisions that vary from the industry standards to meet customer requests and interest. Meat cutting is also shifting in response to the rigorous muscle research funded by the beef industry to locate new value-added cuts. Two steaks, the top blade, aka flatiron, and shoulder tender, aka teres major, are recent success stories, propelled to popularity by restaurants and chefs. Excavated from the chuck, these single-muscle cuts were found through a series of university-based studies to test for color, connective tissue quantity, flavor, juiciness, and tenderness. So far, the new cuts from the bottom round, like the Western Griller, have proved less popular. Ongoing research of the terra incognita will likely bring more beef discoveries—and new cut names—down the road.

PURE BEEF CUT GUIDE

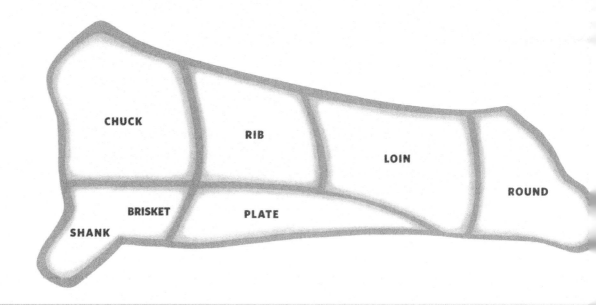

CHUCK

Cuts for braising (chapter 5, page 100); slow roasting or smoking (chapter 8, page 197); simmering (chapter 9, page 224); or in charcuterie (chapter 10, page 251). In addition, Shoulder Tender and Top Blade Steaks are suited to grilling or pan searing (chapter 7, page 162)

CHUCK ROAST (BONE-IN)

CHUCK ROAST (BONELESS)

SHORT RIBS (BONELESS)

SHOULDER TENDER

TOP BLADE STEAK

ARM POT ROAST

CROSS RIB ROAST

STEW BEEF

GROUND BEEF*

RIB

Cuts for roasting (chapter 8, page 197) or grilling or pan searing (chapter 7, page 162).

RIB ROAST (BONE-IN)

RIB STEAK (BONE-IN)

RIB STEAK (BONELESS)

RIB-EYE ROAST

BACK RIBS

*for all ground beef preparations see chapte (page 68) and chapter 10 (page 251)

LOIN

Cuts for quick cooking (chapter 6, page 132); roasting (chapter 8, page 197); or grilling or pan searing (chapter 7, page 162).

STRIP LOIN STEAK (BONE-IN)

STRIP LOIN STEAK (BONELESS)

STRIP LOIN ROAST

T-BONE STEAK

TENDERLOIN STEAK (FILET MIGNON)

TENDERLOIN

SIRLOIN CAP (CULOTTE)

TOP SIRLOIN STEAK

FLANK STEAK

SIRLOIN FLAP (BAVETTE)

TRI-TIP ROAST

TOP SIRLOIN ROAST

SHANK

Cuts for braising (chapter 5, page 100) or simmering (chapter 9, page 224).

SHANK

MARROW BONES

STEW BEEF (ALSO FROM OTHER PRIMALS)

BRISKET

Cuts for braising (chapter 5, page 100); slow roasting or smoking (chapter 8, page 197); simmering (chapter 9, page 224); or in charcuterie (chapter 10, page 251).

BRISKET (POINT)

BRISKET (FLAT)

ROUND

Cuts for quick cooking (chapter 6, page 132); or roasting (chapter 8, page 197); or charcuterie (chapter 10, page 251).

TOP ROUND STEAK

TOP ROUND ROAST

EYE ROUND

CUBE STEAK

GROUND BEEF*

SIRLOIN TIP STEAK

SIRLOIN TIP ROAST

TOP ROUND ROAST

PLATE

Cuts for braising (chapter 5, page 100) or in charcuterie (chapter 10, page 251).

SHORT RIBS

STEW BEEF

GROUND BEEF*

Cuts for quick cooking (chapter 6, page 132) or grilling or pan searing (chapter 7, page 162).

SKIRT STEAK

HANGER STEAK

I understand why there is so much confusion over beef cuts every week when I receive the circular from Joseph Family Foods market. London broil is on sale one week, but what is it, exactly? When I was growing up, it meant flank steak, but now it usually signifies a top-quality top round steak. Care for a New York steak? That can be a boneless steak from the sirloin or from the strip loin. How about a pot roast? That name gets slapped on any chuck roast. It's enough to make anyone stick to steaks and burgers.

Many people try to learn beef cuts by studying those cut charts printed in every meat book—the diagram of a steer in profile with dotted lines separating it into big sections with pictures of meats orbiting around it. I spent hours studying those beef charts, but it never sank in. Even if I memorized a few facts, such as that the cross rib roast is cut from just above the brisket or that the top round is the inside of the cow's leg, it didn't relate to what I did in the kitchen.

One day it dawned on me that learning beef cuts is just like that joke about eating an elephant. You have to do it in small bites. Nobody starts with a whole cow, even people like me who get a year's supply of beef in one lump delivery. When the bulk of boxes arrive containing one- to five-pound vacuum-sealed packages, it does not resemble any animal, only a jumbled meat section at the supermarket.

If I could learn the animal cut by cut, I reasoned, perhaps I could work my way toward understanding the whole. I focused on one cut at a time—the one I wanted to cook. At first, I referred to the cut chart only to locate the general area it came from, which steered me toward a slow cooking method, like braising or slow-roasting, or toward a fast cooking method, like pan-searing or high-heat roasting. The fact is, other than the rib and loin primals—the tender middle section—most beef cuts prefer gentle heat, so it wasn't hard to catch on. Piece by piece, I learned each cut's attributes and cooking qualities, and began to recognize them by their shapes, fat contours, and bones, if any. It all came slowly, by handling the meat myself. Once I'd sliced a top round roast into steaks, deboned a rib roast, and ground my own beef from chuck roast trim, the cut chart started to make sense.

Butchering for Home Cooks

Butchering a gigantic beef carcass takes years to master, but anyone can start small. Hands-on practice and repetition are the steps to progress. Everyone feels tentative at first (even professional chefs who are only used to ready-to-cook steaks), but give it a try—you can't hurt the meat. To prepare yourself, watch a video demonstration online (that's how I learned to clean and trim beef heart, and now I've got it down) or find a butchery class near you. You could even try asking an amenable butcher if you may observe during a slow period in the shop. With guided instruction, you'll not only become more familiar and confident handling all the beef you cook, you'll approach the meat counter empowered with enough information to talk with the butcher and make your purchases. The skills in this list are useful for anyone. Just equip yourself with the largest cutting board you can find (I use plastic so that I can sterilize it in the dishwasher) and good-quality (that doesn't mean expensive) knives. Have a flexible five- or six-inch boning knife (A) for trimming fat and removing bones, a chef's or utility knife (B) for chopping and slicing raw meat , and a long-bladed slicer for cooked meat (C).

No matter the knife, a sharp edge will make you more proficient. Only a well-honed knife lets you make the gliding, smooth strokes that produce clean cuts and keep you safe from slippage. To maintain sharpness, make a habit of running the blade along the steel—the long lance that comes with every knife set—ten to twelve times every time before you use it. (It's just one of those pesky things, like flossing regularly). If your knife has grown too dull to cut cleanly into a piece of paper towel held up with one hand, it's time to sharpen your knife. Use any one of the no-brainer sharpeners on the market and store it in the knife drawer as a reminder to practice what the butchers teach. Or, you can pay to have your knives professionally sharpened.

For reference purposes only, I've organized this list alphabetically by topic. Skim it to find the essentials. Take note of special occasion skills, including tying a roast, boning, and cutting your own steaks—among many others—so that you can come back to them when you have an opportunity to try them out.

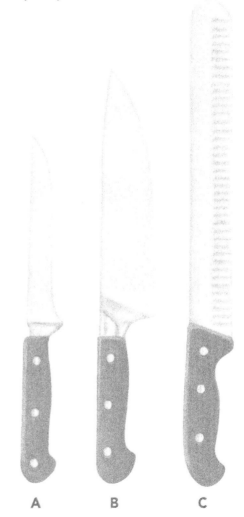

A　　B　　C

BONING

To remove bones before cooking, use a flexible boning knife. Use the blade to feel and hear where it scrapes against the bone and follow the contours to trim off all the meat as cleanly as you can. Short ribs, if you have some on hand, are a great way to practice boning raw meat, and you can use the meat to braise or grind it for hamburger patties or sausage. A four-bone rib roast is the ultimate challenge, not because it is difficult but because it's a precious piece of meat. Use a boning knife to pry around the rib bones, then slice with long shallow strokes along the backbone to free the whole rib-eye muscle.

To bone a cooked steak or roast for easy slicing, let it rest first. Use a boning knife to separate the meat from the bone and switch to a slicing knife to make serving slices. Be sure to collect any bones in the freezer for future stock making.

BUTTERFLYING

To prepare a roast—small or large—with a rounded shape for stuffing, place the meat on your cutting board running away from you the long way. Hold your boning knife parallel to and one inch above the cutting board. Use the tip of the knife to make one long cut down the full length of the roast about one inch deep. Use the fingers of your other hand to pry the cut open and repeat the cut over and over again, keeping the one-inch thickness of the meat until it unrolls to lie flat.

If the meat is flat like flank steak, position a chef's knife, eight inches or longer, to divide its thickness in half. Keep the blade parallel to the cutting board. With the palm of your non-cutting hand on top of the steak to hold it firmly, slice through the meat using long, shallow strokes to come within one to one-half inch of the edge (see illustration below). It will open like a book.

In all cases, smooth slicing—not a sawing motion—prevents raggedness, but, once rolled and tied, even your first efforts will be quite presentable.

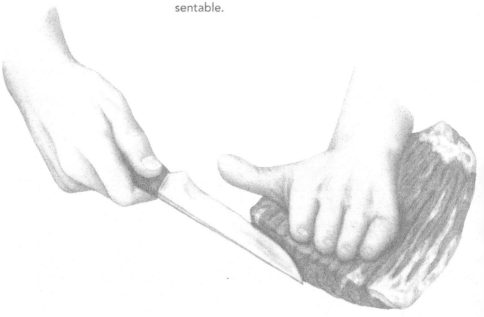

CHOPPING AND MINCING

To dice meat for tacos, empanadas, or dishes that call for sautéing or stir-frying chopped meat, chill the steak in the freezer for twenty minutes. Use a chef's or utility knife to slice the meat ¼ inch thick (see illustration **A** below). Turn each slice on its side and cut it into ¼-inch strips, then cut these strips across ¼ inch thick to make even ¼-inch dice (see illustration **B** below). You'll get more consistent cuts if you chop the meat by hand, though you may use a food processor when you're not concerned about uniformity. When using a food processor, first cut the meat into 1-inch cubes and then pulse it in the machine with rapid-fire bursts until the meat is finely chopped but before it gets puréed.

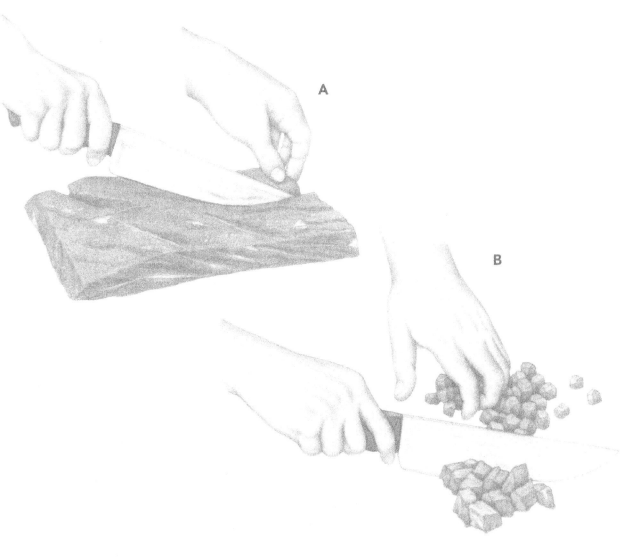

A

B

CLEANING OFFAL

HEART: Cut the heart in half or into quarters if you'll be cutting it into strips. Use a boning knife to trim off all of the outside fat and the vessels from the interior chambers until what remains is pure maroon muscle. Cut into strips for marinating and grilling, slice very thin or chop to stir-fry or sauté it.

KIDNEYS: Fresh kidneys, when you can get them, have a mild odor; soak them in a bowl of cold water for two to four hours to diminish it. Use a paring knife to trim off the thin outer membrane, cut in half to remove the vessels, and cut the kidney along the segments to make bite-size pieces.

TONGUE: Trim the underside and base of the tongue before simmering or curing to make corned tongue. Once you've cooked it until a wooden skewer slides through the tongue with ease, let the meat cool just until you can handle it and peel off all of the skin with your fingers while it's still warm. Slice, cube, or dice the tongue to eat it as is or to pan-fry, sauté, or grill it.

CUTTING STEAKS

FROM A BLADE CHUCK ROAST: Typically used for pot roast, this cut has two tender steaks—top blade (aka flatiron) and chuck-eye—that you can prize out yourself to cook with a high-heat method. Blade chuck is recognized by the slender bone running through it and is the first cut off the chuck primal next to the rib section. To free the top blade steak, aka flatiron, simply run your knife blade along the bone (freeze the bone to make stock later). Cook it as a steak or slice it into strips for satay. The chuck-eye is the more rounded collection of muscles above the bottom bone (the chine bone). To remove it, cut along the fat seam just above it and trim off the bone; you now have a premium grilling steak. What remains is a tougher strip of meat that you can braise whole, cube for stew meat, or grind.

FROM A BONELESS ROAST: Cutting your own steaks from boneless rib-eye, strip loin, sirloin, sirloin tip, aka round tip, and top round roast is a smart way to save money. Use a chef's knife with an eight-inch or longer blade and decide on the thickness—¾ inch is a thin steak that cooks quickly, 1 inch is a nice standard, 1½ inches is the thickest I like. Tip the blade forward and push straight down through the meat, ideally in a single, smooth motion (see illustration below).

FROM A THICK T-BONE OR PORTERHOUSE: You can get two medallions from a single steak that's at least 1½ inch thick. By cutting along the bone to remove it (freeze the bone to make stock later), you'll get one tenderloin and one boneless strip loin. If you like, trim the fat to make a pleasing shape to grill or sauté.

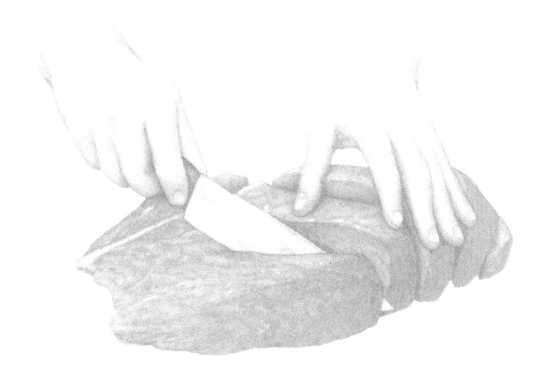

CUTTING STEW MEAT

To cut your own beef for stew, trim the exterior fat from any chuck roast, brisket, or sirloin tip roast, aka round tip roast. (Round roasts, I have consistently found, make dry stew meat; reserve them for slow-roasting, stir-frying, chopping, or grinding.) Depending on the size of the serving pieces you want, or to control the timing (smaller cubes will cook in less time), use a chef's or utility knife to cut the meat into strips one-half to three inches wide. Crosscut the strips into cubes, making them as uniform as you can for even cooking (see illustration below). As you cut, trim away any excess fat and discard it.

Use this same method for cutting your own kebab meat.

GRINDING BEEF

Set up a hand-cranked or electric meat grinder with the blade and the plate size called for in the recipe. Cut the meat into one-inch cubes and chill it well, or freeze it for twenty minutes. Push the cubes into the feeder tube and collect the grind in a cold metal bowl. Only use a food processor for grinding whole muscle meat cuts, since the blade will not sever sinew (a fact I learned the hard way when I ground short ribs in the food processor only to create an inedible burger). Process up to eight ounces at a time, pulsing the beef just until it becomes finely chopped.

SLICING AGAINST THE GRAIN

Cutting across the meat fibers for serving makes the meat easiest to chew. The grain is more visible when the meat is raw, so take a long look before you cook it. After cooking, slice off the end of the steak or roast and examine it carefully. If you see long strands of meat running parallel to one another, you're cutting *with* the grain. Stop, turn the meat ninety degrees, and start again. If your first slice looks like the cut end of a thick rope, you're slicing *against* the grain and all is well.

TRIMMING

Exterior fat is the easiest to remove with any sharp knife. Exterior fat insulates and bastes beef while it cooks, so it's a good idea to leave it at least ¼ inch thick when using high-heat methods with the tenderest cuts.

Some steaks, including hanger steak and some top blade steaks, aka flatiron, have a thin line of gristle running through them. It will not break down during cooking, so you'll need to decide whether to slice it out before or after cooking. Either way, you need to cut all the way through the meat to make two thin steaks.

Silver skin, or elastin, is a shiny, skin-thin fat that does not break down during cooking. It's common on tenderloin and flank steak, and you may find traces of it on other cuts as well. To trim it off, slip a boning knife just under the silver skin and make a short slice to lift a piece of it up for a handle. Grab the handle with your free hand and pull, while slicing in the opposite direction to remove a thin strip (see illustration below). Repeat this two-step process until you've removed it all.

FOR SHORT RIBS: To reduce the amount of defatting after cooking, trim the exterior fat on short ribs to ¼ inch. With the blade of a boning knife parallel to the cutting board, slip the tip into the fat and cut away strips of fat, repeating until the exterior fat is as thin as you want it.

FOR SKIRT STEAK: This cut sometimes comes with a thin, papery membrane attached, which is easy to peel off by hand. Use a boning knife to slice under the membrane to free up one end and make a handle. Put your palm flat on the free end of the skirt steak and pull on the handle firmly to strip off the membrane.

FOR STEW BEEF: Cut the beef into cubes and remove any surface fat with a slice of your knife.

FOR STEAKS AND ROASTS: Trim off fat after cooking, depending on your taste, by tracing your knife between the fat and the lean muscle. On large roasts, you may choose to leave the fat cap in place before serving, since many people enjoy eating it, especially when it's beautifully browned.

TYING A ROAST

Tie up a roast when you want to maintain an even shape for uniform cooking or need to contain a stuffing. Knot strands of butcher's twine or place silicone bands (Sources, page 270) along the roast, evenly spaced every two to three inches, to secure it. When the roast is cooked, clip off the twine or bands with kitchen shears while the meat rests so they won't get in the way of slicing.

Beef Cooking Basics

When beef meets heat, many biochemical changes occur within the proteins and fats. Much of what transpires is within your control, and an understanding of basic meat science in beef cookery can help you become more self-assured and versatile in handling any cut. These principles hold true no matter if the beef you buy is grassfed, natural, organic, or standard commodity (and they apply to other meats, including veal, game, lamb, and pork).

SLOW METHODS

Braising, stewing, simmering, slow roasting, and smoking call for low temperatures (typically below 300°F) and long cooking times (often an hour or more). Most of these techniques rely on moisture—either added in the form of water or stock or the liquid present within the muscle—to convey the heat that melts the collagen beginning at 150°F. Slow-roasting and smoking are dry-heat methods that heat the meat gradually so that the proteins do not bind up and harden as they do when blasted with heat.

FAST METHODS

Grilling, roasting, broiling, pan searing, sautéing, and stir-frying employ high temperatures (typically over 400°F) for short time periods (often ten minutes or less). The surface browns rapidly and heat radiates toward the meat's interior, which causes the muscle fibers to contract and lose moisture. In the dry heat conditions in the oven or on the grill, the muscle fibers squeeze out water within the protein cells while the fats soften and begin to melt. Short cooking preserves moisture and leaves the meat juicy. Monitoring the internal temperature prevents the meat from reaching above 149°F, the stage where protein hardening begins and meat fibers toughen.

SOUS-VIDE, A MODERN SLOW METHOD

This temperature controlled, hot water immersion technique is the ultimate in slow cooking. Restaurant chefs love sous-vide—a cooking technology that originated in France and means "under pressure"—because it allows them to calibrate the doneness of a steak to medium-rare, for example, and then keep it ready to serve for hours. Like poaching, sous-vide does not achieve high enough temperatures to brown meat, so chefs sear or use a blow torch to sear their steaks.

I've cooked sous-vide enough to recognize that it works wonders on meat fibers and fat while preserving every drop of juice. Sealed in a vacuum packaging and submerged into water anywhere from 132°F to 145°F depending on the cut, the beef cooks ever so slowly—up to 72 hours—and precisely. The downside is that this modern method requires specialized equipment, longer cooking durations and critical calibrations of time and temperature compared to traditional cooking techniques. Although you won't find sous-vide among the recipes in *Pure Beef*, anyone with a taste for cooking adventure can explore the range of equipment options online (from the high-tech SousVide Supreme methods) and apply them to any beef cut covered in the book.

The Cut-Cook Connection: A Nose-to-Tail Guide

To cook beef with confidence and consistency, you do not need a complete cow anatomy course. All you need to know is whether the cut you have in hand is naturally tender or tough. If it's one of the tough cuts from the ends of the cow, you want a slow method that releases the meat bundles from the fats that bind them. If it's one of the tender middle cuts, you can use a fast method that creates tasty surface browning while cooking the interior as quickly as possible. (Not to confuse matters, but you can also use slow methods with the tender cuts. In general, we stick to high-heat methods whenever possible for that unbeatable browning effect. See Essential Browning, page 61.)

So, how do you tell the tough and slow from the tender and fast?

The most useful tool for understanding beef cuts is one I learned from meat scientist Bob Dickson, who taught butchery for twenty-five years at Oregon State University: Our own bodies. I'd often notice how in conversations about meat cuts with experts, they'd slap their thigh or reach around to their shoulder blade, but Bob put it all together for me. Granted, we are not remotely related to *bos Taurus,* but the physiology is less important than the activity that each body part gets in the course of a day.

In the simplest terms, exercised muscles are tough, while supportive muscles are tender. Just as in cows, our midsections contain the least-used muscles, so they are the tenderest muscles in our bodies. Tender muscles have more intramuscular fat and fine fibers gently stretched like a hammock. Those tough muscles at our active upper and lower extremities are threaded with rubbery connective tissue and have thick, coarse fibers from a lifetime spent contracting in exertion. These basic body parts—the two tough ends and the long tender middle—relate to the four major sections of the cow called primals: the chuck in the front and round in the rear are the tough ends; the rib and loin are the tender middles.

THE TOUGH ENDS

Chuck is the term used for the shoulder on beef cattle. As on our own bodies, the shoulder contains a complex network of highly active muscle groups. They allow a wide range of motion while supporting our necks and heads, even when we're at rest. For cows that spend their lives hoisting a fifty-pound head up and down to eat, these are the heavy-lifting muscles, riddled with the connective tissues that make them some of the toughest cuts. They are also among the tastiest.

As established by the North American Meat Processors Association, the chuck primal consists of the neck to the first five of the thirteen rib bones, down to just above the elbow. This is a big area on a broad-shouldered animal, and makes up 29 percent of the total yield from a whole beef carcass. If the label on a large roast reads "chuck," you have one of the classic pot roast cuts. You can trust it in any slow method that cooks the collageny connective tissue over low, moist heat with ample time, especially braising and stewing, which are explored in chapter 5. Slow-roasting and smoking are two dry-heat methods (the moisture from *within* the meat cooks the collagen) ideal for chuck roast and are covered in chapter 8. Much of the chuck ends up as trim or, in butcher's parlance, "the grind," which makes excellent ground beef, the basis for a range of dishes in chapter 4. While most chuck cuts are too sinewy for fast methods, there are rare exceptions, such as the new steaks like top blade, aka flatiron, in chapter 7.

Round is the name for the cattle's hindquarters. It corresponds to our buttocks and upper thighs, which consist of large, lean muscle groups that get loads of exercise (even though it may not seem like it). In cattle, these muscles work all day, every day standing and ambling around while out with the herd. Toughness is only part of the issue with the round. Its leanness—a lack of intramuscular fat—coupled with thick muscle fibers makes this primal one of the most challenging for cooks. At the same time, cuts from this primal are the most economical.

The round is the second largest of all the primals but yields the most beef per animal with little fat going to waste. It begins at the hip joint and reaches all the way to the hock. Many retail round cuts from the thigh are sold as roasts. They include top round (the inner thigh and most tender) and bottom round (the outer thigh and the least tender), and eye round (a not-so-tender muscle that sits between them). Slow-roasting is the best cooking method for these boneless, lean, and flavorful roasts (along with thin slicing, as in deli-style roast beef, to optimize tenderness), which is addressed in chapter 8. Round roasts are never used in this book for pot roast or stew because they turn out stringy and dry; only sirloin tip roast, aka round tip roast, a cut that sits at the juncture of the loin and the round, results in braises and stews worth eating and is included in chapter 5.

There are just three exceptions to this slow-cooking rule of thumb for the round primal—sirloin tip, top round, and mechanically tenderized round steaks. Both sirloin tip steaks, aka round tip steaks, and top round steaks can handle the fast, high-heat cooking methods of grilling or pan-frying, provided they are cooked quickly to medium rare. Cubed, Swiss, or pounded steaks from the round are suitable, though still chewy, options for pan-frying and are the popular chicken fried steak cut. Chapter 7 includes several examples. Once sliced into slivers, chopped, or minced, the round cuts are also perfect for stir-frying, the ultimate fast and hot method picked up in chapter 6. What doesn't become a round roast or steak gets ground to make extra-lean ground beef for recipes in chapter 4 and chapter 10.

THE TENDER MIDDLE

Rib is the name for the primal cut containing most of the rib cage. On our bodies, it would extend from just below the sternum to the floating ribs, wrapping around the back. It plays a supportive role in cattle, too, encasing their vital organs and staying relatively stationary. The main muscle called the rib-eye hugs the spine and wears a cap of flat muscle. Fine grained and tender with constellations of fat, it is one of the most revered cuts on the whole carcass, sold for a premium as roasts or steaks.

The smallest primal, the rib, begins where the chuck is cut off at the fifth rib and ends at the twelfth. It is also the most uniform, with a ladder of rib bones and a cylinder of lean muscle capped with a blanket of fat. When the tips of the meaty rib bones are cut into short ribs, it presents a monumental seven-bone rib roast, which is often divided into one four-bone and one three-bone roast. Or, the back ribs can be removed so it becomes the boneless rib roast often called prime rib. Both of those imperial, special-occasion roasts are included in chapter 8. Most rib sections get sliced into steaks. Cut with the bone in, they are called rib steaks; without, they become rib-eyes. (This is one way a single cut goes by many names.) You'll find this supreme steak in chapter 7.

In roast or steak form, rib cuts take to fast cooking methods because they're naturally tender and marbled. Marbling—the wisps of intramuscular fat within the muscle—insulates the proteins and bastes the meat internally for high-heat grilling or roasting. Seared to a burnished brown with a perfectly pink interior, rib has become the ideal, what most people picture when they think about eating beef.

Loin is a long primal on the mid-section that follows the backbone from the last rib to the base of the sacrum. As we know too well, it's difficult to exercise the abdomen enough. The same goes for cattle, and it results in tender muscles that are the most desired on the entire beef carcass. Like luxury real estate, this primal commands top dollar.

On the beef cut chart, the loin extends from the thirteenth rib to the hip joint, excluding the belly. Two valuable muscles sit on either side of the loin bones: the tenderloin and the loin eye muscle. When the whole primal is cut into cross sections, you get the famous T-bone or porterhouse steaks, each containing a portion of both the tenderloin and loin eye muscles separated by bone. Often the tenderloin is removed whole to be sold as a roast or sliced into medallions, the famous filet mignon. What remains on the bone is called the strip loin, which is cut into another pricey steak—the strip loin steak, aka New York strip—bone in or boneless. Like the rib primal, the loin's lean, fine muscle fibers and marbling qualify it for any fast method. Steaks from this primal are included in chapter 7 and roasts in chapter 8.

The rear section of the loin is the sirloin, a jumble of muscles that become less tender as they near the round primal. The top sirloin is the most valuable of all, another fine roast or steak for fast methods of roasting, grilling, or pan-searing. The sirloin section also produces less costly but tasty and interesting steaks, including tri-tip, flank, and sirloin flap, aka bavette. Collected into a category called "bistro steaks," they get appropriate high-heat cooking treatments in chapter 7. Sirloin steaks are also good for cutting into chunks, strips, and cubes for grilling or broiling as used in the global cuisine recipes to be found in chapter 6.

MINOR PRIMALS

The brisket, foreshank, and plate are the industry names for the upper chest, front leg, and underbelly, respectively. Bony or with strata of fat, these are the least valued sections. But, for the motivated cook, there are interesting and valuable uses for these lesser parts.

Of all these, the brisket is the meatiest. In fact, this muscle is one ranchers use to gauge fat gain (they also measure at the pelvis and the top of the tail). A plump brisket is one sign that the animal is finished and ready for slaughter. The classic barbecue, corned beef, and pastrami cut, brisket demands slow cooking. There are two briskets per animal, and each is shaped like a torpedo. The tip is called the point, and it has a band of fat running through it; the flat is more uniform and lean under its fat cap. There are slow-cooking recipes for brisket in chapters 5, 8, and 10.

The foreshank is one tough cut, and what doesn't end up ground is simmered slowly to make exceptional stocks and soups. Likewise, the short ribs that are cut from the plate contain a lot of bone and cartilage. Only slow cooking brings forth their rewards. Both cuts are featured in chapter 9.

The plate contains the diaphragm—the thin skirt steak on the sides with the thicker hanger steak suspended in the middle. Both have become popular bistro-style steaks—coarse-grained, chewy, and flavorful—ideal for a fast sizzle on the grill, and are included in chapter 7.

BONES

Stripped of all the major muscles and cut through with band saws, the gigantic beef carcass becomes a weighty pile of bones. They have little market value, but are a plentiful and inexpensive resource for cooking. Chapter 9 explores their uses in depth.

There are three types of useful bones: meaty bones, collagen-rich bones, and marrow bones. Meaty bones, namely oxtail, short ribs, and shank, deliver loads of flavor into a simmering liquid over time. With the meat left on the bone or picked off, they yield just enough for a meal. Knuckle bones contain the most collagen, which gives body along with beefiness to the water in which they simmer for hours. But other beef bones make excellent stock, too, especially once roasted until the proteins brown delectably. For some, the marrow within the humerus and femur bones is a delicacy. These hollow bones are cross cut into sections to access the fatty beef essence within. Soaked and then roasted, marrow can be spread on toast, dabbed on a just-seared steak, or swirled into braised and stewed dishes—or a risotto (page 247)—to great effect.

OFFAL

Also known as organ meat, offal is becoming more accepted in this country as people embrace nose-to-tail eating, but you have to search for it (it's even last in this list). Most of the offal from slaughterhouses goes to the export markets of Asia and South America where they are delicacies.

Cooking with organ meats is the final frontier of beef cookery. To handle, clean, and trim these slippery parts takes some getting used to. Part of the problem is that offal resembles the living animal part, whereas a steak does not. Take tongue. Ignore the nubby taste buds and simmer it gently, peel it while it's warm, slice it thin, and you have at your disposal one of the beefiest cuts to eat as is, to bread and fry into cutlets, or to dice for tacos.

It's unfortunate that squeamishness (my own included) can get in the way of enjoying offal like beef heart—the leanest, meatiest muscle there is. Trimmed and thinly sliced, it can stand up to potent marinades for quick high-heat grilling or stir-frying, and it can be roasted. Kidneys, too, have a smooth texture, and are good seared in a skillet or slipped into a stew. Only beef liver, although I tricked it out with bacon and booze, was too mealy to chew and too potent to swallow though ground it makes great dog food. As for tripe, I did not find any available from grassfed beef producers who do not, as yet, have the processing options to utilize "everything but the moo." All the rest, you'll encounter here and there throughout the recipe chapters, most often listed under "More Choice Cuts."

GET A LITTLE TENDERNESS

Most beef cuts are not naturally butter-knife tender, but there are many ways for resourceful cooks to enhance that quality. All of them manipulate the connective tissues that bind the meat fibers.

Slow cooking is the most common and effective way to break down the connective tissues gradually until the meat is fall-apart tender. You can achieve this through simmering meat in a liquid, baking it in a low oven, or smoking it for hours. Mechanical tenderizing *before* cooking, by scoring, piercing, or pounding, also severs the tough connective tissues and does advance work so that your teeth don't have to. (Still, a cube steak will never trick your mouth into believing that it's chewing rib-eye.) Hand chopping or slicing beef cuts very thin for a satay or stir-fry achieves the same tenderizing result. The ultimate tenderizing method is grinding, which takes care of any toughness and leaves you with easy-to-chew ground beef ready for anything, from grilling to stewing to sausage-making.

Contrary to popular belief, marinating is not an effective method for tenderizing the tougher cuts. Marinades with an acidic ingredient, like lemon juice or vinegar, affect only the surface area of the meat. If exposed for too long, the meat can become unpleasantly mushy. The only success I've had tenderizing with marinades is with open-grained meats like skirt, which absorbs moisture readily, and when the beef is sliced very thin as in Coca-Cola Jerky (page 269). Overall, marinades are best as flavor boosters.

Finally, slicing against the grain is key to a tender eating experience. And for coarse-grained cuts, such as flank and sirloin flap steak, aka bavette, make those slices thin.

PART TWO

COOKING WITH GRASSFED BEEF

Grassfed beef is widely lauded as a healthier meat option. But those praises turn to criticism when you get it into the kitchen where it's gained an undeserved reputation for being tough, gamey, and dry. As a result, the advice for cooking grassfed beef is rife with warnings:

Don't cook it over high heat!

Don't cook it past medium rare!

Don't salt the meat before cooking, or it will be dry!

I took some of these tips to heart when I read them repeatedly. They caused me to doubt my own experiences, and so I tested them all. I avoided searing my steaks, cooking roasts past medium rare, and salting the meat before cooking it. Not one of these techniques made the meat perform better or become more tender or juicy, and I missed the salt and alluring brown crust. Most surprising of all was that while *some* cuts of the leanest grassfed beef may take less time to cook than their conventional counterparts, *other* fatty cuts can take longer.

This experiment restored my trust in the methods that have produced fantastic results for the nearly ten years I've been cooking only grassfed beef. I detail those guidelines in this section and implement them in every recipe, but, to sum it up:

season it well; brown it whenever you'd like; use an appropriate cooking method; and cook it shy of the serving temperature you want.

Before I get into these basic cooking principles, it needs to be said that not all grassfed is created equal. Like other artisanal products, including bread, cheese, and wine, grassfed beef is not consistent from producer to producer, place to place, or year to year. Some ranchers have devined the magic formula for producing pasture-raised beef that is out of this world. (To this day, no one has pinpointed whether it's the genetic line, the soils, the grasses, the age at slaughter, or a host of other variables that make exceptional muscle meat. Likely, it is a combination of all those facets.)

Your first mission is to find grassfed beef you adore (How to Taste Artisan Beef, page 34) through the best source available to you—and there are many more all the time. Once you have high-quality beef in hand, you can cook it to your satisfaction. I've worked with dozens of brands that vary by breed, age at slaughter, finishing feed, and brand to ensure that the cooking principles laid out here succeed in every instance.

Skillful cooking of grassfed beef begins by matching each cut with the proper slow or fast method (The Cut-Cook Connection, page 53). Nearly every end cut, from the shoulder to the cheeks and the rump to the oxtail, is tough and needs low, slow cooking. Only the middle parts—all the places you could reach if you were mounted on a steer—can handle the hot and fast cooking of a flaming grill or smoldering cast-iron pan. This holds true for grassfed beef as well as natural and organic beef from any breed or source.

But grassfed beef *is* different. Its composition, textures, and tastes are unlike conventional, grain-finished beef and more like wild game. To cook it well requires fine-tuning standard cooking methods to preserve its moisture, highlight its tenderness, and complement its distinctive flavors.

Unique Beef

It's funny how strange regular beef looks to me now, especially in its raw state. Side by side, grassfed and generic commodity beef don't even look like the same meat: grassfed is red as a beet instead of rosy pink from increased myoglobin pigments; it is nearly fat-free where most beef is fat-streaked and marbled; the meat is compact and firm like a relaxed bicep muscle, not slack and yielding. Finally, the cuts from grassfed beef are smaller—sometimes dramatically, by as much as 40 percent by weight—a convenient form of portion control for anyone who wants to eat less meat.

What sets grassfed beef apart in the kitchen is its leanness, which makes it more sensitive to heat. From the outside fat cover on the muscles to its internal marbling, fat protects muscle fibers from heat. Grain-fed beef, well insulated by its fat, can be cooked at higher temperatures for longer periods of time without catastrophe. In grassfed beef lacking any extra fat insurance, timing is everything.

Beef is up to 75 percent water, but lean beef has a lower water-holding capacity than fattier beef. The moisture trapped inside the meat combines with fat to create sensations of juiciness in your mouth. It also affects perceptions of the meat's tenderness, which explains why grassfed beef got a reputation for being tough when it was only dry.

Prolonged cooking of grassfed beef contracts the muscle fibers and rapidly squeezes out the juices to the point meat scientists aptly call protein hardening. This is why, when grilling steaks or hamburgers, the longer the meat is cooked, the tougher and less juicy it becomes. Cooking methods and times that preserve the moisture present within the meat are critical to good eating.

All of these qualities affect your chewing experience, since lubrication from both fat and moisture increases the sensations of tenderness in your mouth. (Super lean beef is called squeaky beef, which nobody likes.) Still, even the most tender grassfed beef cuts will not be as soft as grain-finished beef, and long-braised cuts, including brisket and pot roast, will retain some texture, not "melt in your mouth." While high-quality grassfed beef can be as tender as grain-finished beef, it will always offer a bit of chew—a trait I consider a bonus, since I *like* to chew.

Size is another factor that distinguishes most grassfed beef from standard commodity beef and shortens cooking times. Whole roasts of grassfed beef are often smaller because the animals gain weight much more slowly over their lifetime on pasture than in feedlots. (Cattle fed high-calorie rations maintain weight gains consistently from month to month while cattle on grass gain only at the height of the grass-growing season.) Beef from some small-framed breeds, such as Corriente, are smaller still.

Your awareness and attention to these physical distinctions will help you to master grassfed beef cookery.

The Salt Supremacy

I believe strongly in salt. The application of salt to meat plays a tremendous role in bringing beef to its full flavor potential. To season beef well—salting it—is the single most effective way to enhance the eating satisfaction of any meat you cook.

In general, I add salt to beef either well in advance of cooking or just before cooking. I use kosher salt to season meat in its raw state. The coarseness of the kosher salt gives me more control, and I can see where I've salted. I use enough salt so that the meat looks as if it has a light dusting of confectioner's sugar. You can also use coarse sea salts, such as *sel gris*, a moist, mineral-rich salt from France that looks like sand from an exotic beach (Sources, page 272).

In order to protect my salt stores from getting contaminated while I'm cooking, I always portion the amount I think I'll need into a small dish. I take a big pinch of the salt between my index finger and thumb, raise my arm about six inches over the meat, and rub my fingers together to sprinkle it on. This is not for show. Salting from on high ensures that the salt disperses more evenly and I get much more control than I ever could from a saltshaker.

I came across one grassfed manifesto in which the author urged home cooks never to salt until the meat was cooked because the salt would draw out precious moisture and make it dry. No one wants dry grassfed beef, least of all me, but I think the trade-off for the small amount of moisture loss is worth it. When salt hits the surfaces of the meat it *does* initially attract the water from within. But, over time, the water reverses its course and draws the salty moisture back into the meat, seasoning it profoundly and enhancing the taste of the meat in the same way a brine does without just making it taste, well, salty.

Here's my rule of thumb. The larger the piece of meat, the sooner it can be salted. I generally salt roasts up to twenty-four hours in advance, while steaks get a dusting of salt fifteen to twenty minutes before they go on the grill. Early seasoning is a principle I cook by, whether I'm making a stew or a skillet supper, a steak, or a smoked brisket. Try it out for yourself, and see what you think.

Good seasoning from salt applies in general cooking too. I didn't write the instruction to taste for seasoning as often as I'd have liked in every recipe. But if you came to one of my cooking classes, I'd pause frequently to let you dip a tasting spoon into the dish to judge for yourself whether it needed more spices, herbs, or most of all, salt. Adopt the habit of tasting from these recipes as you go from step to step, and I promise that your cooking will improve instantly and immeasurably.

For those who have health concerns and follow a sodium-reduced diet, cut the salt called for in the recipes by 25 to 50 percent. If you salt when the instructions specify, the amount of salt you do use will go a long way toward enhancing the whole dish.

Essential Browning

In its raw state, beef is lackluster in flavor, but heat changes everything. During cooking, meat undergoes a wonder of physical and biochemical changes that still enthrall meat scientists. The heat-induced transformations are so complex—rearranged proteins, enzyme hyperactivity, and water distribution, to name a few—it's not fully understood how they turn bland muscle into tempting meat. But it's something we all witness in the kitchen whenever we see beef change in color and texture, shrink, and develop aromas that prove irresistible to all our senses.

The one topic that the experts and home cooks comprehend concretely is browning, famously known as the Maillard reaction for the early twentieth-century French scientist who first identified it. I don't need to convince you that browned meat tastes incredible, but achieving good browning is an acquired skill. Many home cooks are tentative about applying the high heat required to kick-start the chain reaction that leads to a well-seared crust. (Years ago, while cooking at my friend Jill's house in Sonoma, California, I turned on the burner to heat a sauté pan and she said, "I didn't know my burner went that high.") Be bold, but not reckless—you'll only end up with tough meat and char—and you'll develop a feel for the high-heat cooking method the Maillard reaction demands.

Any of the tender cuts from the middle section of the cow—the rib and the loin primals (The Tender Middle, page 54)—respond well to the intense dry-heat of grilling, roasting, and broiling. However, I rarely broil because it's hard to monitor the meat during the final sensitive cooking stages and easy to overcook it. When I can't grill, I use a skillet on the stovetop instead to fry hamburgers and steaks—either in a little oil or on a bed of salt (Salt-Seared Steak with Chard-Gorgonzola Gratin, page 194).

For tough cuts that are best braised, I depend on browning as a first step to creating an all-important flavor layer that builds during simmering. Called combination cooking because it uses dry and moist heat (the initial browning of beef, or bones, or both, followed by simmering in liquid) makes the most splendid pot roasts, soups, and stews.

It's worth mentioning that while browning is the most straightforward way to reach beef's full eating potential, it's not the only way. You'll find plenty of recipes in this book, especially with meat cuts that are best cooked with low, slow heat, that do not depend on the Maillard reaction.

Timing and Doneness

There is no general timing guideline that holds true for each and every cut of grassfed beef. It's important to be attentive while cooking and to use all your senses—and, tools, especially a reliable instant-read thermometer—to judge the moment when the meat is done. There is no crime in under-cooking beef; you can always cook it longer if needed. But you can never cook it less, and over-cooking is by far grassfed's greatest pitfall.

None of this means that you shouldn't cook grassfed beef over high heat. I crank up the heat to grill steaks and hamburgers and roast larger cuts over 400°F to create the all-important crust that makes them mouthwatering. But I *am* vigilant about timing. When grilling, I don't leave the meat unattended, and I use a timer or watch the clock set for the minimum amount of time it should take for medium rare. With a poke of my index finger, I can test hamburgers and steaks to gauge their firmness. (You can pick this trick up in a single cooking session simply by touching your meat when it's raw and several times as it cooks so that you can feel with your own fingers how the meat firms up. With a few more cooking sessions, you'll have it down.) You can use an instant-read thermometer instead (slide it into thin cuts from the side), or when in doubt, take the meat off the heat and knick it with a sharp knife for a visual check. Always take into account that no matter how small the cut of meat is, its internal temperature will continue to climb once you remove it from the heat source (Give It a Rest, page 203). And, note that grassfed beef appears more red or pink than grain-fed when cooked to the same temperature.

To cook any cut of grassfed beef to medium or beyond, I switch from direct, high heat to indirect or low heat—or even off the heat to rest—the moment it hits medium rare. Then, I stand by for the last few minutes until it reaches the final cooking temperature minus a few degrees to compensate for carry-over cooking. For example, when grilling, I slide the meat to the coolest part of the grill, put on the cover, and create an oven to finish cooking. When searing steak in a skillet, I slip it into a 300°F oven. More often, the residual heat from the pan is all it takes to bump the meat from medium rare to medium. When roasting in the oven, I turn the oven off but keep the roast inside. A low-heat finish is the key to grassfed beef cooked to your liking.

Cooking with grassfed beef is often about what you do *not* have to do. One dramatic difference I've found is how little excess fat there is. With roasts and steaks, little trimming is required. With stocks and soups, I end up with mere spoonfuls of fat to skim and only a thin layer, often less than one-quarter inch on top, when they're chilled. When browning chuck roasts, beef cubes for stew, or ground beef, it's rare that I have to pour off any fat before proceeding with the recipe. Less fat also means less overall shrinkage in the meat, which means more value for you.

Favorite Flavor Pairings

Mineral, wild mushroom, sweet grass, game, and umami (profound savoriness) are some of the words used to describe the tastes of grassfed beef. They also serve as clues for flavor pairings, which form the basis for this quick reference guide. These are ingredients I've found to have an affinity to grassfed beef in particular, which has a more pronounced flavor than conventional beef and doesn't get easily masked. I naturally veer toward these staples whenever I'm devising a dish for dinner, and you will encounter examples of their usage throughout this book. Refer to it for your own creations, either singly or in combinations that play up the unique, resplendent qualities of great meat (Sources, page 270).

- Anchovies, whole packed in salt or paste, plus fish sauce and Worcestershire
- Arugula
- Chiles, fresh, roasted, and puréed
- Coffee, ground for rubs or brewed for stews
- Fresh herbs, especially thyme, rosemary, and bay leaves
- Fresh ginger
- Horseradish, especially freshly grated, and wasabi
- Juniper berries, whole for broths, crushed for rubs
- Miso, soy sauce, and oyster sauce
- Mushrooms, especially wild, including morels and porcinis
- Mustard, smooth or coarse
- Paprika, sweet, hot, and smoked
- Sea salt, including sel gris, smoked, flake, and other finishing salts
- Shallots, fresh or sautéed
- Sichuan peppercorns, toasted and ground
- Spirits, including brandy and whiskey
- Sumac, the mild and tart rust-colored fruit from the Middle East
- Tart fruits, including cranberries, figs, apricots, and tamarind
- Warm spices, especially allspice, cinnamon, and cloves
- Wine, especially red, and fortified wines, such as port and Madeira

Frozen Beef

Grassfed beef is a seasonal product, available in most parts of North America from June to November. In other months, you'll only find frozen, and if you buy your beef directly from a rancher or through a meat-buying collective, frozen is what you get.

Fresh meat has long been the standard, but the reality is, especially for grassfed, frozen is better. It allows the ranchers to determine the best time of year to slaughter their animals—typically after the height of the grass-growing season in late summer or early fall. The beef can be aged, butchered, packaged, and stored for future sales without any concerns about compromising the meat's quality or safety. (According to food industry experts, good packaging and a freezer below 0°F are the most important conditions for preserving meat for up to one year.) One meat scientist also mentioned that freezing can improve grassfed beef's tenderness because the ice crystals puncture the meat fibers, though it does purge additional water once thawed. (FYI: the red liquid in the bag is not blood but water colored red from myoglobin, a protein pigment in muscles.)

For all the benefits, defrosting is a challenge from both practical and food safety standpoints. It requires planning ahead to defrost meat and preventing its temperature from climbing above 40°F within four hours of cooking. Remembering to defrost your meat will become habitual once you become a loyal customer to your favorite grassfed rancher.

CAN I COOK FROZEN BEEF?

Ideally, you will start with a piece of meat that is defrosted all the way to the center. Yet three of my rancher friends have confided in me that they cook frozen beef all the time. One admitted, "I just stick it frozen in the oven and it comes out great." "How long?" I asked. "All day," came the reply. Of course, frozen beef will cook eventually—taking four to five times as long as a defrosted piece of beef. What you sacrifice is some control over the doneness, unless you're cooking a tough piece of meat, like chuck roast. The critical downside is the increased potential for bacteria to grow during the long period when the beef is in the temperature danger zone of 41°F to 140°F. So, for pot roasting, large roasts, and soups, when the finished temperatures will be well above 165°F, it may turn out just fine. In all other cases, change your menu.

How to Defrost

For optimum food safety, beef should be left at room temperature for no more than four hours. So, defrosting on the countertop is not a safe option. However, there are three recommended methods for defrosting frozen meat, listed here in order of speed.

• DAYS: REFRIGERATOR DEFROSTING

This is the safest, most foolproof and effortless way to defrost your meat. Put the packaged meat in a container to catch any drips and place it on the lowest shelf in the refrigerator with no other foods, raw or cooked, beneath it. It will take a minimum of two days for a pound of ground beef and up to four days for a three-pound roast. When I plan meals for the week, I pull beef from the freezer to defrost at its own pace to use within five or six days. It is amazing how long it takes for meat to defrost in the refrigerator, and it will sometimes still be partially frozen in the center. Whenever necessary, I use the Cold Water Bath method to complete defrosting.

• HOURS: COLD WATER BATH

Submerging frozen beef in cold water is the method many restaurateurs use for quick defrosting. Place the meat in a container at least four times the size of the cut for good circulation. Fill the container with cool water (below 70°F) and change the water every 30 to 45 minutes. A pound of ground beef or steak will defrost within two hours. You can expedite the process by letting a trickle of cool water run over the meat. Because of the water waste, I am reluctant to do this except in an urgent situation. It is most effective with steaks and other small cuts or packages of meat or to finish defrosting larger roasts.

• MINUTES: MICROWAVE

This is the riskiest defrosting method, to be reserved for when you're in a pinch. Wait until just before you are about to cook the meat, because the microwave can heat the meat to unsafe temperatures (above 40°F). Microwaves also heat the meat very unevenly and can even start to cook it, especially ground beef or the tips of steaks. Larger pieces of meat over two pounds that are still frozen in the center fare best. Use short bursts of the defrost setting on your microwave, turn the meat frequently, and cook it immediately.

About the Recipes

I created every recipe in *Pure Beef* using locally sourced grassfed beef, but you can use these recipes with any beef. Depending on the technique and the size of the cut, the cooking times may vary slightly, and you may find the need for more trimming before cooking and de-fatting before serving.

Beginning with the most abundant (and cheapest) cuts, the chapters proceed from ground beef, chuck, and round to steaks and roasts, and conclude with bones and trim. There are recipes for every cut—from the most popular rib-eyes to little-known beef cheeks. This recipe collection offers appetizing examples of nose-to-tail eating and a model for putting beef in balance on your table.

My goal was to make the other components of each dish equal to or greater than the beef. Overall, I reduced beef portion sizes in general and supplemented with beans, potatoes, and grains. Many of the recipes include side dishes to suggest ways to complete the meal; the more side dishes you add, the less prominent the beef becomes. With steaks, I suggest specific ways to serve less meat in combination with seasonal vegetables and salads. With roasts, it's hard to get beef off center stage (sometimes meat is the point, and that's okay on occasion), but I hope that you'll apply what you learn in the other chapters and use your own appetite—adding salads, cut fresh vegetables, and fruits—to create truly fulfilling meals.

Each chapter covers a range of cooking methods suitable to the category of meat cuts included. The first recipe in each chapter is a learning recipe for those who are new to cooking with grassfed—or any—beef and want to follow a foundational recipe such as meatloaf, grilled steak, stir-fry, roast beef, or stock. The recipes that follow within each chapter illustrate technique variations for the appropriate beef cut. Typically, I recommend the specific cut I find least expensive and best suited to the job; you'll find other recommendations listed under "More Choice Cuts." Some of these cuts (or their names) may be unfamiliar to you (see the Pure Beef Cut Guide, pages 42-43). I hope that you'll ask for them wherever you buy beef. Customer requests have a big impact, not only at the individual retailer, and can travel far up the supply chain.

In addition to high-quality meat, these recipes will benefit from the best ingredients you can find and afford. Whenever possible I choose produce that is local or regional and organic. I use eggs from chickens that ranged free and dairy products labeled "pastured," meaning that the butter, milk, and cream comes from cows that grazed on grasses, never in feedlots. Likewise, the pork meat used in these recipes comes from locally raised pigs, and the pork fat I use for charcuterie is supplied by my butcher. But I'm no purist. I depend on shredded mozzarella, boxed breadcrumbs, and pre-washed spinach, which you'll encounter in the recipes. With the same eye toward convenience, the recipes list substitutions wherever possible, from canned beans to frozen vegetables.

RECIPE INGREDIENTS:

BLACK PEPPER is freshly and finely ground (it really *does* make a difference).

CHOPPED ONIONS are diced ½ inch. One medium onion yields about 2 cups (8 ounces) chopped.

EGGS are large, preferably from free-ranging local chickens.

FLOUR is unbleached and organic.

FRESH HERBS are chopped and lightly packed and, if possible, locally grown.

MILK can be whole, part-skim, or non-fat unless otherwise specified.

PARMESAN CHEESE is preferably Parmigiano-Reggiano.

SALT is fine salt, preferably sea salt, unless kosher is specified (The Salt Supremacy, page 60).

VEGETABLE OIL is any mild-flavored cooking oil, including sunflower (my favorite), canola, corn, safflower, or olive. For stir-frying, good-quality peanut oil contributes flavor and smells heavenly.

CHAPTER 4
GREAT GROUND BEEF

For years, I failed to recognize the wonders of ground beef. Then one day I owned about thirty pounds of it.

Growing up, ground beef was a given. My mother bought the pink-and-white-flecked meat on a Styrofoam tray every week, and it appeared on my plate as brown crumbles in spaghetti sauce or rounded into meatballs. As an adult, I thought of it as cheap meat— characterless, limiting, and mundane—but cooking all that grassfed ground beef from my first cow-share gave me plenty of opportunities to recognize how wrong I was.

Ground beef is the most plentiful beef cut there is. More than one-third of every carcass gets ground from the trim produced when breaking the animal down into manageable pieces. It comes from every part of the cow, making ground beef the very definition of nose-to-tail eating. Ground is also the most affordable and accessible way to try one of the artisan beef brands on the market, be it natural, organic, or grassfed. One pound can feed several people, but cheapness is only part of its value.

Ground beef is a marvel. For creative cooks, it is the most versatile meat cut there is, with no preference for being grilled or fried, simmered or baked, braised or broiled.

Chances are, the last time you ate ground beef was in the form of a hamburger. This chapter kicks off with a learning recipe for a 100 percent grass-fed hamburger that will guide you through all of the steps from shaping to grilling—along with a whole-wheat bun that it deserves. From there you'll be primed for Thai-Style Hamburger Wraps (page 75) and Feta-Stuffed Sliders with Tahini-Yogurt Sauce (page 84).

This chapter then ventures beyond the hamburger to explore the world of cooking with ground beef. Its inspiration ranges from old-time cookbooks that treasured frugality to international cookbooks where ground beef is called "mince." You'll find exciting variations on meatloaf, including Miso-Glazed Meatloaf (page 77) and one dressed up in puff pastry for Poor Man's Beef Wellingtons (page 80). Along with satisfying meatball dishes, casseroles and stews, there are updated versions of time-tested recipes, such as Indian-Spiced Stuffed Peppers (page 98) and Lemony Chard Bundles (page 94).

Skillet suppers like Joe's Special (page 83) can sustain you midweek, while weekend projects like Beef Ravioli with Sage Butter Sauce (page 96) are their own reward. In cooking—or browsing— your way through this chapter, you'll see, as I did, that ground beef is valuable and practical, and when given its full due, can be quite extraordinary.

Ground Beef Choice Cuts:

All ground beef is made from trim passed through a meat grinder, generally twice, to produce minced meat. It comes from all of the cuts and is blended for varying lean/fat blends, ranging from 70 percent lean/30 percent fat (the highest fat limit by law) to 96 percent lean/4 percent fat. The ground beef from grassfed beef averages about 85 percent lean/15 percent fat, but you won't find this information on the package. (If you're curious, ask the rancher, since some have their beef sampled and know the composition.) It makes an excellent all-purpose ground beef.

Conventional ground beef is labeled according to fat content. Some packages include additional labels of "ground chuck," "ground round," and "ground sirloin" to indicate the primal source for the meat used. However, these ground beef types range in fat within the legal limits, so read the labels attentively.

LEAN contains no more than 22 percent fat and goes as low as 15 percent fat. A higher fat content makes extra-juicy hamburgers, but you may want to discard any excess fat after browning it for use in other dishes.

EXTRA LEAN contains less than 15 percent fat and goes as low as 4 percent fat (sometimes labeled super lean). Use 90 percent or leaner for meatloaf and stuffings where liquids, breadcrumbs, and egg lend moisture to the mix. It's also the choice for jerky (Peppered Hamburger Jerky, page 268), where leanness is essential for preservation.

GROUND BEEF SAFETY TIPS

Although I trust in the source for the beef I buy, I still play it safe in the kitchen with all raw meat, especially ground beef. Grinding greatly increases the surface area, making ground beef more susceptible to bacterial growth, unlike a roast, which only has a limited surface area exposed.

Temperature is one of the main firewalls to maintain safety, and it's critical to keep ground beef chilled below 40°F. When I'm making hamburgers, I take the beef out of the refrigerator only when I'm ready to form the patties. If I haven't started the grill yet or won't cook them within fifteen to twenty minutes, I cover the patties and put them back into the refrigerator.

Sanitation is the other key to food safety. Hot, soapy water, and preferably a sanitizing solution, will help to prevent food-borne illness. I have two strategies for avoiding cross-contamination—the spread of bacteria to other foods, cutting boards, and other work surfaces. When I'm making meatloaf or meatballs, I collect all my ingredients first and add the ground beef last. I mix with one hand, so that I can keep the other one clean in case I need to turn on a water faucet, open a drawer, or answer the phone. If all goes well, I won't have to pause to wash my hands until after I've patted the meatloaf into the pan or rounded the meatballs. Afterwards, I dispatch any utensils, bowls, and the cutting board into the dishwasher for sanitizing and spray my work counter with a light solution of one teaspoon bleach to one quart of water.

CUSTOM-GROUND HAMBURGERS

Freshly ground beef is the ultimate burger experience. In New York City and Las Vegas restaurants, custom-ground hamburgers go for eighteen dollars and up. The key is the grind—a top-secret blend of ground beef specialized for each restaurant that can include a combination of chuck, short ribs, brisket, and even spendy dry-aged steaks.

It's simple to create your own signature burger using a meat grinder (hand-crank or electric). You can also chop the beef in a food processor or by hand so long as the meat you choose has no sinew (e.g., short ribs) to cut through.

One of my favorite blends is chuck roast with short ribs—two cuts with exceptional flavor. Play around with your own favorites to make the very best burger you've ever had—for *much* less than eighteen bucks.

If you like steak tartare, grinding or chopping your own is the way to go, so that it's very fresh. Tenderloin is the classic cut for tartare, but don't ignore other even tastier choices, including top blade steak, aka flatiron, or shoulder tender, aka teres major, both exquisite cuts from the chuck.

PERFECT GRASSFED HAMBURGERS

The perfect hamburger begins before you put it on the grill. If you pay attention to how you handle the meat, how you shape it, and when you salt it, you'll get burgers with just the right loose, tender texture and the right size for the bun.

My ideal is a one-third pound burger, evenly shaped about one inch thick and four inches across. Handling the ground beef just enough, but not too much, I pat it into a neat disk, round the edges, and make a depression in the center so that it doesn't inflate into a hamburger ball while cooking. I cook my burgers to medium rare over high heat. If you like medium or medium well, just be sure to finish cooking the burger away from the flame.

Serve this burger on the best bun you can find. If you're lucky enough to have a bakery making its own hamburger buns, stock up. Or, bake and freeze a batch of homemade Whole-Wheat Hamburger Buns (recipe follows) to pull out whenever that burger craving hits you. An excellent homemade ketchup (recipe follows) along with your choice of lettuce leaves, tomato, and onion slices—what have you—puts this burger over the top.

Makes 6 servings

....

2 POUNDS GROUND BEEF, 75 TO 85 PERCENT LEAN
KOSHER SALT
6 HAMBURGER BUNS (RECIPE FOLLOWS)
KETCHUP (RECIPE FOLLOWS)

Prepare a gas or charcoal grill for high heat (425°F to 475°F), scrape the grate clean, and oil it lightly. Line a baking sheet with parchment paper and spoon some salt into a small bowl. Divide the ground beef into 6 mounds on the baking sheet. Scoop up a mound in each hand and judge their weight as best you can. If they seem about the same, put one of the mounds down and pick up another one, again judging its weight against the first. Continue in this fashion with each of the mounds, and add or subtract some of the ground beef to make them as equal as you can. (For complete accuracy, use a scale with a piece of plastic wrap over the plate).

Use both hands to gently press one mound into a 1-inch-thick disk about 4 inches wide. Then, rotate it between your palms to even up the edges without smashing it. Put the disk back on the parchment paper and use your thumb to make a quarter-sized impression about ¼-inch deep in the center. Repeat with the 5 remaining mounds of ground beef and season both sides of the patties with the kosher salt. (If you will not be grilling the hamburgers within the next 15 to 20 minutes, cover and refrigerate.)

When the grill is so hot that you can only hold your hand 4 inches above it for 5 seconds or less, place the patties on the hottest part of the grill. Cook them for 3 to 3½ minutes, then flip and cook for 3 to 3½ minutes more for medium rare. (For medium, slide the burgers to the coolest part of the grill—or turn it off. Close the lid, and cook for 1 to 3 minutes longer.) Discard the parchment paper from the baking sheet and arrange the cooked hamburgers on it. If desired, grill the buns, cut side down, for 1 to 2 minutes, and serve with ketchup and your favorite toppings.

WHOLE-WHEAT HAMBURGER BUNS

The perfect grassfed burger needs a worthy bun—and good ones are hard to find. To make this whole-wheat bun, I called on my bread baking training in France and Mel Darbyshire, head baker of the Grand Central Baking Company in Portland. It is tender to the bite and moist but stands up to a substantial burger. The user-friendly dough can be mixed by machine or hand. It rises once before you pat it flat and stamp out rounds—just like making biscuits. The second rise occurs in short order before baking, cooling, and splitting them to eat within a day, or to freeze for up to one month.

Makes 8 (4-inch) buns

....

2 CUPS (9 OUNCES) WHOLE-WHEAT FLOUR

2 CUPS (9 OUNCES) ALL-PURPOSE FLOUR,
    PLUS MORE FOR DUSTING

2 TABLESPOONS SUGAR

2¼ TEASPOONS INSTANT OR ACTIVE DRY YEAST

1½ TEASPOONS SALT

1½ CUPS WARM MILK (75°F TO 80°F)

1 TABLESPOON VEGETABLE OIL

1 EGG

2 TEASPOONS FLAX SEEDS OR SESAME SEEDS

To mix the dough, whisk the whole-wheat flour, all-purpose flour, sugar, yeast, and salt in the bowl of a stand mixer, a food processor, or a large mixing bowl. In a large measuring cup, whisk together the milk, oil, and egg. Pour the liquids into the dry ingredients and stir together with a few strokes of a rubber spatula to form a rough dough.

If using a stand mixer, attach the dough hook and mix on medium speed for 8 minutes. The dough will clear the sides of the bowl, but may stick to the bottom. Using the spatula, scrape the dough hook and the bottom of the bowl to collect the dough into a ball.

If using a food processor, use the dough blade and pulse the machine until the dough comes together in a ball. Run the machine for 1 minute to knead it.

If kneading by hand, work the spatula firmly through the dough to collect as much of the flour as you can. Scrape the dough onto an unfloured countertop. Set a kitchen timer for 12 minutes and knead rhythmically but not hurriedly. The dough will become very elastic and will be tacky. Using the spatula, collect the dough, including any scraps from the counter and your hands, into a ball. Flour your hands and place the dough back into the bowl.

Cover the bowl with plastic wrap and leave it at room temperature for 1½ to 2 hours until the dough doubles in volume.

To shape and bake the buns, line a large baking sheet with parchment paper. Dust the counter with flour and tip out the dough, scraping the bowl with a rubber spatula to release it in one large clump. Flour your hands and press the dough ¾ inch thick. Dust a biscuit cutter about 3½ inches in diameter to cut out 8 circles, collecting the dough and patting it down again 1 to 2 times until all the dough gets used. Space them onto the baking sheet and press them with your palm so that they are 4 to 4½ inches wide. Let them rise uncovered for 30 to 45 minutes until they are about 1½ inches high.

Preheat the oven to 350°F with the racks centered in the oven. Brush the tops of the buns lightly with water and sprinkle with the flax seeds. Bake until they are golden brown, 16 to 18 minutes. Cool to room temperature before splitting with a bread knife and store at room temperature or in the freezer in a resealable plastic bag.

LARDO KETCHUP

I've searched for ages for a ketchup recipe that was better than bottled, and I found it in an unexpected place: a Portland food cart called Lardo. Chef Rick Gencarelli serves this outstanding ketchup with fries that accompany every one of his pork-lover's sandwiches. One dip and I was smitten.

Makes 1 cup

....

1 TABLESPOON VEGETABLE OIL

1 SMALL ONION, CHOPPED

2 GARLIC CLOVES, MINCED

½ TEASPOON SWEET PAPRIKA

⅛ TEASPOON CAYENNE

⅛ TEASPOON GROUND ALLSPICE

⅛ TEASPOON GROUND CINNAMON

1 HEAPING TEASPOON TOMATO PASTE

¼ CUP PACKED LIGHT BROWN SUGAR

¼ CUP APPLE CIDER VINEGAR

1 (14.5-OUNCE) CAN WHOLE PEELED TOMATOES, DRAINED

Heat the oil in a small saucepan over medium heat. Add the onion and garlic and cook until the onion turns translucent, about 3 minutes. Add the paprika, cayenne, allspice, and cinnamon and cook until the spices are fragrant, about 1 minute. Add the tomato paste and cook for 30 seconds. Add the brown sugar, vinegar, and tomatoes, and bring the mixture to a boil. Reduce the heat to low and cook until the mixture is reduced to a thick tomato sauce, 45 to 50 minutes. If you have an immersion blender purée the mixture right in the saucepan, or cool to room temperature and transfer it to a blender and purée until very smooth. Transfer the ketchup to a glass container and chill in the refrigerator for 2 hours. Store for up to 2 weeks.

DELUXE PIMENTO CHEESEBURGERS

There are many great American cheeses to melt onto a deserving hamburger, including aged goat, farmhouse Cheddar, and blue. But the ultimate cheeseburger in my book is one made with the Southern spread called pimento cheese. (I also use it to make the best grilled cheese sandwiches.) Based on a recipe by Atlanta chef Scott Peacock, this pimento cheese mixture offers so much cheesy, oniony, spiciness to a cheeseburger that I find no other condiments are required.

Makes about 1⅓ cups

....

1½ CUPS GRATED EXTRA-SHARP CHEDDAR CHEESE

¼ CUP MAYONNAISE

2 TABLESPOONS FINELY CHOPPED ROASTED RED PEPPER

1 TEASPOON GRATED ONION

PINCH OF CAYENNE

Combine the grated cheese, mayonnaise, red pepper, onion, and cayenne in a small mixing bowl until well blended and creamy. Taste and if it needs a bit of salt, add a pinch. Cover and refrigerate the cheese spread until about 20 minutes before you're ready to use it.

When the burgers are nearly cooked to your liking, slide them to the coolest part of the grill so that you don't risk overcooking them. Put 2 heaping tablespoon-sized dollops on top, close the grill lid or cover the pan, and heat until melted.

INSIDE-OUT HAMBURGERS

Hamburgers stuffed with savory ingredients are more than a novelty: they're practical, economical, and an insurance plan for moist burgers. This approach also bulks up the burgers, so you need less meat for a good-sized burger that fits the bun. And, you won't ever overcook your grassfed burger waiting for the cheese to melt. Take care while flipping because these burgers are a bit delicate.

To form these burgers, put the ingredients listed into a medium mixing bowl. Break up one pound of ground beef into the bowl and gently mix it together as if you're making meatloaf but with a gentle hand to avoid compacting the meat. Shape the mixture into four 4-inch wide and ¾-inch-thick hamburger patties. Season them well with kosher salt on both sides before grilling, pan-searing, or broiling.

Blue Cheese-Bacon:

5 ounces bacon (about 4 strips), chopped and fried until crisp

3 ounces aged blue cheese, cut into ¼-inch cubes and chilled (about ½ cup)

Served with Herb Aïoli (page 187)

Mushroom-Cheddar:

½ cup cooked chopped mushrooms

3 ounces Cheddar cheese, cut into ¼-inch cubes and chilled (about ½ cup)

Served with Harissa (page 129)

Green Chile-Monterey Jack:

1 (4-ounce) can diced green chilies, well drained

3 ounces Monterey Jack cheese, cut into ¼-inch cubes and chilled (about ½ cup)

Served with Avocado-Tomatillo Salsa (page 151)

THAI-STYLE HAMBURGER WRAPS

When I read about a Thai hamburger at a hip LA restaurant, I had to create one for myself. These hamburgers are mixed and shaped in advance to let the sweet and spicy flavors work their way through the ground beef, which takes only twenty minutes. Wrapped inside crisp lettuce leaves and topped with quick-pickled onions and tomatoes, it's a fresh take on good old burgers that's perfect for gluten-free and carb-conscious friends.

Line a baking sheet with parchment paper. Combine the shallot, ginger, lemongrass, brown sugar, fish sauce, lime juice, sweet chile sauce, basil, and salt in a large mixing bowl. Break up the ground beef into the bowl and knead the ingredients with a rubber spatula or your hands until thoroughly blended. Portion the ground beef mixture into 6 equal mounds, weighing them in your hands two by two, and adjust to make them as equal as possible.

Working with one mound of ground beef at a time, use both hands to press it gently into a 1-inch-thick oval. Put the patty on the parchment paper and use your thumbs to make a nickel-sized impression ¼-inch deep in the center. Repeat with the remaining ground beef mixture. Cover and chill in the refrigerator to marinate for about 20 minutes—much longer and the beef starts to get mushy.

Prepare a gas or charcoal grill for high heat (425°F to 475°F), scrape the grate clean, and oil it lightly. Place the onion into a small bowl and pour the seasoned rice wine vinegar over it and add just enough water to cover. Marinate for 15 to 20 minutes, drain, and set the onion aside on a platter along with the sliced tomato, lettuce leaves, and cilantro.

When the grill is so hot that you can only hold your hand 4 inches above it for 5 seconds or less, place the patties on the hottest part of the grill. Cook them for 3 to 3½ minutes, then flip and cook them for 3 to 3½ minutes more for medium rare. (For medium, slide the burgers to the coolest part of the grill—or turn it off. Close the lid, and cook for 1 to 3 minutes longer.)

Discard the parchment paper from the baking sheet and arrange the cooked hamburgers on it. Brush them with the sweet chile sauce, serving any extra sauce in a small dish on the side. To serve, place 1 lettuce leaf on each plate and put a hamburger on it, then top with a tomato slice, pickled onion, and cilantro. Fold the lettuce over the hamburger to eat as a wrap or use a knife and fork.

Makes 6 servings

....

1 SMALL SHALLOT, MINCED

1-INCH PIECE GINGER, PEELED AND VERY FINELY CHOPPED (1 TABLESPOON)

1 STALK LEMONGRASS, MINCED

2 TEASPOONS PACKED LIGHT BROWN SUGAR

1 TABLESPOON FISH SAUCE

1 TABLESPOON LIME JUICE

¼ CUP SWEET CHILE SAUCE, PLUS ADDITIONAL FOR SERVING

6 FRESH THAI BASIL LEAVES, FINELY CHOPPED

¾ TEASPOON SALT

1½ POUNDS GROUND BEEF, 75 TO 85 PERCENT LEAN

1 RED ONION, VERY THINLY SLICED

¼ CUP SEASONED RICE WINE VINEGAR

1 MEDIUM RIPE TOMATO, SLICED

6 LARGE TENDER LETTUCE LEAVES, SUCH AS BIBB OR RED LEAF

6 CILANTRO SPRIGS, FOR SERVING

HAMBURGER STEAKS
IN ONION CREAM SAUCE

Commonly known as Salisbury steak, this recipe dates from a time when a hamburger was considered a luxury item. Based on Julia Child's *Mastering the Art of French Cooking*, it is served on a plate without the bun to be eaten with a fork and knife. It makes a comforting wintertime supper I enjoy with a glass of red wine and steamed broccoli to share some of the cream sauce.

For other departures from the standard hamburger, use this recipe to build two old-school fast food favorites. To make a loco moco, mound steamed white rice with the cooked patty, pour on the sauce, and gild it all with a fried egg. To make a patty melt, skip the cream sauce and sandwich the cooked hamburger, the onions, and slices of sharp Cheddar with rye bread, then cook in a hot buttered skillet until toasted on both sides.

Makes 4 servings

....

2 TEASPOONS EXTRA-VIRGIN OLIVE OIL

1 LARGE ONION, CHOPPED

¼ CUP ALL-PURPOSE FLOUR

2 TABLESPOONS LIGHTLY PACKED FINELY CHOPPED
    FRESH PARSLEY

1 TEASPOON FRESH THYME OR ½ TEASPOON
    DRIED

½ TEASPOON WORCESTERSHIRE SAUCE

1¾ TEASPOONS SALT, DIVIDED

¼ TEASPOON BLACK PEPPER

1 POUND GROUND BEEF, 85 TO 90 PERCENT LEAN

1½ TABLESPOONS UNSALTED BUTTER

1½ CUPS HALF-AND-HALF

⅛ TEASPOON GROUND NUTMEG

Heat the oil in a large skillet over medium-low heat. When it slides across the pan, add the onion and cook, stirring occasionally, until it is caramel colored, about 8 minutes. Transfer the onion into a small bowl and set it aside.

Spread the flour on a large dinner plate. Combine the parsley, thyme, Worcestershire sauce, 1¼ teaspoons of the salt, and pepper in a large mixing bowl. Break apart the ground beef into the bowl and gently knead the ingredients with a rubber spatula or your hands until the mixture is well blended. Divide it into 4 equal shares and shape into 4 oval patties ¾ inch thick. Dust them with the flour and leave them on the plate.

Melt the butter in the skillet over medium-high heat. When the butter foams, shake any excess flour from the patties and cook them until they are well browned, 3½ to 4 minutes per side for medium rare. (For medium, reduce the heat to low and cook the patties for 1 to 3 minutes more.) Transfer the patties onto a clean plate, cover them with aluminum foil, and keep them in a warm place near the stove.

Reduce the heat to medium low, add the half-and-half and the reserved onion, and simmer until the cream sauce coats a spoon, about 10 minutes. Season with the remaining ½ teaspoon salt and nutmeg and taste for salt. Serve each patty with a generous spoonful of the hot cream sauce.

MISO-GLAZED MEATLOAF

with Quick Pickled Cucumber Salad

I'm going to come right out and say it: this meat-loaf "frosted" with miso is not as pretty as a picture. But, it's a fabulous way to taste the complex interaction among the amino acids in miso and beef. It produces that captivating fifth flavor called umami (in addition to hot, sour, salty, and sweet). An American-style *hambaagu* with miso is a popular snack food in Japan, and I translated it into a meatloaf patted thin for lots of glazing surface area. Miso, a salty, intensely flavored fermented soybean paste, lifts a simple meatloaf mixture onto a higher plane. Red miso ranges in color depending on the grain blends and fermentation time, and I used a mild, pale-colored brand. Serve portions over steamed short-grain white rice with Quick-Pickled Cucumber Salad (recipe follows) on the side.

Preheat the oven to 350°F and have a square 8-inch baking pan on hand.

Whisk the miso with 1 tablespoon of the sake, the ponzu, if using, and the sugar in a small bowl until smooth. Combine half of the miso mixture in a large mixing bowl with the onion, egg, soy sauce, breadcrumbs, and the remaining tablespoon of sake. Break up the ground beef and pork into the bowl and knead the ingredients together gently using your hands until thoroughly blended. Transfer the ground beef mixture into the baking pan, gently pressing it evenly and into the corners.

Use a rubber spatula to spread the remaining miso mixture evenly over the top of the meatloaf. Bake until the meatloaf pulls away from the sides of the pan and an instant-read thermometer registers 155°F, 35 to 40 minutes.

Makes 4 servings

....

¼ CUP MILD RED MISO (SOURCES, PAGE 272)

2 TABLESPOONS SAKE, DIVIDED

1 TABLESPOON PONZU SAUCE, OPTIONAL

1 TEASPOON SUGAR

1 SMALL ONION, VERY FINELY CHOPPED

1 EGG, BEATEN

2 TABLESPOONS SOY SAUCE

⅔ CUP COARSE, DRY BREADCRUMBS

1 POUND GROUND BEEF, 85 TO 90 PERCENT LEAN

4 OUNCES GROUND PORK

QUICK-PICKLED CUCUMBER SALAD

Makes 4 servings

....

2 LARGE CUCUMBERS, PEELED

¼ CUP RICE WINE VINEGAR

2 TABLESPOONS SUGAR

1 TEASPOON SOY SAUCE

PINCH OF RED PEPPER FLAKES

Slice the cucumbers in half lengthwise and use a teaspoon to scrape out the seeds. Slice them very thin on the diagonal and put them into a bowl. In a separate bowl, whisk the rice wine vinegar, sugar, soy sauce, and pepper flakes until the sugar dissolves. Pour the dressing over the cucumbers, stir, and let the flavors develop at room temperature for about 30 minutes while the meatloaf bakes.

PURE BEEF MEATLOAF

Traditionally, meatloaf is a combination of beef, pork, and sometimes veal. I love the firmness and meatiness of this 100 percent beef meatloaf, where the taste of grassfed beef isn't lost in the mix. In the time it takes for my oven to preheat, I assemble and shape this meatloaf into a free-form log so the sides and the top crisp and brown. (If you tend to like your hamburgers medium well to well, this mix is great for burgers with built-in moisture insurance.)

In the dead of our mountain winter, meatloaf is my family's favorite with Oven Steak Fries (page 188) and Beet-Carrot Slaw (page 121). For myself, I rewarm any leftover slices to make an open-faced sandwich on whole-wheat toast topped with Tangy Barbecue Sauce (page 223) and pickled jalapeños. Try the variation with quinoa to make it gluten-free and nutty-tasting. Both meatloaf mixtures can be used for meatballs described in the variation.

Makes 6 servings

1 CUP FINE, DRY BREADCRUMBS

1 SMALL ONION, FINELY CHOPPED

1 GARLIC CLOVE, MINCED

½ CUP TOMATO SAUCE

1 TABLESPOON MOLASSES

1 EGG, BEATEN

½ CUP LIGHTLY PACKED CHOPPED FRESH PARSLEY

1¼ TEASPOONS SALT

½ TEASPOON BLACK PEPPER

1½ POUNDS GROUND BEEF, 85 TO 90 PERCENT LEAN

3 SLICES BACON, CUT IN HALF, OPTIONAL

Line a rimmed baking sheet with parchment paper and set it aside. Preheat the oven to 375°F.

Combine the breadcrumbs, onion, garlic, tomato sauce, molasses, egg, parsley, salt, and pepper in a large mixing bowl. Break up the ground beef into the bowl and and knead with a rubber spatula or your hands until well blended. Mound the meat mixture onto the prepared baking sheet and use your hands to shape into a log, roughly 8 inches long and 4½ inches wide. Drape the bacon slices over the top of the meatloaf with the edges touching, if using.

Bake until it is well browned, sizzling on the bottom, and an instant-read thermometer registers 155°F, 40 to 45 minutes. Cool for 10 minutes for better slicing.

VARIATION: GLUTEN-FREE MEATLOAF

¾ CUP QUINOA
¼ TEASPOON SALT

Bring 1 cup of water to a boil in a small saucepan over high heat. Add the quinoa and salt, reduce the heat to low, cover, and steam for 10 to 14 minutes until the water is absorbed and the quinoa is tender to the bite. Transfer the quinoa into a bowl, cool to room temperature, and use it in place of the breadcrumbs in the recipe.

VARIATION: MEATBALLS

Use either the standard or gluten-free meatloaf mixture to shape meatballs, large (1¼ inches in diameter and 2 ounces each) or small (1 inch in diameter and 1 ounce each). Arrange them in a single layer on an ungreased baking sheet and preheat the oven to 375°F. Bake the large meatballs for 20 to 22 minutes and the small meatballs for 15 to 17 minutes. Alternatively, you can fry the meatballs in a large skillet over medium heat, working in batches and turning them 2 to 3 times until browned and cooked through.

POOR MAN'S BEEF WELLINGTONS

I made it a mission to bring beef wellington down to size simply because I love puff pastry, but rarely have any tenderloin on hand, the traditional meat secreted inside a beef wellington. And, I made them into single-serving sizes to offer more pastry per beef bite. They're as cute as cupcakes.

In my view, meatloaf is a superior choice for Wellington because it's far more economical and hard to overcook. Besides, it's fun to dress up meatloaf with a mushroom-bacon topping all wrapped up in a puff pastry crust. With steamed vegetables on the side, you have a princely meal fit for company. I enjoy these as is, but if you fancy a sauce, follow the instructions to make the sauce for Porcini-Rubbed Tenderloin with Saba Sauce (page 207) omitting the saba or serve with some homemade ketchup (page 73).

There are three main steps involved—cooking the mushroom filling, mixing the meatloaf, and wrapping it in the puff pastry assembly. You can do any of these steps, or all of them, one day in advance.

Makes 8 servings

....

MUSHROOM FILLING:

4 OUNCES BACON (ABOUT 3 STRIPS), CHOPPED

1 LARGE SHALLOT, FINELY CHOPPED

1 POUND CREMINI MUSHROOMS, FINELY CHOPPED

⅓ CUP DRY RED WINE

3 GARLIC CLOVES, MINCED

½ TEASPOON SALT

¼ CUP LIGHTLY PACKED CHOPPED FRESH PARSLEY

MEATLOAF:

1½ CUP ROLLED (OR OLD-FASHIONED) OATS

½ CUP LOW-SALT BEEF STOCK (SHORT ORDER STOCK, PAGE 226; ROASTED BEEF STOCK, PAGE 228)

3 EGGS

1 TABLESPOON DIJON MUSTARD

2 TEASPOONS CHOPPED FRESH THYME OR 1 TEASPOON DRIED

2 TEASPOONS SALT

½ TEASPOON BLACK PEPPER

⅛ TEASPOON GROUND NUTMEG

1¾ POUNDS GROUND BEEF, 85 TO 90 PERCENT LEAN

8 OUNCES GROUND PORK

1 (17-OUNCE) PACKAGE FROZEN PUFF PASTRY, THAWED

To prepare the mushroom filling, line a small bowl with paper towel. Heat a large skillet over medium-low heat and cook the bacon until the fat melts and the bacon browns, about 5 minutes. Use a slotted spoon to remove the bacon to the paper towel-lined bowl.

Drain all but 1 tablespoon of bacon fat and increase the heat to medium. Cook the shallot for 1 minute until fragrant, then increase the heat to medium high. Add the mushrooms and cook until they have released their liquid, about 4 minutes. Add the wine, garlic, and salt and cook, stirring occasionally, until the mushrooms brown in spots, 7 to 8 minutes. Stir in the reserved bacon and the parsley and transfer to a bowl. Chill the mushroom mixture in the refrigerator until completely cooled, about 15 minutes.

To make the meatloaf, combine the oats, stock, 2 of the eggs, mustard, thyme, salt, pepper, and nutmeg in a large mixing bowl. Break up the ground beef and pork into the bowl and knead the ingredients together gently using your hands until thoroughly blended.

Line a 6-ounce ramekin or a large muffin tin with plastic wrap so that it overhangs by a couple of inches. Gently pack it with the meatloaf mixture to mold it, then lift up the overhanging plastic wrap

release a miniature meatloaf. Repeat to make 8 meatloaf rounds. Chill them until ready to use.

Prepare an egg wash by whisking the remaining egg with 1 tablespoon of water and set it aside along with a pastry brush. Roll out each of the 2 sheets of the puff pastry on a lightly flour-dusted counter top into squares 15 x 15 inches and cut each into 4 equal pieces to make a total of 8 squares.

To make each meatloaf Wellington, put 2 heaping tablespoons of the mushroom mixture in the center of each puff pastry square. Place each meatloaf round on top of the mushrooms and brush the edges of the puff pastry with the egg wash. Wrap the puff pastry around the meatloaf, overlapping the bottom and pleating the sides. Invert the meatloaf so that the seam side is down on an ungreased baking sheet and brush it all over with the egg wash. Use a paring knife to cut a small X in the center of the puff pastry dough about ¼-inch deep. Chill the wrapped meatloaves for at least 25 minutes and up to 1 day in advance.

When you are ready to bake, preheat the oven to 400°F with a rack positioned in the center of the oven. Bake the meatloaves until the crusts are deeply golden brown and an instant-read thermometer registers 155°F, 30 to 35 minutes. Cool on a rack for 15 minutes and serve.

BABY MEATBALLS IN TOMATO-BASIL SAUCE

These two-bite meatballs, tender with ricotta, simmer in a simple tomato sauce. They lend their flavors to the sauce and save you the step of browning them first, so you can have dinner ready in twenty minutes. This is the way to enjoy a spaghetti and meatball supper any day of the week or a meatball sandwich on toasted ciabatta.

Makes 6 servings

....

TOMATO SAUCE:

2 TABLESPOONS EXTRA-VIRGIN OLIVE OIL

3 GARLIC CLOVES, MINCED

¼ TEASPOON RED PEPPER FLAKES

1 (28-OUNCE) CAN CRUSHED TOMATOES

½ CUP DRY RED WINE

½ CUP LIGHTLY PACKED CHOPPED FRESH BASIL OR
    1 TABLESPOON DRIED

MEATBALLS:

1 GARLIC CLOVE, MINCED

½ CUP WHOLE MILK RICOTTA

⅔ CUP FINE, DRY BREADCRUMBS

1 EGG, BEATEN

¼ CUP LIGHTLY PACKED CHOPPED FRESH PARSLEY

¼ CUP FINELY GRATED PARMESAN CHEESE

1 TEASPOON SALT

¼ TEASPOON BLACK PEPPER

1 POUND GROUND BEEF, 85 TO 90 PERCENT LEAN

To make the tomato sauce, heat the olive oil over medium heat in a large saucepan. Add the garlic and the pepper flakes and cook until they sizzle and become fragrant, about 1 minute. Add the tomatoes, wine, and basil and bring to a simmer.

To prepare the meatballs, have a large dinner plate and a tablespoon-sized scoop or two teaspoons on hand. Combine the garlic, ricotta, breadcrumbs, egg, parsley, Parmesan cheese, salt, and pepper in a medium mixing bowl. Break up the ground beef into the bowl and knead the ingredients with a rubber spatula or your hands until thoroughly blended. Use the rounded scoop or spoons to make ½-ounce knobs of the ground beef mixture, the size of a large gumball, and space them around the plate. Moisten your hands with water and roll the meatballs into uniform spheres.

To cook the meatballs, gently plop each one into the simmering sauce. Spoon the sauce over their tops, cover the pot, and simmer over low heat for 18 to 20 minutes, until the meat changes color all the way through (cut one in half to test).

JOE'S SPECIAL

A lot of people take credit for creating this dish, a winning combination of ground beef, mushrooms, and spinach made famous in San Francisco. To make my own version, I strived to get the texture of the eggs just the way I like them, a little like a frittata with well-seasoned ground beef, heavy on the spinach, and melted Monterey Jack on top. It's a lifesaving one-skillet dish for a late-night supper or a sleep-in Sunday brunch served with hot buttered toast. Pass the hot sauce.

Makes 6 servings

....

1 TABLESPOON EXTRA-VIRGIN OLIVE OIL

1 MEDIUM ONION, CHOPPED

8 OUNCES MUSHROOMS, SLICED

12 OUNCES GROUND BEEF, 85 TO 90 PERCENT
   LEAN

2 GARLIC CLOVES, MINCED

½ TEASPOON DRIED MARJORAM OR OREGANO

1¼ TEASPOONS SALT

¼ TEASPOON BLACK PEPPER

1 POUND FRESH BABY SPINACH OR 1 (10-OUNCE)
   BAG FROZEN CHOPPED SPINACH, THAWED
   AND DRAINED

10 EGGS

1 TEASPOON WORCESTERSHIRE SAUCE

2 CUPS GRATED MONTEREY JACK CHEESE

Heat the oil in a large skillet over medium high. When it shimmers add the onion and cook, stirring occasionally, until it begins to brown, about 6 minutes. Add the mushrooms and leave them to cook until they release their liquid and brown in spots, about 8 minutes. Add the ground beef, break it up with a wooden spoon, and season it with the garlic, marjoram, salt, and pepper. Cook, continuing to break up the ground beef until it is evenly browned, about 4 minutes. Mound the spinach on top of the beef, cover, and steam until the spinach wilts. Uncover, stir the spinach into the ground beef, and cook until the pan is nearly dry.

Reduce the heat to low and preheat the broiler. Beat the eggs in a bowl with the Worcestershire sauce. Pour the eggs into the skillet, allow the eggs to set on the bottom of the skillet for 1 minute, and then stir to make large curds with puddles of eggs in between. Leave the eggs to set on the bottom for 1 minute longer then stir once more. Turn off the heat but leave the skillet on the burner. Sprinkle on the cheese and place the skillet under the broiler until the eggs are no longer liquid and the cheese is melted, about 2 minutes.

FETA-STUFFED SLIDERS
WITH TAHINI-YOGURT SAUCE

These mini-burgers are inspired by the Turkish grain-enriched stuffed meatballs called *kibbeh* with a feta surprise in their centers. Shaped into mini-burgers called sliders, baked, pan-fried, or grilled, they're dolloped with the zesty yogurt sauce and sprinkled with sumac, a citrusy, rust-colored spice common in Middle Eastern and North African cooking that is simply fabulous with beef. Presented between pita triangles for the bun, they're fun to serve as a casual dinner or party appetizer.

Makes 6 to 8 servings as a main dish;
12 to 16 as an appetizer
....

YOGURT SAUCE:

¾ CUP (5 OUNCES) PLAIN, THICK YOGURT,
    PREFERABLY GREEK-STYLE

2 TABLESPOONS TAHINI (SESAME SEED PASTE),
    STIRRED UNTIL SMOOTH

1 GARLIC CLOVE, MINCED

2 TEASPOONS LEMON JUICE

⅛ TEASPOON SALT

¼ CUP FINELY CHOPPED FRESH MINT

SLIDERS:

1 CUP BULGUR

½ CUP GRATED ONION

1½ TEASPOONS GROUND CUMIN

1¼ TEASPOONS SALT

1 TEASPOON SWEET PAPRIKA

⅛ TEASPOON CAYENNE

1½ POUNDS GROUND BEEF, 75 TO 85 PERCENT
    LEAN

2 OUNCES FETA CHEESE

5 PITA BREADS, CUT INTO QUARTERS FOR SERVING

2 TABLESPOONS COARSELY GROUND SUMAC FOR
    SERVING, OPTIONAL (SOURCES, PAGE 272)

Make the yogurt sauce by stirring together the yogurt, tahini, garlic, lemon juice, salt, and mint in a small serving bowl until well blended. Thin it with 1 tablespoon cool water to make 1 cup. Taste for lemon juice and salt and set it aside to let the flavors develop until ready to serve. (You can make this up to 1 day ahead and store it in the refrigerator overnight, then let it sit at room temperature for 1 hour before serving.)

To make the sliders, bring a teakettle of water to a boil. Put the bulgur in a large mixing bowl and stir in 1 cup boiling water. Cover the bowl with plastic wrap and leave it to swell and absorb all the water, about 15 minutes. Add the the onion, cumin, salt, paprika, and cayenne to the bulgur and stir to combine. Break up the ground beef into the bowl and gently mix with a rubber spatula or your hands to blend it thoroughly.

Preheat the oven to 350°F and lightly grease a baking sheet. Break the feta into marble-sized pieces to have enough for each slider. Use a ¼-cup measuring cup to portion the ground beef mixture. Moisten your hands and shape the portions into balls, and use your thumb to press a piece of feta into the center of each. Press the balls into ¾-inch patties about 2½ inches wide and space them on the baking sheet. You'll have 18 to 20 sliders.

Bake the patties until they are walnut brown, 15 to 17 minutes and remove them with a metal spatula (the bulgur tends to grab a little bit). Alternatively, pan-fry them in 1 tablespoon of olive oil in a skillet over medium-high heat or grill them on a preheated medium-high charcoal or gas grill (375°F to 425°F)for 3 to 3½ minutes per side.

To serve the sliders, sandwich each one inside a pita triangle with a sprinkle of sumac and a spoonful of the reserved yogurt sauce.

SHEPHERD'S PIE

Around here, shepherd's pie is an old stand-by that sheepherders like my friend Pam Royes and her husband Skip cooked years ago on tiny wood-burning stoves in their camps in Hell's Canyon. (They always ate beef, not lamb, which technically makes this cottage pie in the United Kingdom, but here it's still shepherd's.) There's nothing more nourishing than golden-browned mashed potatoes blanketing a belly-warming, well-seasoned ground beef filling. The art of this dish is its simplicity of ingredients, provided they are market fresh and the ground beef is top quality. I serve this to friends straight from my favorite four-inch-deep cast-iron pot accompanied by nothing more than a leafy green salad.

Makes 6 servings

....

FILLING:

2 TABLESPOONS UNSALTED BUTTER

1 LARGE ONION, CHOPPED

2 CARROTS, CHOPPED

1 POUND GROUND BEEF, 85 TO 90 PERCENT LEAN

1¼ TEASPOONS SALT

⅛ TEASPOON BLACK PEPPER

2 TABLESPOONS ALL-PURPOSE FLOUR

1¾ CUPS LOW-SALT BEEF STOCK (SHORT ORDER STOCK, PAGE 226; ROASTED BEEF STOCK, PAGE 228)

1 CUP FROZEN GREEN PEAS

TOPPING:

2 POUNDS RUSSET POTATOES (ABOUT 3 LARGE), SCRUBBED AND QUARTERED

3 GARLIC CLOVES, PEELED

½ CUP WARM MILK

3 TABLESPOONS UNSALTED BUTTER, SOFTENED

1¼ TEASPOONS SALT

⅛ TEASPOON BLACK PEPPER

PINCH OF GROUND NUTMEG

1 EGG, BEATEN

To make the filling, melt the butter in a large, deep, oven-safe skillet over medium heat. Add the onion and carrots and cook, stirring occasionally, until the onion softens and begins to brown, about 8 minutes. Add the ground beef, salt, and pepper and break up the beef into crumbles. Cook, stirring, until the beef is no longer pink.

Add the flour and stir until it absorbs all the moisture in the pan, about 1 minute. Stir in the stock, scraping the bottom of the pan to incorporate all of the flour. Reduce the heat to low and simmer until the carrots are tender, about 10 minutes. Take the skillet off the heat, taste for salt and pepper, and stir in the peas. (You can prepare the shepherd's pie filling up to 2 days in advance and reheat on the stovetop before proceeding with the recipe.)

Meanwhile, make the topping by putting the potatoes and garlic cloves in a stockpot and adding enough cool water to cover them by 1 inch. Bring the water to a boil over medium-high heat then reduce the heat to low and simmer the potatoes until they are fork tender, 15 to 20 minutes. Drain the potatoes well, setting aside the garlic cloves, and return them to the pot to steam dry for 5 minutes.

Put the milk and butter into a large mixing bowl. Slip the skins from the potatoes and pass them through a ricer or food mill or hand mash them in the bowl, blending in the reserved garlic cloves, butter, and milk until smooth. Season the mashed potatoes with the salt, pepper, and nutmeg and taste them for seasoning. Whisk in the egg until the mashed potatoes are smooth and light.

Preheat the broiler to medium high with the top rack placed 8 inches below the element. Spread and smooth the mashed potatoes over the top of the filling to make the top "crust." Broil the shepherd's pie until the top is evenly golden brown, 8 to 10 minutes.

MORE CHOICE CUTS:

Top round steak, chopped finely by hand, will bring great texture to the filling, and it can be used just like the ground beef in this recipe.

Leftover pot roast (page 104) or roast beef (page 110), anywhere from 12 to 16 ounces, can be chopped and mixed into the filling once the gravy has thickened.

REAL TAMALE PIE

For several years, I hosted a tamale party once a year and my canning and gardening friends joined in the labors. We learned why Mexican families make tamales only at holiday time. Individual tamales are labor intensive. Since my family loves them, I looked for a speedier way, and the result was this pie.

Made with a masa harina crust you shape with your hands, this pie contains a mild ground beef filling chunky with squash, pinto beans, and the sweet surprise of golden raisins. (If using dried beans, you'll need to cook them in advance.) The crust bakes up tender and light, a wonderful switch from the standard cornbread topping. Serve this pie for a carefree dinner with friends accompanied by sour cream, avocado wedges, and salsa, such as Roasted Corn Salsa (page 175).

Makes 8 servings

....

DOUGH:

2 CUPS (10 OUNCES) MASA HARINA

1 TEASPOON BAKING POWDER

¾ TEASPOON SALT

1½ CUPS LOW-SALT BEEF STOCK (SHORT ORDER STOCK, PAGE 226; ROASTED BEEF STOCK, PAGE 228), CHICKEN STOCK, OR WATER

⅔ CUP (4½ OUNCES) LARD OR VEGETABLE SHORTENING

FILLING:

1 TABLESPOON VEGETABLE OIL

1 MEDIUM ONION, CHOPPED

1 POBLANO OR GREEN PEPPER, SEEDED AND CHOPPED

1½ POUNDS GROUND BEEF, 85 TO 90 PERCENT LEAN

2¼ TEASPOONS SALT

1½ TEASPOONS GROUND CUMIN

1 TEASPOON DRIED OREGANO, PREFERABLY MEXICAN

½ TEASPOON GROUND CINNAMON

¼ TEASPOON CHILE POWDER

2 GARLIC CLOVES, MINCED

1 (14-OUNCE) CAN DICED TOMATOES WITH THEIR JUICE

½ POUND SMALL CHAYOTE OR ZUCCHINI SQUASH, CHOPPED

1½ CUP COOKED PINTO BEANS OR 1 (15-OUNCE) CAN PINTO BEANS, DRAINED AND RINSED

½ CUP GOLDEN RAISINS, CHOPPED

For the dough, mix the masa harina, baking powder, and salt in a large mixing bowl. Heat the stock in a pot over medium-high heat until warm. Mix it into the dry ingredients with a fork to make a soft dough. Beat the lard in a standing mixer with the paddle attachment on high speed until smooth and light, about 2 minutes. Add the masa dough and beat on medium speed for 5 minutes to make a thick, fluffy, and tacky dough. Cover the dough with plastic wrap and let it rest at room temperature for 30 minutes.

Meanwhile, make the pie filling. Heat the oil in a large skillet over medium heat. Add the onion and pepper and cook, stirring occasionally, until the onion turns translucent, about 3 minutes. Add the ground beef, salt, cumin, oregano, cinnamon, and chile powder. Cook, breaking up the ground beef into small clusters, until it turns brown. Add the garlic and tomatoes and reduce the heat to low. Simmer until it is as thick as chili, about 5 minutes. Stir in the chayote, pinto beans, and raisins and set aside to cool slightly.

Preheat the oven to 400°F. Spoon the ground beef mixture into a 13 x 9-inch baking dish. Dampen your hands and press the masa onto a piece of wax paper or plastic wrap into a rectangle roughly 13 x 9 inches. Flip it over on top of the pie filling and peel off the paper or plastic. Use your fingers to pinch the crust to the edges and patch any cracks. Bake the pie until the masa dough is springy to the touch in the center and looks dry on the surface, 25 to 30 minutes. Cool for 15 minutes on a wire rack before cutting into serving pieces.

BOLOGNESE MEAT SAUCE

For me, there is no better partner for pasta than this decadent and thick Italian meat sauce. It's really a stew of ground beef braised in wine, milk, and beef stock. A touch of porcini mushrooms highlights the earthy flavors of the beef, especially grassfed. Boiled spaghetti, taglietelle, or bucatini, which is hollow, all handle this substantial sauce well. Serve any of them showered with freshly grated Parmigiano-Reggiano. For two gluten-free options, try spaghetti squash described in the variation or the make-ahead Polenta Torta (recipe follows).

Makes 4 cups

....

1 OUNCE DRIED PORCINI MUSHROOMS

3 TABLESPOONS EXTRA-VIRGIN OLIVE OIL

2 OUNCES PANCETTA OR BACON, FINELY CHOPPED (ABOUT ½ CUP)

1 MEDIUM ONION, FINELY CHOPPED

1 CARROT, FINELY CHOPPED

1 CELERY STALK, FINELY CHOPPED

1 POUND GROUND BEEF, 85 TO 90 PERCENT LEAN

¼ TEASPOON RED PEPPER FLAKES

3 GARLIC CLOVES, MINCED

1¼ TEASPOONS SALT

⅛ TEASPOON BLACK PEPPER

2 TABLESPOONS TOMATO PASTE

½ CUP DRY WHITE WINE

¾ CUP WHOLE MILK

1 CUP LOW-SALT BEEF STOCK (SHORT ORDER STOCK, PAGE 226; ROASTED BEEF STOCK, PAGE 228) OR WATER

Bring a teakettle of water to a boil. Put the dried mushrooms in a small bowl, cover with 1 cup boiling water, and let them soak for 20 minutes. Drain the mushrooms, reserving the soaking liquid, and chop them finely. Strain the soaking liquid and set it aside.

Heat the oil in a large saucepan over medium heat. Add the chopped mushrooms, pancetta, onion, carrot, and celery and cook until the pancetta and vegetables begin to brown, stirring occasionally, about 12 minutes. Add the ground beef, pepper flakes, garlic, salt, and pepper and cook, breaking up the ground beef with a wooden spoon, until it changes color, about 5 minutes. Stir in the tomato paste and cook, stirring occasionally, until the meat begins to brown in the bottom of the pan, about 12 minutes.

Reduce the heat to low, pour in the wine, milk, stock, and the reserved mushroom soaking liquid. Use the spoon to scrape the bottom of the pan clean. Simmer the sauce partially covered until it is very thick, 1½ to 1¾ hours.

NOTE: **When tossing this sauce with pasta, reserve ¼ cup of the pasta cooking water to splash in if it seems too dry or "tight."**

VARIATION: SPAGHETTI SQUASH BOLOGNESE

While the Bolognese is simmering, split, seed, and microwave a medium spaghetti squash (about 3 pounds) one half at a time for 12 minutes on high heat or bake cut side down on a baking sheet at 350°F until you can pierce it with a fork, about 1 hour. Use a fork to scrape the flesh into long strands into a medium mixing bowl. While it's still warm, toss it with 2 tablespoons of unsalted butter or olive oil and serve it in place of pasta topped with the Bolognese Meat Sauce.

POLENTA TORTA

Made in layers, like lasagna (only gluten-free), this torta sandwiches Bolognese Meat Sauce (page 90) within golden layers of polenta. It's baked in a springform pan and unmolded to reveal its eye-catching layers. This torta is actually unfussy to make and can be fully assembled up to two days in advance. It makes a light yet richly flavored meal, so I serve it with a simple spinach salad tossed with balsamic vinaigrette.

Makes 8 servings
....

1½ CUPS POLENTA OR COARSE CORNMEAL

1¼ TEASPOONS SALT, DIVIDED

½ CUP LIGHTLY PACKED CHOPPED FRESH BASIL, DIVIDED

3 CUPS (ABOUT 15 OUNCES) BOLOGNESE MEAT SAUCE (PAGE 90), DIVIDED

2 CUPS GRATED MOZZARELLA CHEESE, DIVIDED

1 (14-OUNCE) CAN CRUSHED TOMATOES, DRAINED

½ CUP FINELY GRATED PARMESAN CHEESE

Bring 4 cups of water to a boil in a large saucepan over medium-high heat. Whisk the polenta with 1½ cups tepid water and ¾ teaspoon of the salt in a medium mixing bowl to prevent lumping. Whisk the polenta mixture into the boiling water until smooth. Reduce the heat to low, cover, and cook the polenta for 30 minutes, stirring vigorously about every 10 minutes.

Meanwhile, oil a 9-inch springform pan. Wrap the bottom with aluminum foil and center it on a baking sheet. Preheat the oven to 375°F.

Mix ¼ cup of the chopped basil into the Bolognese sauce. Working while the polenta is still hot and spreadable, dollop one-third of it into the prepared pan. Use a rubber spatula to smooth it all the way to the edges into a layer about ½ inch thick. Spoon on 1½ cups of the Bolognese sauce and smooth it into an even layer not quite to the edges. Sprinkle on 1 cup of the mozzarella cheese. Repeat the layers by smoothing ½ of the remaining polenta on top of the meat, adding the remaining 1½ cups Bolognese sauce, and topping it with the remaining 1 cup of mozzarella. Complete the torta with a layer of the remaining polenta. Mix the tomatoes and the remaining ¼ cup chopped basil together in a bowl and pour it over the top. Sprinkle on the Parmesan cheese.

Bake the torta uncovered until the edges are bubbling and the cheese is melted and beginning to turn golden, 20 to 25 minutes. (If you made the torta in advance and it has been refrigerated, bake it for an additional 15 minutes). Let the torta stand for 15 minutes before removing the sides of the springform pan and slicing into wedges.

CHIPOTLE AND CORN SLOPPY JOES

I have fond memories of eating mild-mannered sloppy joes—that thick ground beef and tomato chili that "slops" out of the bun—in my youth. When I grew up and learned about chipotles, the smoked jalapeño that gives anything a full-flavored kick, I couldn't live without it in this recipe. Follow the great American tradition and serve this to a crowd on a Sunday during football season on Whole-Wheat Hamburger Buns (page 72), or treat this as you would any chili: spoon it over rice or biscuits, wrap it in tortillas, or make nachos. You can also turn it into a taco salad by serving it over chopped romaine with salsa, sour cream, and, if you dare, pickled jalapeño slices.

Heat the oil in a large skillet over medium-high heat. When it shimmers, add the onion and cook, stirring occasionally, until translucent, about 2 minutes. Add the ground beef, and cook, breaking it up with a wooden spoon until it is no longer pink, about 5 minutes. Add the garlic, chipotle, tomatoes, tomato paste, corn, cumin, cinnamon, oregano, and salt and stir until well blended. Reduce the heat to low and simmer until it is thickened and there are no puddles of liquid, 9 to 10 minutes. Taste for seasoning before serving.

NOTE: Chipotle peppers are most readily available in a 7-ounce can labeled "chipotles in adobo sauce." Add some of the sauce along with the chopped chile if you like more heat.

Makes 6 servings with leftovers

1 TABLESPOON VEGETABLE OIL

1 SMALL ONION, FINELY CHOPPED

1 POUND GROUND BEEF, 85 TO 90 PERCENT LEAN

2 GARLIC CLOVES, MINCED

1 CHIPOTLE, FINELY CHOPPED*

1 (14-OUNCE) CAN DICED TOMATOES,
     WITH THEIR JUICE

1 HEAPING TABLESPOON TOMATO PASTE

1 (10-OUNCE) PACKAGE FROZEN CORN KERNELS
     (ABOUT 2½ CUPS)

1½ TEASPOONS GROUND CUMIN

½ TEASPOON GROUND CINNAMON

¼ TEASPOON DRIED OREGANO

¾ TEASPOON SALT

LEMONY CHARD BUNDLES

There is no leafy green I love more than Swiss chard. I use it to wrap up this Greek-style stuffing with beef, pork, and plenty of fresh parsley and dill to make handsome dark-green chard rolls. Once the rolls come out of the oven, I douse them with the simply made lemon sauce. Serve these rolls with orzo or rice pilaf on the side.

Makes 6 servings

....

ROLLS:

12 LARGE SWISS CHARD LEAVES, ROUGHLY
    9 INCHES LONG

1 SMALL ONION, VERY FINELY CHOPPED

2 GARLIC CLOVES, MINCED

¼ CUP LIGHTLY PACKED CHOPPED FRESH PARSLEY

3 TABLESPOONS LIGHTLY PACKED CHOPPED FRESH
    DILL OR 1 TEASPOON DRIED

1¼ TEASPOONS SALT

⅛ TEASPOON BLACK PEPPER

8 OUNCES GROUND BEEF, 85 TO 90 PERCENT LEAN

6 OUNCES GROUND PORK

4 TABLESPOONS SALTED BUTTER, MELTED

LEMON SAUCE:

1 TEASPOON CORNSTARCH

1 TABLESPOON FRESHLY SQUEEZED LEMON JUICE

2 EGG YOLKS

¼ TEASPOON SALT

½ CUP LOW-SALT BEEF STOCK (SHORT ORDER
    STOCK, PAGE 226; ROASTED BEEF STOCK, PAGE
    228) OR WATER

To make the chard rolls, bring a large pot of salted water to a boil over medium-high heat. Use a paring knife to trim the thick stems from the base of each chard leaf, notching into the leaf to cut off the widest part. Chop the stems into 1-inch lengths and put them into an 8- or 9-inch square baking dish. Use tongs to dip each leaf into the boiling water for 30 seconds, shake to drain, and drape them around the edge of a colander to drain and cool. Repeat this procedure with the remaining chard leaves.

Put the onion, garlic, parsley, dill, salt, and pepper in a large mixing bowl. Break up the ground beef and pork into the bowl and use a rubber spatula or your hands to mix it well.

Preheat the oven to 350°F. Work with one chard leaf at a time with the rib side up. Place ¼ cup of the ground beef mixture at the base of the leaf and press it into a log about 4 inches wide. Roll up the leaf around it, tucking in the sides, and rolling all the way to the tip. Place the chard roll on top of the chard stems in the baking dish with the seam side down. Repeat with the remaining leaves and crowd them into the baking dish. Drizzle them with the melted butter. (You can prepare them up to this point 1 day ahead.) Cover the baking dish securely with aluminum foil and bake until the chard is easily pierced with a fork and the meat is cooked through to 155°F on an instant-read thermometer, 40 to 45 minutes.

Meanwhile, make the sauce by whisking the cornstarch with the lemon juice in a small mixing bowl until smooth. Add the yolks and the salt and whisk until smooth and lightened in color. Bring the stock to a boil over medium-high heat in a small saucepan. Drizzle some of the hot liquid into the cornstarch mixture and whisk rapidly. Put the saucepan over low heat and whisk all of the cornstarch mixture into the saucepan. Cook without boiling until it thickens, about 1 minute. Spoon the sauce over the chard rolls just before serving with a portion of the chard stems.

VARIATION: CABBAGE ROLLS

If you prefer cabbage, boil a small, cored Savoy or green cabbage in plenty of salted water until the outer leaves can be peeled away, about 4 minutes. Since the leaves are larger, make 8 rolls (instead of 12). Roll, bake, and sauce as directed.

BEEF RAVIOLI

with Sage Butter Sauce

When a day comes along that I have time for a kitchen project, I often opt for making homemade ravioli. This recipe makes thirty large ravioli (I plan on five per serving) to freeze for a dinner party or an extra-special weeknight supper down the road.

Mix the pasta dough and let it rest while you make the uncooked filling. Roll the dough into sheets using a pasta machine, or with a confident hand using a rolling pin, then fill, seal, and boil, or freeze for up to three months. Boil them directly from the freezer to serve at your whim in sage butter sauce or slip one into a bowl of Crystal Clear Consommé (page 231) for an impressive first course light on the beef.

Makes 6 servings for a main course;
15 servings for an appetizer

....

PASTA:

4 CUPS (18 OUNCES) ALL-PURPOSE FLOUR, PLUS
    ADDITIONAL FOR DUSTING

6 EGGS, BEATEN

FILLING:

1 GARLIC CLOVE, PEELED

1 SMALL ONION, CHOPPED

1 SMALL CARROT, CHOPPED

1 CELERY STALK, CHOPPED

1 EGG

1 CUP FINELY GRATED PARMESAN CHEESE, PLUS
    ADDITIONAL FOR SERVING

8 OUNCES GROUND BEEF, 85 TO 90 PERCENT LEAN

½ TEASPOON SALT

⅛ TEASPOON BLACK PEPPER

SAGE BUTTER SAUCE:

12 TABLESPOONS SALTED BUTTER, CHILLED, CUT
    INTO CUBES, AND DIVIDED

¼ CUP FINELY CHOPPED FRESH SAGE

FRESHLY GROUND BLACK PEPPER

MORE CHOICE CUTS:
Leftover pot roast or braises, cooled and chopped, are ideal ready-made ravioli fillings.

To make the pasta dough by hand, put the flour in a bowl and make a well in the center. Pour the eggs in the center and use a fork to whisk the flour into the eggs, working progressively toward the outer rim of the bowl to gradually incorporate the flour into a dough. When you have a rough dough, begin kneading it with your hands. Once the dough is fairly smooth, dust the counter with flour and lift the dough from the bowl, discarding all the raggedy bits of flour. Knead the dough until it is satiny smooth and firm, 10 to 12 minutes. Dust the dough with flour, wrap it in plastic, and let it rest for 30 minutes at room temperature.

To make the pasta dough in a food processor, put the flour and eggs in the food processor bowl fitted with the plastic dough blade. Attach the cover and turn on the machine until a dough forms, about 1 minute. If there is stray flour, add 1 teaspoon water at a time through the feed tube to make a cohesive dough slightly tacky to the touch. Knead the dough by hand on a lightly floured counter until it is satiny smooth. Dust the dough with flour, wrap it in plastic, and let it rest for 30 minutes at room temperature.

To make the filling, purée the garlic, onion, carrot, celery, egg, and Parmesan in a food processor, scraping down the sides once or twice, until very finely chopped. Add the ground beef, salt, and pepper and pulse 8 to 10 times until it is minced and well blended. (You can make the filling up to 1 day in advance and store it in the refrigerator until ready to use.)

Fill a small bowl with water and have a pastry brush on hand. Sprinkle a baking sheet with flour and set it aside. Dust the counter lightly with all-purpose flour. Cut the dough into 4 pieces, keeping the unused dough covered. Roll the dough through a pasta machine into wide strips according to the manufacturer's instructions, progressively making them thinner until your hand is a shadow behind the sheet of pasta. Alternatively, roll out the dough by hand, dusting the counter lightly as needed to make an even, ultra-thin sheet you can almost see through.

Use a round cutter about 3 inches in diameter to cut circles spaced as closely together as you can. Dust the circles very lightly with flour to prevent sticking and keep them covered to prevent them from drying out while you continue to roll out and cut the remaining dough.

Place level tablespoon-sized dollops of the filling on half of the pasta circles, brush the edges lightly with water, and top with another circle of pasta. Use your fingers to push air pockets away from the mounds of filling and press to seal the edges well. Gently pat the top of each ravioli to spread the filling out and so each one looks like a hat. Arrange them in a single layer on the baking sheet. (To freeze, put the baking sheet in the freezer until the ravioli are solid. Transfer into resealable freezer bags for storing.)

To cook the ravioli, bring a large pot of salted water to a boil over medium-high heat and have a colander set into a large bowl on hand. Reduce the heat to low so that the water is simmering steadily and slip the ravioli into it. Simmer gently until the ravioli float to the surface, 3½ to 4 minutes. Collect them with a slotted spoon and let them drain in the colander briefly. Reserve ¼ cup of the pasta water.

Meanwhile, make the sauce by melting 6 tablespoons of the butter in a large skillet over low heat. Add the sage and cook until fragrant, about 2 minutes. Ladle ¼ cup of pasta water into the pan, bring it to a simmer, and whisk in the remaining 6 tablespoons of butter to make a light sauce. Slip the drained ravioli into the pan and shake it to coat them with the sauce before serving with black pepper and grated Parmesan to taste.

INDIAN-SPICED STUFFED PEPPERS

Baked stuffed peppers are often ho-hum to me, but these offer a harmony of enlivening flavors. Inspired by Julie Sahni's ground beef recipe in *Classic Indian Cooking*, I spiced up the filling with coriander and cumin and perfumed the tomato sauce with garlic and ginger. This filling calls for quinoa (*keen-wah*), a marvelous, quick-cooking, high-protein grain. The peppers are lovely over a bed of simply sautéed greens, such as kale. You can also use the filling to give new life to summer's supersized zucchini as detailed in the variation.

Makes 6 servings

....

FILLING:

2 TABLESPOONS VEGETABLE OIL

1 MEDIUM ONION, CHOPPED

1 TABLESPOON GROUND CORIANDER

1½ TEASPOONS GROUND CUMIN

¼ TEASPOON RED PEPPER FLAKES

1 POUND GROUND BEEF, 85 TO 90 PERCENT LEAN

1½ TEASPOONS SALT

1¼ CUPS QUINOA

8 SMALL RED, YELLOW, OR GREEN BELL PEPPERS

SAUCE:

1 (28-OUNCE) CAN WHOLE PEELED TOMATOES, DRAINED

2 GARLIC CLOVES, PEELED

1-INCH PIECE GINGER, PEELED

¾ TEASPOON SALT

To make the filling, heat the oil in a large skillet over medium heat. Add the onion, coriander, cumin, and pepper flakes, and cook, stirring now and then, until the onion softens and the spices smell toasted, about 6 minutes. Add the ground beef and the salt and cook, breaking it up into clusters with a spoon, until it is no longer pink. Reduce the heat to low and add the quinoa and 1½ cups water. Cover and simmer until the quinoa plumps and most of the liquid is absorbed, about 25 minutes.

Meanwhile, cut off the tops of the peppers and use a teaspoon to remove the seeds and ribs. Take a very thin slice off the bottom of each pepper to stabilize them and arrange them in a 13 x 9-inch baking dish. Pack them with the ground beef mixture. (You can prepare them to this point up to 2 days in advance.)

Preheat the oven to 375°F.

To make the sauce, purée the tomatoes, garlic, ginger, and salt in a blender or with an immersion blender to make a smooth sauce. Dollop it on top of each pepper and let it spill down the sides. Cover the baking dish securely with aluminum foil and cook until the peppers are fork tender, 35 to 40 minutes.

VARIATION: STUFFED ZUCCHINI ROUNDS

Use large zucchinis weighing 2 pounds or more. Trim the ends and cut the zucchini into 4-inch rounds. Stand each round up on end and use a small round cutter to punch out the seedy center, leaving at least a ½-inch wall. Alternately, use a paring knife to carve out the centers and discard them. Arrange the zucchini cylinders on end in the baking dish and fill, sauce, and bake as directed.

CHAPTER 5

SLOW SIMMERED FEASTS

I credit my Dutch oven casserole, the cobalt blue one I bought at a yard sale for twenty dollars, with producing the most wonderfully tender beef I've ever eaten. The amazing thing is that the beef was a chuck roast, one of the toughest cuts on a cow.

My oval Dutch oven, which usually sat unused in the cupboard above my stove, was the only pot large enough to contain the plate-size, bony cut labeled "arm roast" I'd pulled from the chest freezer one Sunday in October. The heavy-bottomed pot browned the meat as dark as walnut skin. I poured in enough water to make the roast look like it was taking a shallow bath, and the lid clunked down with authority. I set it into a low oven, got caught up in weekend tasks, and hours passed. What emerged from that pot was a miracle only heat, time, and a solid pot could create: the complete transformation of the un-chewable and sinewy into a succulent feast.

Since then, I've come to think of slow-simmered dishes as the most convenient, stress-free, and satisfying of all. In an old community cookbook, I found a recipe called "Stay-A-Bed Stew," a name I now apply to anything that cooks unattended on the stovetop or in the oven. It's widely known as braising.

The recipes in this chapter all use this remarkable old-world method. You'll encounter a compendium of pot roasts, stews, and other meals of luscious meats steeped in their own gravy, from homey Boston Baked Beans with Brisket (page 120) to singular Heavenly Green Stew (page 117). Stuffed with root vegetables or beans, baked inside a flaky crust, or served with a raft of buttermilk biscuits, these are stand-alone meals where a crisp, brightly dressed salad is a nice, but nonessential, counterpoint.

The standard way to braise involves browning the meat, which heightens beef's most savory compounds, before adding stock, wine, water, or a combination. The liquids carry those flavors as they melt the fat connecting the meat fibers, until those fibers fall apart with a fork's prodding. Grassfed Pot Roast with Parsnips, Carrots, and Fingerlings (page 104) exemplifies this classic method written for first timers. It serves as a model for browning the meat and the steps involved in building layers of flavor through the choice of liquid, vegetables, herbs, and the timing and judicious use of salt.

Other recipes illustrate variations on the essential technique where the meat is seared in the oven, a better choice for rounded roasts, which brown more evenly with less splattering and attention. Some of these braised meats are not browned until the very last step. In Tomato-Braised Beef Cheeks with Wilted Spinach and Oven Polenta (page 113), a final blast in a hot oven crisps the beef and sauce to a veneer. This braise-and-glaze technique also creates the syrupy sauce of Rolled Cranberry-Glazed Beef Brisket with Braised Red Cabbage (page 107), a pot roast worthy of centerpiece status on the holiday table.

These are recipes to make when you have the time, in anticipation of the days when you don't—try them for Sunday suppers, holidays, potlucks, or a workday when everything else feels like too much. Pot roasts, stews, and other simmered beef dishes all freeze well, defrost in the microwave, and reheat in the oven, tasting better than the day you made them. Their leftovers are a treasure trove of comforting meals, from Potato-Pot Roast Croquettes (page 106) to Last-Minute Beef Ragù (page 112). Meals that took hours to cook one day or a month ago give you a break when you need it, so that you can take a breath, lift your spoon, and just eat.

Braising Choice Cuts

The very best braising cuts come from the forequarter, predominantly the chuck primal. "Pot roast" is a cooking term applied to labels on chuck roasts, as in "boneless pot roast." Although these well-exercised muscles rife with intermuscular fat become exceptionally tender through slow simmering, grassfed retains more texture than grain-finished beef even when thoroughly cooked. Absent from this list are any cuts from the round (with the exception of sirloin tip roast) because they are disappointingly dry and stringy when braised and are best reserved for the quick-cooking recipes in chapter 6 or the slow roasts in chapter 8.

BEEF CHEEKS are palm-sized muscles prized from the pockets of cheekbone. These heavily worked muscles are loaded with flavor and broth-enriching collagen and are conveniently portion sized for braising.

BRISKET is the large, flat pectoral muscle with long, thick muscle fibers and a fat cap on one side. It is sold whole or in halves: the "flat" is the leaner squared-off cut; the "point" or "nose" is tapered and has a layer of fat running through it. One of the premium pot roast cuts, brisket is also ideal for smoking and brining and poaching for corned beef (chapter 10, page 264).

CHUCK ROAST is a general term for any flat-sided and thick (usually three to five inches) cut from the chuck, or shoulder. It contains several muscles groups with grains running in different directions bound by seams of connective tissue. Sold under many different names, all have the clue "chuck" on the label. Chuck roasts are commonly boneless, and some of them come rolled and tied in netting. Others contain bones, which contribute flavor to the braising liquid. Look for the superlative blade roast, the arm roast with a tell-tale round bone in the center, and the 7-bone pot roast, distinguished by a thin, curved bone that looks like the number "7." All chuck roasts turn tender after low, slow cooking, whether in a braise or in a low oven (chapter 8, page 198).

FLANK is a thin abdominal muscle from the bottom sirloin with thick meat fibers running in the same direction. One of the few cuts that adapts equally well to high or low-heat cooking, it is a very lean (though not inexpensive) option for braising that shreds beautifully.

SHORT RIBS are the meaty bones from the chuck, or shoulder, rib primals, and plate. English-style ribs are cut into roughly 4-inch lengths that may come in four-bone sections (you can cut through the intercostal meat to make single-bone servings). Flanken or Korean-style are very thinly sliced cross-cut short ribs (about ¼ inch). You can also buy boneless short ribs. Most braising recipes call for the thicker English style, which benefit from trimming some of the exterior fat (Trimming, page 51) before use.

SIRLOIN TIP ROAST, aka round tip roast, is a relatively tender, boneless roast that lies between the sirloin, or hip, and the round, or hindquarter. Leaner than chuck roasts, it is the only cut from the round I recommend for braises and stews. It is also one of the most versatile cuts for both slow and fast cooking methods.

TONGUE is a collagen-laden whole muscle that requires hours of slow-simmering to become tender, and is often corned. Once cooked and peeled, tongue can be eaten as is, thinly sliced or chopped for tacos, or breaded and fried to make cutlets or fritters.

THE BEST STEW BEEF

While you can buy pre-cut stew beef, there are many reasons why I prefer to cut my own. Primarily, I like to know exactly what beef I'm getting. Packaged meat labeled "stew meat" generally comes from the chuck or the round, but I prefer the chuck by far. Round cuts turn dry even after hours of cooking in a liquid because these single muscles have little of the intermuscular fat that "melts" during slow cooking.

By cutting my own stew beef, I can also control the size and trim off all the fat. For dishes like Richard Olney's Beef Bourguignon (page 126), which I like to serve in wide bowls with a knife and fork, I cut a chuck roast into large chunks. When making Two-Bean Chili Colorado (page 130) and other dishes eaten with a spoon, I cut the beef into bite-size cubes.

Size also lets me adjust the timing of any stew. If I have two hours or more, larger pieces are no problem, but if I want the stew done within ninety minutes, I cut the beef into ½-inch cubes and get dinner done on time.

Doing it yourself instead of buying packaged "stew meat" also saves money, and, because cut meat has more surface area exposed to potential contamination, it can give you peace of mind if you have food safety concerns. This goes for "fajita meat" and "kebab meat," too, which you can cut yourself from a good-sized steak or small roast (page 50).

SLOW COOKER CONVERSION

I don't often use a slow cooker, but I appreciate the convenience it offers to people who can't be at home to tend a simmering pot. Many of the braises and stews in this chapter, and many stocks and soups in chapter 9 can be adapted for slow cookers with a six-quart capacity.

Read through the recipe first because most of them involve browning—either in a skillet before simmering or in the oven afterwards—which will require additional cookware. You'll brown in a skillet and then capture the flavor in the browned bits on the skillet's surface by scraping it clean with a little added liquid and pouring it all into the slow cooker. For recipes calling for browning *after* simmering, you'll need to transfer the meat to an oven-safe pan. Only you can decide if the slow cooker offers you a convenience.

Other adjustments you'll need to make include reducing the stock or other liquid called for in the recipe by one-quarter to one-half because there is less evaporation in a slow cooker. Also, reserve herbs and spices for the last hour of cooking to preserve their punch, and taste and fine-tune the seasonings before serving. I've found these general time guidelines below hold true—provided that you start checking the beef's doneness on the early side because you *can* overcook a braise—tailored to manufacturer's recommendations and your own experience:

Pot roast, short ribs, and beef stock: 10 to 12 hours on low or 5 to 6 hours on high.

Stews and soups: 6 to 8 hours on low or 3 to 4 hours on high.

GRASSFED POT ROAST

with Parsnips, Carrots, and Fingerlings

A superlative pot roast is one of life's essentials, and this recipe covers all you need to make it your own. Patient browning makes all the difference, especially if you use water in place of good beef stock. Once the stovetop work is done, the oven does nearly all the rest, simmering the meat to succulence and bathing it all in a velvety sauce that's perfect with a spike of mustard, if you like. I stuff the pot with root vegetables, including sweet parsnips and waxy fingerling potatoes, in good proportion to the beef. There's always enough for last-minute company, or to provide leftover beef for the Potato-Pot Roast Croquettes (recipe follows) on another night.

Makes 6 servings with leftovers

1 (3- TO 3½-POUND) BONELESS CHUCK ROAST

KOSHER SALT

1 TABLESPOON VEGETABLE OIL

1 MEDIUM ONION, THICKLY SLICED

3 TABLESPOONS ALL-PURPOSE FLOUR

3 CUPS LOW-SALT BEEF STOCK (SHORT ORDER STOCK, PAGE 226; ROASTED BEEF STOCK, PAGE 228) OR WATER

1 TABLESPOON WORCESTERSHIRE SAUCE

1½ TEASPOONS SALT

¼ TEASPOON BLACK PEPPER

1 TEASPOON CHOPPED FRESH THYME LEAVES OR ½ TEASPOON DRIED

2 BAY LEAVES

3 LARGE CARROTS, PEELED

2 LARGE PARSNIPS (ABOUT 1 POUND), PEELED

1½ POUNDS FINGERLING POTATOES

1 TABLESPOON WHOLE-GRAIN MUSTARD (PAGE 234), OPTIONAL

Preheat the oven to 300°F. Pat the beef dry and season it liberally with the kosher salt on both sides. Heat the oil in a large Dutch oven over medium-high heat. A splatter screen reduces clean up. When it shimmers, add the beef and cook undisturbed until the underside is deeply browned, about 10 minutes. Turn the beef and brown the other side, about 10 minutes more.

Using tongs, remove the meat from the pot and set it aside on a dinner plate. There should be just a film of fat in the pot; if necessary, pour out any excess. Reduce the heat to medium, add the onion and cook, stirring occasionally, until it browns, about 6 minutes. By now, the bottom of the pot will be darkened from the meat bits stuck to it. Add the flour and cook for 1 minute, stirring, until the flour is absorbed. Pour in the stock and Worcestershire sauce. While the liquid comes to a boil, use a wooden spoon to scrape the film of flour and the browned bits from the bottom of the pot. Add the salt, pepper, thyme, bay leaves, and the beef, along with any juices from the plate, to the liquid. The surface of the beef will be just above the liquid. Cover the pot securely and place it in the oven for 2½ hours.

Meanwhile, cut the carrots and parsnips by dividing the slender part from the thicker end. Slice the slender end into 1-inch rounds; cut the thick ends lengthwise and crosscut them into 1-inch crescents. Cut the potatoes into 2-inch-long segments.

Turn the beef over and fit the carrots, parsnips, and potatoes around the beef, pushing them into the liquid so that they are partially submerged. Cover the pot and continue braising, stirring the vegetables once, until the beef shreds readily with a fork and the vegetables are very tender 1 to 1½ hours more for a total of 3½ to 4 hours.

Transfer the pot roast to a cutting board, scoop the root vegetables into a warmed serving bowl, and discard the bay leaves. If necessary, skim any fat from the gravy with a ladle. (If serving this the next day, chill the gravy in the refrigerator and lift off the layer of fat.) Stir in the mustard, if using, and taste for seasoning.

Slice the pot roast thickly, or, for leaner servings, divide it along the natural seams, trim off the fat, and cut it into serving pieces. Arrange the beef in the center of the vegetables in the serving bowl and pour the gravy over all.

MORE CHOICE CUTS:

Bone-in chuck roast makes a ready substitute for boneless— just pull away the bones, trim any fat, and slice the chunks before serving.

Brisket is a terrific cut to pot roast, a bit fattier than chuck roast with a grain that generally runs in the same direction for easy slicing.

POTATO-POT ROAST CROQUETTES

These crisply coated, fluffy potato cakes are just one reason we hoard leftover pot roast in my house. Little did I know that we're not alone: clever cooks from Japan to Ireland shape mashed potatoes and cooked meat into cakes, then batter and fry them. The result is a thrifty bistro-style supper. I shape the croquettes to the size of duck eggs, pan-fry them until golden brown all the way around, and we devour them with a salad of escarole in mustardy vinaigrette.

Makes 4 servings

....

1½ POUNDS RUSSET POTATOES (ABOUT 3 MEDIUM), PEELED AND QUARTERED

1 TABLESPOON SALT

2 EGGS

¼ TEASPOON BLACK PEPPER

1 CUP COARSE, DRY BREADCRUMBS

5 OUNCES LEFTOVER POT ROAST (PAGE 104), COOLED AND COARSELY SHREDDED (ABOUT 1 CUP)

¾ CUP VEGETABLE OIL

Put the potatoes in a saucepan, and add cool water to cover. Bring the water to a boil over medium-high heat, add the salt, reduce the heat to medium low, and simmer until they are fork tender, about 20 minutes. Drain and return them to the pan to steam dry for 5 minutes. Mash the potatoes using a potato ricer, grater, or masher, the smoother, the better. Beat 1 of the eggs, add it to the potatoes along with the pepper, and stir just to blend them in.

Beat the remaining egg in a small bowl. Put the breadcrumbs into a pie plate or wide, shallow bowl. Scoop and lightly pack the potato mixture into ¼-cup measuring cup. Tap it out into the palm of your hand and flatten it into a pancake. Press about 1 tablespoon of the shredded pot roast into the center of the pancake, then fold the potato over to enclose it. Use your hands to pack and smooth the potato into an egg shape. Repeat with the remaining potatoes and meat; you'll get 10 to 12 croquettes. Dip each croquette into the egg, letting the excess drip off, and roll it in the breadcrumbs, pressing lightly for an even coat. Place them on a dinner plate and chill them in the refrigerator for at least 10 minutes. (They'll also hold in the refrigerator for 12 hours to fry the next day.)

Fit a rack into a baking sheet and preheat the oven to 250°F. Heat the oil in a medium skillet over medium-high heat and have a slotted spoon on hand. When a droplet of the egg sizzles instantly in the skillet, shallow-fry the croquettes 4 at a time so that you have enough space to roll them over. Use the spoon to roll them around gently. When the underside is golden brown, turn the croquettes over and fry the other side. Drain them on the rack, put them in the oven to keep them warm, and fry the second batch. The croquettes will hold in the warm oven for 30 minutes.

ROLLED CRANBERRY-GLAZED BEEF BRISKET

with Braised Red Cabbage

This festive garnet-glazed roast makes pot roast worthy of a Christmas or New Year's Eve dinner. Braised in whole cranberries, brown sugar, and ginger, the beef drinks in a tangy sweetness. It's an unusual combination, but I'm always looking to include these beloved little fruits in my cooking outside of Thanksgiving. Yet I nearly abandoned the idea until I was browsing through my 1952 *Joy of Cooking* and found a cranberry pot roast, which emboldened me to try out my own. The cranberries' natural pectin creates a chunky, chutney-like sauce to garnish the beef, which I like to serve with Braised Red Cabbage (recipe follows) and baked mashed butternut squash.

Brisket, with its long fibers and loads of collagen, is one of the best pot-roasting cuts there is. The flat cut is the leaner, thinner part of a whole brisket (the point end has a fat layer running through it). I trim it well, then roll it up and tie it using the silicone bands (Sources, page 273) in place of butcher's twine, which allows me to serve this brisket in lovely rounded slices.

Makes 6 servings with leftovers

BRISKET

1 (3½- TO 4-POUND) FLAT CUT BRISKET

KOSHER SALT

1 (12-OUNCE) BAG FRESH OR FROZEN
    CRANBERRIES

1 MEDIUM ONION, CHOPPED

¾ CUP PACKED LIGHT BROWN SUGAR

1 TEASPOON GROUND GINGER

½ TEASPOON BLACK PEPPER

¼ TEASPOON GROUND CLOVES

1 CUP LOW-SALT BEEF STOCK (SHORT ORDER
    STOCK, PAGE 226; ROASTED BEEF STOCK, PAGE
    228) OR WATER

1 CUP ORANGE JUICE

1 BAY LEAF

CONTINUES ▶

Preheat the oven to 500°F. Cut 5 (14-inch) strands of butcher's twine or have 5 large silicone bands on hand. Trim any fat from the underside of the brisket, pat it dry, and season it liberally on both sides with the kosher salt. Roll it up tightly the long way with the fat on the outside and tie it with the butcher's twine or secure it with silicone bands. Put the roast in a Dutch oven or other deep and heavy pot just large enough to contain it. Roast it uncovered in the hot oven until dark walnut brown, about 20 minutes.

Meanwhile, mix the cranberries, onion, brown sugar, ginger, pepper, cloves, stock, orange juice, and bay leaf in a medium saucepan and bring it to a boil over medium-high heat.

Reduce the oven temperature to 325°F and pour the cranberry mixture over the beef. Cover the pot and cook the beef until you can shred the meat easily with a fork, 2 to 2½ hours.

Raise the oven temperature to 400°F. Transfer the beef to a clean oven-safe serving dish and remove the twine or bands. Strain the sauce, reserving the cranberry mixture, and pour the sauce over the beef. Discard the bay leaf. Roast the beef uncovered in the oven until it forms a shiny glaze and the sauce is syrupy, 12 to 15 minutes. Slice the beef ½ inch thick and spoon the cranberries all around it before serving with the braised cabbage, if desired.

MORE CHOICE CUTS:
Boneless chuck roast that comes rolled and tied is also ideal for this dish.

Sirloin tip roast, aka round tip roast, is a leaner choice than chuck for braising and slices easily and handsomely.

BRAISED RED CABBAGE

Makes 6 servings

....

2 POUNDS RED CABBAGE (ROUGHLY 1 MEDIUM HEAD)

1¼ TEASPOONS SALT

2 TABLESPOONS UNSALTED BUTTER

1 TABLESPOON EXTRA-VIRGIN OLIVE OIL

1 CUP DRY RIESLING OR WHITE WINE

FRESHLY GROUND BLACK PEPPER

Quarter the cabbage, cut out the core, and slice it into ¼-inch ribbons. When ready to cook, toss the cabbage with the salt in a large bowl. Heat the butter and olive oil in a large skillet over medium-high heat. When the butter foams, add the cabbage in large handfuls and cook until each batch wilts, making more room in the pan. Pour in the wine and cover. When you see steam escaping from the pan, reduce the heat to low and cook until the cabbage is very tender and only a film of liquid remains, 30 to 35 minutes. Taste for salt, season it with the pepper, and cover to keep it warm.

ROAST BEEF BRAISED IN ZINFANDEL

with Winter Herbs and Potato Gnocchi

This is a meat and potatoes dinner that I love to make for dinner guests. Sirloin tip roast, aka round tip roast, is the only cut from the round primal that likes a long braise to produce moist slices of beef. Because it is nicely shaped and boneless, it's ideal for slicing whole. I treat the beef with a moist rub of garlic and fresh herbs for up to two days before browning it in a hot oven and slow-cooking it in red wine. Like all pot roasts, it demands so little active work time, I can get my hands involved in making the Potato Gnocchi (recipe follows). Or, serve it with slices of artisan bread to sop up the winey juices.

Makes 6 servings

....

3 TABLESPOONS EXTRA-VIRGIN OLIVE OIL

4 GARLIC CLOVES, PEELED AND SMASHED

2 TABLESPOONS FINELY CHOPPED FRESH THYME

2 TABLESPOONS FINELY CHOPPED FRESH ROSEMARY

1 TABLESPOON FINELY CHOPPED FRESH SAGE

1 TABLESPOON KOSHER SALT

1 (2½- TO 3-POUND) SIRLOIN TIP ROAST

1 MEDIUM ONION, THICKLY SLICED

2 FENNEL BULBS, CORED AND THICKLY SLICED

12 OUNCES CREMINI MUSHROOMS, STEMS TRIMMED AND CUT IN HALF

1 (750-ML) BOTTLE ZINFANDEL OR OTHER DRY RED WINE

2 BAY LEAVES

4 TABLESPOONS CHILLED UNSALTED BUTTER, CUT INTO ½-INCH CUBES

Make an herb paste by muddling together the olive oil, garlic, thyme, rosemary, sage, and salt in a mortar and pestle or a small mixing bowl with a wooden spoon. Rub the herb paste all over the roast, wrap in plastic wrap, and refrigerate for at least 12 hours and up to 2 days.

Preheat the oven to 450°F with the rack positioned in the lower half of the oven. Place the roast in a Dutch oven and roast uncovered until the garlic and herbs in the rub change color and the beef surface is nicely browned, about 20 minutes. Remove from the oven and reduce the temperature to 300°F.

Scatter the onion, fennel, and mushrooms around the roast. Pour the wine over the meat and vegetables and tuck in the bay leaves. Cover and braise until you can shred the meat easily with two forks, 2½ to 3 hours.

Reduce the oven temperature to 250°F. Use tongs to lift the beef from the pot onto a cutting board and cover to keep it warm. Scoop the vegetables from the broth with a slotted spoon onto a serving platter and keep warm in the oven. Discard the bay leaves. Place the pot with the braising liquids over medium heat, bring to a simmer, and reduce until it is syrupy and reduced to about 1 cup, about 20 minutes. Remove it from the heat, whisk in the butter to make a glossy sauce, and taste for salt.

To serve, slice the beef ½ inch thick against the grain and arrange it on the bed of vegetables. Spoon some of the sauce over the meat slices to moisten them and pass the rest at the table to serve with the gnocchi, if desired.

POTATO GNOCCHI

If you can make mashed potatoes, you can make gnocchi, tender potato pillows that turn velvety in any sauce. I make it even easier by baking the potatoes in the oven while the Roast Beef Braised in Zinfandel slow cooks. To speed things up, you can also microwave them. A food mill or ricer makes the smoothest potato puree for gnocchi. I break from tradition by using a melon baller to portion and shape them, which yields more consistently sized gnocchi that are perfectly bite sized (i.e., not too big).

To make the gnocchi well in advance, or save extra for another meal like the Last-Minute Beef Ragu (page 112), freeze the gnocchi for up to 3 months, and boil them straight from the freezer as instructed.

Makes 6 servings

. . . .

1¾ POUNDS RUSSET POTATOES (ABOUT 4 MEDIUM)

1 CUP (4½ OUNCES) ALL-PURPOSE FLOUR, PLUS
    ADDITIONAL FOR SHAPING

1 TEASPOON SALT

1 EGG, BEATEN

OLIVE OIL FOR GREASING THE BOWL

MORE CHOICE CUTS:

Boneless chuck roasts, which are sometime rolled and tied, are less lean than sirloin tip roast, may take an additional 30 to 60 minutes cooking time.

Brisket, rolled and tied according to the instructions in the recipe for Rolled Cranberry-Glazed Beef Brisket (page 107) works great here, too.

Pierce the potatoes 3 to 4 times with a fork and bake them on the rack alongside the braising beef or in a preheated 350°F oven until they can be stabbed straight through with a fork, 1 to 1½ hours. Alternatively, microwave the potatoes according to the settings on your microwave until fork tender.

When the potatoes are cool enough to handle, cut them in half, use a spoon to scoop out the flesh, and pass it through a food mill or ricer into a large mixing bowl. Alternatively, use a hand masher to mash the potatoes in the bowl, taking care to mash them well. Sift the flour and salt over the potatoes and add the egg. Use a fork to combine the ingredients into a supple, non-sticky "dough." Cover the dough with plastic wrap and let it rest for 15 to 30 minutes.

Dust a baking sheet with flour and have a small bowl of flour on hand. Use a melon baller or a 1 teaspoon measuring spoon to portion the potato into tiny rounds and flick each ball of dough from the melon baller with your thumb to leave a small cup. Dust the melon baller and your thumb frequently to keep the dough from sticking. As you shape them (expect some irregularity), arrange the gnocchi in a single layer on the baking sheet and set them aside. (To freeze the gnocchi, freeze them directly on the baking sheet until firm, about 2 hours. Then, package them in a resealable freezer bag for storage for up to 3 months.)

To cook the gnocchi, bring a large pot of salted water to a boil over high heat and grease a large mixing bowl with olive oil. Drop half of the gnocchi into the pot and use a slotted spoon to capture them about 30 seconds after they bob to the surface, draining them well. Toss them with the olive oil in the bowl and repeat with the remaining gnocchi.

LAST-MINUTE BEEF RAGÙ

This is a meal built on leftovers. The braised meat from any pot roast becomes the foundation for a traditional pasta sauce that simmers for only 20 minutes. This recipe prepares enough ragù for the full one-and-a-half-pound batch of Potato Gnocchi (page 111) or one pound of pasta, fresh or dried. Wide, short papardelle is an Italian standard for this type of meaty sauce. Stout hollow pastas, like penne rigate (with ridges) and campanelle are good, too.

Makes 4 to 6 servings
....

2 TABLESPOONS EXTRA-VIRGIN OLIVE OIL

1 MEDIUM ONION, CHOPPED

10 TO 12 OUNCES RESERVED LEFTOVER POT ROAST
    (PAGE 104), COARSELY SHREDDED

4 GARLIC CLOVES, PEELED AND VERY THINLY
    SLICED

1½ CUPS LOW-SALT BEEF STOCK (SHORT ORDER
    STOCK, PAGE 226; ROASTED BEEF STOCK,
    PAGE 228)

1 (28-OUNCE) CAN WHOLE PEELED TOMATOES,
    DRAINED

1 TABLESPOON TOMATO PASTE

½ TEASPOON SALT

¼ TEASPOON RED PEPPER FLAKES

1½ POUNDS GNOCCHI (PAGE 111), OR 1 POUND
    FRESH OR DRIED PASTA

GRATED PARMESAN CHEESE

FRESHLY GROUND BLACK PEPPER

Heat the olive oil in a large skillet over medium heat and bring a large pot of salted water to a boil over high heat. Add the onion to the skillet and cook until lightly browned, stirring occasionally, about 6 minutes. Add the pot roast, garlic, and stock and simmer steadily for 10 minutes until the liquid reduces by half. Crush the tomatoes with your fingers as you add them to the skillet, and stir in the tomato paste, salt, and pepper flakes. Reduce the heat to low and simmer until thickened, 15 to 20 minutes, and taste for salt.

Meanwhile, boil the gnocchi as directed in the recipe on page 111 or the pasta in boiling salted water until tender to the bite. Serve immediately in warmed pasta bowls with a ladle of the ragù sprinkled with Parmesan and black pepper to taste.

TOMATO-BRAISED BEEF CHEEKS

with Wilted Spinach and Oven Polenta

"What do you want with beef cheeks when there are plenty of perfectly good cuts?" my butcher Kevin teased me. It's true that cheeks are the most overworked cow muscle there is. Once braised, they are fine-grained and rich, which makes them worth seeking out. I've savored these nuggets of beef—like mini-pot roasts—in restaurants, so I had to try them at home.

This recipe is remarkable for more than using an unusual beef cut. Instead of the classic braising technique, you simmer the cheeks first until they are nearly melting and then brown them under the broiler, giving them a burnished, almost crisp finish on the outside. The creamy Oven Polenta (recipe follows) bakes in the oven alongside the beef, and the spinach cooks while they broil. Serve this in pasta bowls to eat all together with soup spoons.

Makes 4 servings

....

4 BEEF CHEEKS (ABOUT 2 POUNDS)

KOSHER SALT

3 TABLESPOONS EXTRA-VIRGIN OLIVE OIL, DIVIDED

1 MEDIUM ONION, CHOPPED

2 GARLIC CLOVES, MINCED

¼ TEASPOON RED PEPPER FLAKES

2 TABLESPOONS TOMATO PASTE

¾ CUP LOW-SALT BEEF STOCK (SHORT ORDER STOCK, PAGE 226; ROASTED BEEF STOCK, PAGE 228) OR WATER

¼ CUP BALSAMIC VINEGAR

1 (14-OUNCE) CAN CRUSHED TOMATOES, DRAINED

¼ TEASPOON GROUND FENNEL SEEDS

1 BAY LEAF

½ TEASPOON BLACK PEPPER

12 OUNCES FRESH SPINACH, STEMMED AND ROUGHLY CHOPPED (ABOUT 8 CUPS)

CONTINUES

Trim the membranes from the exterior of the beef cheeks with a flexible, thin-bladed knife, leaving intact the seam of collagen inside the meat. Pat the cheeks dry and season them liberally with the kosher salt on both sides. Preheat the oven to 300°F.

Heat 2 tablespoons of the olive oil in a medium Dutch oven over medium heat and cook the onion until it turns translucent, about 3 minutes. Add the garlic and pepper flakes and cook until fragrant, about 1 minute. Add the tomato paste and spread it around the pan. Cook until it darkens in color, about 2 minutes. Stir in the stock, vinegar, tomatoes, fennel seeds, bay leaf, and black pepper and bring to a simmer. Nestle the beef cheeks into the sauce in a single layer. Cover and braise in the oven for 3 to 3½ hours.

When the beef pulls apart readily with a fork, remove the pot from the oven and turn the broiler on high. Transfer the beef cheeks from the braising liquid into a small skillet greased with the remaining 1 tablespoon of olive oil. Broil, watching closely, until the beef cheeks are nearly blackened on the surface, about 3 minutes.

To cook the spinach, bring the tomato braising sauce to simmer over medium-low heat. Spoon off any pools of fat. Add the spinach and stir it into the sauce. Cover and cook until wilted. Taste for seasoning and discard the bay leaf. Serve each beef cheek over the spinach, sauce, and the polenta, if using, in warmed wide bowls.

OVEN POLENTA

Start making this before you begin the Tomato-Braised Beef Cheeks with Spinach (page 113), or any other braise or stew. It cooks alongside and will wait for hours kept warm in a low oven.

Makes 4 servings

....

1 CUP POLENTA

½ TEASPOON SALT

2 TABLESPOONS UNSALTED BUTTER

1 CUP FINELY GRATED PARMESAN CHEESE

Preheat the oven to 300°F with the rack positioned in the lower half of the oven. Bring 3 cups of water to a boil over high heat. Place the polenta and salt in a 2-quart oven-safe casserole dish and whisk in 1 cup of cool water until smooth. Whisk in the boiling water until the polenta is smooth. Cover the dish with a tight-fitting lid or aluminum foil and place in the oven to cook for 1½ to 2 hours, stirring every 30 minutes. When the polenta is swelled, glossy, and pulls away from the sides of the pan when stirred, remove it from the oven and stir in the butter and Parmesan. Cover and keep warm until ready to serve.

MORE CHOICE CUTS:

Boneless short ribs, rich in collagen like beef cheeks, are superb in this braise. Check them for doneness after 2½ hours of braising and spoon off any excess fat from the tomato sauce before cooking the spinach.

Meaty beef shank is also excellent if you're game to eat around the bone and they braise in about 2 hours.

WHISKEY POT PIE

Using a single pot, this beef pie simmers on the stovetop ever so briefly before it finishes cooking in the oven beneath a golden brown crust. The alcohol in the whiskey cooks off, leaving an unbeatable flavor. Suet-Butter Pie Crust (recipe follows) makes the flakiest crust I know, but you can substitute your favorite homemade or purchased dough for the top crust. To go straight from the stovetop to the oven, you'll need a deep oven-safe skillet, ideally ten inches wide and at least two inches deep.

Makes 6 servings

....

3 TABLESPOONS ALL-PURPOSE FLOUR

1 TEASPOON SALT

1 POUND STEW BEEF, CUT INTO 1-INCH CUBES

1 TABLESPOON SALTED BUTTER

1 TABLESPOON VEGETABLE OIL

1 LEEK, GREEN AND WHITE PARTS CHOPPED

2 MEDIUM CARROTS, CHOPPED

3 TABLESPOONS LIGHTLY PACKED CHOPPED FRESH PARSLEY

2 TEASPOONS LIGHTLY PACKED CHOPPED FRESH THYME OR ½ TEASPOON DRIED

⅛ TEASPOON BLACK PEPPER

2½ CUPS LOW-SALT BEEF STOCK (SHORT ORDER STOCK, PAGE 226; ROASTED BEEF STOCK, PAGE 228) OR WATER

5 TABLESPOONS WHISKEY

2 TABLESPOONS DIJON MUSTARD

1 MEDIUM POTATO (ABOUT 8 OUNCES), PEELED AND CUT INTO ½-INCH CUBES

1 (9-INCH) UNBAKED PIE DOUGH SUCH AS SUET-BUTTER PIE DOUGH (RECIPE FOLLOWS)

FLOUR FOR DUSTING

Whisk the flour with the salt and toss it with the beef cubes until they are well coated. Heat the butter and oil in a large and deep oven-safe skillet over medium-high heat. When the butter foams, add the beef cubes and cook, turning them 2 to 3 times, until well browned, about 8 minutes.

Add the leek and carrots and cook until the whites of the leek turn translucent, about 3 minutes. Add the parsley, thyme, pepper, and the stock and stir, scraping up the browned bits on the bottom of the pan. Reduce the heat to low, stir in the whiskey and mustard, and cover.

Simmer the stew for 30 minutes. The beef will still be firm, but become tender while baking. Taste the beef for salt and pepper, then stir in the potatos, and let the stew cool slightly while you prepare the crust.

Preheat the oven to 350°F. Roll out the pie dough on a lightly floured countertop into a circle at least ¼ inch thick. Trace a paring knife around a dinner plate a little larger than the circumference of your skillet to make the round top crust. Lift the crust up gently and center it on top of the beef filling. It will sink down and invert neatly up the sides of the skillet. Use a paring knife to make 4 slits in the top of the crust for vents. Bake the pie until the crust is golden brown and some of the gravy is bubbling up around the edges, 60 to 70 minutes. Let it cool for 20 minutes before serving.

> **MORE CHOICE CUTS:**
> Kidneys, if you're partial to them, belong in this pie along with the beef. About 8 ounces, trimmed (page 51) and cut into 1-inch chunks, will do nicely if you cook them with the beef and bake as directed.

SUET-BUTTER PIE DOUGH

This is the flakiest pie dough I've ever made, one I keep at the ready in my freezer for potpies and turnovers as well as for dessert pies. This is a stiff dough that's easy to work with and patch if it cracks. Suet is the brittle, dense white fat that surrounds the kidneys. You can request it through a custom butcher (Sources, page 270). Simply separate the fat from any membrane and grate it using a large box grater. Stored in the freezer until the occasion calls for it, suet brings fantastic flavor to pie dough but softens quickly at room temperature, even more so than butter. Measure the suet and keep it chilled until you're ready to make the dough. For easiest handling, be sure to chill the dough well before rolling it out.

Makes 2 (9-inch) crusts

....

3 CUPS (13½ OUNCES) ALL-PURPOSE FLOUR

1 TABLESPOON CHOPPED FRESH THYME OR
    1 TEASPOON DRIED, OPTIONAL

1 TEASPOON SALT

1 CUP (2 STICKS) UNSALTED BUTTER, CUT INTO
    ½-INCH CUBES AND CHILLED

½ CUP (3½ OUNCES) BEEF SUET, LARD, OR
    VEGETABLE SHORTENING, CHILLED

⅓ CUP COLD WATER

To make the dough in a food processor, combine the flour, thyme, if using, and salt in the processor bowl and pulse 2 to 3 times to blend. Add the cold butter cubes and suet and pulse 4 to 5 times in 2-second bursts until the flour looks like coarse cornmeal.

Pour the water in through the feed tube and pulse 6 to 8 times more until the mixture collects into a dough.

To make the dough in a stand mixer, put the flour, thyme, if using, and salt in the bowl and stir with the paddle attachment. Add the cold butter cubes and suet and stir on low speed until the flour mixture resembles coarse meal. Add the water and stir until it collects into a dough.

To make the dough by hand, combine the flour, thyme, if using, and salt in a large mixing bowl. Use a pastry blender or two table knives to cut the cold butter cubes and suet into the flour until it resembles coarse cornmeal. Add the water and stir with the pastry blender or a fork until it collects into a dough.

Turn the dough out onto a lightly floured countertop and smear it once or twice on the counter using an open palm to collect any scraps. Divide the dough into 2 equal pieces (each enough for 1 9-inch pie), shape each piece into a disk, and wrap with plastic wrap. Refrigerate for at last 30 minutes before rolling. Store the extra pie dough in the freezer for up to 1 month.

HEAVENLY GREEN STEW

These tender beef chunks in a pool of warmly spiced spinach-yogurt sauce form the most exciting rendition of beef stew I've ever had. Called *saag gosht*, it's a one-dish meal to relish over steamed basmati rice. The beef plays second fiddle to fresh spinach wilted and puréed to become the braising sauce. The stew's most alluring qualities come largely from garam masala—the Indian spice blend of coriander, cardamom, cumin, cinnamon, cloves, and black pepper. The spiciness and intensity of garam masala can vary greatly, so be sure to taste your blend or make your own as I do based on Julie Sahni's master recipe from *Classical Indian Cooking* (see note).

Makes 6 servings

....

4 TABLESPOONS VEGETABLE OIL, DIVIDED

2 MEDIUM ONIONS, CHOPPED

3-INCH PIECE GINGER, PEELED AND VERY FINELY
    CHOPPED (3 TABLESPOONS)

6 GARLIC CLOVES, MINCED

2 TEASPOONS GROUND CORIANDER

2 TEASPOONS GARAM MASALA*

12 OUNCES FRESH BABY SPINACH OR 1 (10-OUNCE)
    BAG FROZEN SPINACH, THAWED

½ CUP PLAIN YOGURT

2 TEASPOONS SALT

2 TO 2½ POUNDS STEW BEEF, CUT INTO 1½-INCH
    CUBES

1 (4-INCH) CINNAMON STICK

2 BAY LEAVES

Heat 2 tablespoons of the oil in a large skillet over medium-high heat. Add the onions and cook, stirring frequently, until they begin to turn caramel colored, about 5 minutes. Add the ginger, garlic, coriander, and garam masala and cook, stirring until fragrant, about 1 minute. Add the spinach and, if it's fresh, cook until it wilts. Transfer the spinach mixture into a food processor. Add the yogurt and salt and purée until very smooth.

Heat the remaining 2 tablespoons of oil over medium-high heat in a Dutch oven. When it shimmers, cook the beef, working in batches so that you don't overcrowd the pan, turning 2 to 3 times until well browned, about 10 minutes per batch. Add the spinach purée to the pot with the beef and stir in 2 cups of water. Add the cinnamon stick and bay leaves. Bring the liquid to a boil over medium heat and scrape the bottom of the pot to release the browned bits. Cover and reduce the heat to low. Simmer on the stovetop until the beef is fork tender, 1¼ to 1½ hours. Discard the cinnamon stick and bay leaves and taste for salt and garam masala before serving.

NOTE: To make 5 tablespoons of garam masala, combine 2 tablespoons ground cumin, 1½ tablespoons ground coriander, 1¼ teaspoons ground cardamom, 1¼ teaspoons ground cinnamon, ½ teaspoon ground cloves, 1¾ teaspoons black pepper and mix well. Store it in an airtight container.

CUBAN-STYLE SHREDDED BEEF AND PEPPERS

(*Ropa Vieja*)

This beef, tomato, and bell pepper stew is as vibrant as the Havana I visited years ago. It involves a two-step method for transforming a whole roast from the chuck into shredded beef for serving with Black Beans and Rice (page 219) or wrapping into a flour tortilla. Though based on the *ropa vieja*, this one doesn't use the traditional flank steak since I prefer to reserve that pricier cut for the grill. Instead, I use a bone-in arm roast that is quite lean for a chuck roast and has a uniform grain. Use any pot roast with a bone to contribute flavor to the broth. Once braised and shredded, the meat stews with tomatoes, more garlic, sliced onion, peppers, and spices to enjoy any way you can dream up.

Makes 6 servings with leftovers

BRAISE:

1 (3½- TO 4-POUND) BONE-IN POT ROAST

1 (28-OUNCE) CAN WHOLE PEELED TOMATOES

1 GARLIC CLOVE, PEELED

1 MEDIUM ONION, CHOPPED

1 MEDIUM CARROT, CHOPPED

1 CELERY STALK CHOPPED

6 WHOLE PEPPERCORNS

1 TEASPOON SALT

1 BAY LEAF

STEW:

1 TABLESPOON OLIVE OIL

1 WHITE ONION, THINLY SLICED

2 TEASPOONS GROUND CUMIN

⅛ TEASPOON CAYENNE

2 GARLIC CLOVES, MINCED

1 RED, YELLOW OR GREEN BELL PEPPER, SEEDED AND THINLY SLICED

½ TEASPOON DRIED OREGANO

1½ TEASPOONS SALT

1 CUP LIGHTLY PACKED CHOPPED FRESH CILANTRO

Place the beef in a Dutch oven that fits it snuggly. Add only the juice from the canned tomatoes, reserving the tomatoes for later, and just enough water to reach the surface of the meat. Add the garlic, onion, carrot, celery, peppercorns, salt, and bay leaf. Cover the pot with the lid ajar and bring it to a boil over medium-high heat. Reduce the heat to low and simmer until the meat shreds readily with a fork, 3½ to 4 hours.

Use tongs to lift the beef from the liquid and place it into a bowl to cool. Strain the liquid and discard the cooked vegetables. Return the liquid to the pot and bring it to a steady simmer over medium heat. Reduce it by half to make about 1 cup, about 15 minutes. When the meat is cool enough to handle, shred it finely with two forks, discarding any fat, cartilage, and bone.

Heat the olive oil over medium-high heat in a large skillet until it shimmers. Add the onion and cook, stirring occasionally, until it turns limp, about 3 minutes. Add the cumin, cayenne, garlic, and bell pepper and continue cooking without browning until the vegetables are very tender, about 6 minutes. Mash the reserved whole tomatoes and add them with the oregano, salt, and the reduced broth. Bring the stew to a simmer and cook for 15 minutes until the tomatoes break down and the flavors mingle. Stir in the shredded meat to reheat it for 5 to 7 minutes, and sprinkle on the cilantro just before serving.

MORE CHOICE CUTS:

Boneless chuck roasts are automatic substitutes for the bone-in arm roast.

Skirt steak, the thin, boneless and lean steak much like flank shreds wonderfully once braised to tenderness.

BOSTON BAKED BEANS WITH BRISKET

and Beet-Carrot Slaw

Every Saturday morning, my mother simmered navy beans for our baked bean supper while we kids watched cartoons. I may not make them on a weekly basis, but I can't live for long without made-from-scratch molasses-sweetened baked beans. These baked beans are modeled after a recipe by Boston chef Jasper White. (You'll need to soak the beans eight to twelve hours in advance.) My innovation is to snuggle a small grassfed brisket down into the beans as they stew. Not a proper Bostonian thing to do, but it makes a fabulous one-pot supper for my family. I serve this dish with Beet-Carrot Slaw (recipe follows), which I make while the beans and meat complete their simmering and achieve that crispy brown glaze I covet.

Makes 6 servings

....

2 CUPS DRY NAVY BEANS, SOAKED FOR 8 TO 12 HOURS, DRAINED AND RINSED

1 MEDIUM ONION, CHOPPED

2 GARLIC CLOVES, MINCED

1 TABLESPOON DRY MUSTARD

½ TEASPOON SWEET PAPRIKA

2 TEASPOONS SALT

½ TEASPOON BLACK PEPPER

1 BAY LEAF

1 (2- TO 2½-POUND) BRISKET, POINT OR FLAT CUT, TRIMMED

⅓ CUP PACKED DARK BROWN SUGAR

⅓ CUP MOLASSES

1 HEAPING TEASPOON TOMATO PASTE

1 TABLESPOON APPLE CIDER VINEGAR

1 TABLESPOON CORNSTARCH

Preheat the oven to 325°F. Combine the beans, onion, garlic, mustard, paprika, salt, pepper, and bay leaf in a Dutch oven. Add 2 cups of water, stir to blend, and bring it to a boil over medium-high heat. Nestle in the brisket and bring the liquid back to a boil. Cover the pot and place it in the oven. Cook until the beans are tender and you can pry off a chunk of the brisket with a fork, 2 to 2½ hours.

Whisk the brown sugar, molasses, tomato paste, vinegar, and cornstarch with ½ cup water and stir it into the beans. Turn the brisket over and continue cooking, uncovered, until the surface of the beans and brisket are mahogany brown, 30 to 45 minutes more for a total of 2½ to 3¼ hours. Skim off any surface fat and taste for salt and pepper. Discard the bay leaf. To serve, separate small portions of the brisket with two forks and serve from the pot along with generous spoonfuls of the beans.

MORE CHOICE CUTS:

Chuck steak is a smaller cut from the shoulder that will fit nicely into this pot of beans and cook to tenderness.

Short ribs, either English style or boneless, add interest to this pot of beans. Spoon off any excess fat pooled on the surface before serving.

BEET-CARROT SLAW

This fresh, crunchy, and colorful beet salad could make a convert out of committed beet naysayers. Raw beets are sweet like carrots and stain everything they touch. To grate them, you might want to use the grating attachment on your food processor or don a pair of plastic food service gloves if you keep them around for seeding jalapeños. Alternatively, choose golden beets or the candy-cane striped variety called Chioggia.

Makes 6 servings

....

1 SHALLOT, FINELY CHOPPED

2 TABLESPOONS RED WINE VINEGAR

1 TEASPOON DIJON MUSTARD

2 TEASPOONS SUGAR

6 TABLESPOONS EXTRA-VIRGIN OLIVE OIL

½ TEASPOON SALT

1/ TEASPOON BLACK PEPPER

1 POUND BEETS, TRIMMED, SCRUBBED, AND
    COARSELY GRATED (ABOUT 4 CUPS)

2 LARGE CARROTS, PEELED AND GRATED
    (ABOUT 2 CUPS)

½ CUP LIGHTLY PACKED CHOPPED FRESH PARSLEY

Whisk the shallot, vinegar, mustard, and sugar together in a large mixing bowl. Drizzle in the olive oil while whisking until well blended. Season with the salt and pepper. Toss with the beets, carrots, and parsley. Let the slaw sit at room temperature for about 30 minutes before serving.

BASQUE CUTLETS BAKED IN RED PEPPER SAUCE

If you've been tempted to try tongue but cold and pickled doesn't appeal to you, this is the just the recipe. The first time I tried it at Epi's Basque restaurant near Boise, Idaho, I became a convert: the thin fried tongue cutlets surprised me with their beefy flavors and were delightful in the mild red pepper-tomato sauce. At Epi's, this dish is served with steamed long-grain white rice.

This recipe, adapted from Epi's original, has three steps: simmering the tongue, making the sauce, and frying the cutlets. You can prepare the tongue and the sauce up to two days in advance, then cook the cutlets and reheat the sauce on the day you plan to serve it.

Don't skip this distinctive recipe if you don't want or can't get beef tongue. Instead, substitute one of the suitable cuts suggested below, and you can jump right into making the sauce and frying the beef.

Makes 6 to 8 servings

....

TONGUE:

1 (2½- TO 3-POUND) BEEF TONGUE, RINSED

4 CELERY STALKS, CUT INTO 4-INCH SECTIONS

1 MEDIUM ONION, PEELED AND QUARTERED

5 GARLIC CLOVES, PEELED

1 BAY LEAF

1 CUP (4½ OUNCES) ALL-PURPOSE FLOUR

2½ TEASPOONS SALT

½ TEASPOON BLACK PEPPER

4 EGGS

1½ CUPS COARSE, DRY BREADCRUMBS

1 CUP VEGETABLE OIL

SAUCE:

10 DRIED CHORICERO OR RED ANAHEIM CHILE PEPPERS, STEMMED

1 TABLESPOON OLIVE OIL

3 GARLIC CLOVES, MINCED

1 SMALL ONION, FINELY CHOPPED

⅓ CUP TOMATO PASTE

2½ CUPS FRESH OR CANNED TOMATO PURÉE

¼ TEASPOON RED PEPPER FLAKES

1½ TEASPOONS SUGAR

1 TEASPOON SALT

¼ CUP LIGHTLY PACKED CHOPPED FRESH PARSLEY

To cook the tongue, place it in a large stockpot with the celery, onion, garlic, and bay leaf. Add enough water to cover the tongue completely and bring it to a boil over medium-high heat. Partially cover the pan, and reduce the heat to low, keeping the meat completely submerged, until you can pierce it easily all the way through with a skewer, 3½ to 4 hours. Cool the tongue in the cooking liquid until it is cool enough to handle. Peel off the skin while the tongue is still warm and trim off any fat and gristle. Cover and refrigerate until it is cold so that it is easier to slice thinly. Discard the cooking liquid.

Meanwhile, make the sauce. Put the chiles in a medium saucepan, cover with water, and bring it to a boil over medium-high heat. Reduce the heat to low and simmer partially covered, for 45 minutes. Drain the chiles and pass them through a food mill into a medium-sized bowl and set it aside.

Heat the olive oil in a large skillet over medium heat, add the garlic, and cook until fragrant, about 30 seconds. Add the onion and cook until translucent, about 3 minutes. Add the tomato paste, tomato purée, pepper flakes, sugar, salt, the reserved chiles, and 1 cup of water. Bring to a boil and simmer steadily for 20 minutes, stirring occasionally, until thick. Taste the sauce for salt and keep it warm over low heat.

To fry the beef cutlets, cut the chilled beef tongue crosswise into slices ¼ inch thick. (Save any pieces too small for frying, chop finely, and add them to the sauce.) Put the flour into a wide, shallow dish and whisk in the salt and pepper. In another wide, shallow dish, beat the eggs, and place the breadcrumbs in a third dish. Line a baking sheet with paper towels.

Heat the oil in a large skillet over medium-high heat. Working in batches, dredge the beef tongue slices in the flour, shaking off excess, dip into the eggs, and press the slices into the breadcrumbs to coat them evenly. Fry until golden brown on each side, 1½ to 2 minutes per side. Drain on the paper towels and continue until you have fried all the slices.

Slip the cutlets into the sauce to reheat them before serving portions of tongue and sauce with a sprinkling of the parsley.

VARIATION: BEEF TONGUE FRITTERS

For an appetizer, simmer, skin, and chill the tongue as directed, skipping the sauce. Slice, flour, and fry the tongue according to the recipe instructions and serve the hot fritters with Herb Aïoli (page 187) or Harissa (page 129).

MORE CHOICE CUTS:

Tenderized steaks, including cube steaks or other round steaks pounded ¼ inch thick (see Chicken Fried Steak with Buttermilk Gravy, page 182), allow you to skip the initial simmering step required for tongue. Make the sauce and fry the beef as directed.

COWBOY COFFEE BEEF STEW

with Whole-Wheat Buttermilk Biscuits

Make-ahead, better-the-next-day beef stew is my potluck standard.
Once, I added some strong leftover coffee to the broth and my rancher
friends told me it was the best stew they'd ever had—strong praise
from grassfed beef producers. My conclusion: coffee combined with
well-browned meats and good broth makes the ultimate stew gravy.
Biscuit dough dropped on the top to bake during the stew's final half
hour in the oven transforms it into a complete country-style meal.

Makes 6 to 8 servings

....

STEW:

2 TABLESPOONS ALL-PURPOSE FLOUR

2 TEASPOONS SALT

½ TEASPOON GROUND ALLSPICE

⅛ TEASPOON CAYENNE

2 TABLESPOONS UNSALTED BUTTER

2 TABLESPOONS OLIVE OIL

2½ TO 3 POUNDS STEW BEEF, CUT INTO ¾-INCH
    CUBES

3½ CUPS LOW-SALT BEEF STOCK (SHORT ORDER
    STOCK, PAGE 226; ROASTED BEEF STOCK, PAGE
    228) OR WATER

½ CUP STRONG BREWED COFFEE

1 BAY LEAF

1 MEDIUM ONION, COARSELY CHOPPED

6 MEDIUM CARROTS, PEELED AND CUT AT AN
    ANGLE ¾ INCHES LONG

1½ POUNDS RUSSET POTATOES (ABOUT 3 MEDIUM),
    CUT INTO 1-INCH CUBES

½ TEASPOON BLACK PEPPER

2 TABLESPOONS CORNSTARCH OR ARROWROOT

BISCUITS:

1½ CUPS (6¾ OUNCES) ALL-PURPOSE FLOUR

1½ CUPS (6¾ OUNCES) WHOLE-WHEAT FLOUR

1 TABLESPOON BAKING POWDER

1 TEASPOON BAKING SODA

2 TABLESPOONS SUGAR

¾ TEASPOON SALT

6 TABLESPOONS UNSALTED BUTTER, CUT INTO
    CUBES AND CHILLED

⅔ CUP HEAVY CREAM

⅔ CUP BUTTERMILK

To prepare the stew, whisk the flour, salt, allspice, and cayenne in a small bowl and set it aside. Preheat the oven to 325°F.

Melt the butter and heat the olive oil in a Dutch oven over medium-high heat until it shimmers. Working in batches so that you don't overcrowd the pan, cook the beef cubes, turning 2 to 3 times until they are walnut brown all over, about 10 minutes per batch.

Reduce the heat to medium and return all the beef to the pot. Sprinkle the reserved flour mixture over it and cook while stirring until fragrant, about 2 minutes. Add the stock, coffee, and the bay leaf. Bring to a boil and use a spoon to scrape the bottom of the pot clean.

Cover the pot and transfer it into the oven for 30 minutes. Add the onion, carrots, potatoes, and pepper, and continue cooking in the oven until the beef and the vegetables are tender to the bite, 1 to 1¼ hours more for a total of 1½ to 1¾ hours.

Meanwhile, make the biscuit dough. Whisk together the all-purpose flour, whole-wheat flour, baking powder, baking soda, sugar, and salt in a large mixing bowl. Using your fingertips or a pastry blender, cut the butter into the flour mixture until it resembles coarse meal. Make a well in the center of the flour and pour in the heavy cream and buttermilk. Stir until the dry ingredients absorb all the liquid and you can collect the dough into a ball.

Remove the stew from the oven and taste it for salt and pepper. Remove and discard the bay leaf. Whisk the cornstarch with 3 tablespoons cool water and stir it into the stew.

Using a ⅓ cup measure as a scoop, portion the biscuit dough and plop the mounds in a single layer on top of the stew. (They'll be touching.) Put the stew back in the oven and bake until the biscuit tops are tinged with brown, an additional 30 to 35 minutes.

RICHARD OLNEY'S BEEF BOURGUIGNON

Julia Child's friend and contemporary Richard Olney never became as famous as The French Chef, but he was just as passionate about provincial French food. His version of beef bourguignon has several key elements that make it a standout, including red wine-marinated beef and brandy and a two-stage browning for the beef. To give this stew some elegance, I separate the most tender of the chuck roasts, the blade chuck roast, along the natural seams into large serving pieces. Use any chuck roast you like for this luxurious version of humble stew I serve with cauliflower purée (see Mashed Potato Mix Up, page 214).

Makes 6 servings

....

1 (3½- TO 4-POUND) BONE-IN CHUCK ROAST

KOSHER SALT

1 (750-ML) BOTTLE DRY RED WINE

¼ CUP PLUS 2 TABLESPOONS EXTRA-VIRGIN OLIVE OIL, DIVIDED

1 TABLESPOON CHOPPED FRESH THYME OR 1 TEASPOON DRIED

1 MEDIUM ONION, SLICED ½ INCH THICK

4 MEDIUM CARROTS, PEELED AND SLICED IN 1-INCH SECTIONS

¼ CUP ALL-PURPOSE FLOUR

⅓ CUP BRANDY

3 GARLIC CLOVES, PEELED AND SMASHED

½ TEASPOON BLACK PEPPER

½ CUP LIGHTLY PACKED CHOPPED FRESH FLAT-LEAF PARSLEY, STEMS RESERVED

1 BAY LEAF

10 OUNCES PEARL ONIONS OR 1 (10-OUNCE) BAG FROZEN PEARL ONIONS

2 TABLESPOONS UNSALTED BUTTER

1 POUND FRESH MUSHROOMS, SLICED IN HALF

Divide the beef along the natural muscle seams into 7 to 8 large sections, cutting any oversized pieces to make them more or less even. Put the beef in a shallow glass or ceramic container that fits the meat snuggly and include the bone. Season it generously with the kosher salt and pour in the wine, the ¼ cup olive oil, and thyme. Cover and marinate the beef in the refrigerator for 3 to 12 hours, turning the beef once. Drain the meat and blot dry with paper towels, reserving the marinade.

Heat the remaining 2 tablespoons oil in a Dutch oven over medium heat. Cook the onion and carrots, stirring occasionally, until they are speckled brown, about 7 minutes. Use a slotted spoon to transfer the vegetables to a bowl and set them aside. Increase the heat to medium high and brown the beef on all sides, about 10 minutes total. Sprinkle the flour over the meat and continue to cook, turning often, until well browned all over, about 6 minutes more. Don't rush this step; taking the time to let the meat develop a dark crust produces the richest sauce.

Preheat the oven to 275°F. Return the vegetables to the pot with the meat, add the reserved bone, marinade, and the brandy. Bring the liquids to a boil and scrape the bottom of the pot clean to release all the browned bits. Reduce the heat to low, and add the garlic, pepper, parsley stems, and bay leaf. Cover the pot and braise it in the oven until a fork readily pierces the meat all the way through, 2 to 2½ hours.

Meanwhile, if using raw pearl onions, you will need to peel them first. Bring a small pot of water to a boil over medium-high heat. Plunge in the onions and boil for 2 minutes. Drain, cool, and trim the root end to pop them from their skins. Melt the butter in a medium skillet over medium-high heat and cook the onions until they are translucent and tender, about 3 minutes. Slide them out of the pan to a large serving dish. Add the mushrooms to the same pan and cook them, stirring occasionally, until they are well browned, about 8 minutes. Put them in the dish with the onions.

Use a slotted spoon to lift the meat and vegetables from the broth into the serving dish with the onions and mushrooms, discarding the bone, parsley stems, and bay leaf. Skim any fat from the stock, strain it through a sieve into a saucepan, and simmer to reduce over low heat until it coats the back of a spoon, about 5 minutes. Taste for salt and pour the sauce over the beef and vegetables in the bowl, sprinkle with the chopped parsley, and serve.

MORE CHOICE CUTS:

Boneless chuck roasts, as long as they are not rolled and tied so that you can cut neat pieces, are perfect substitutes.

Sirloin tip roast, aka round tip roast, is the lean and boneless cut from the round that you can cut into serving pieces of any size to braise.

Beef cheeks or boneless short ribs will enrich the sauce with their collagen and will need 30 to 60 minutes more cooking time to become tender.

CHICKPEA-BEEF TAGINE

with Harissa

I am a fanatic for chickpeas (aka garbanzo beans), and I created this North African-inspired stew to get as many chickpeas as beef into every bite. (If using dried chickpeas, you'll need to soak them eight to twelve hours in advance.) You build layers of flavor into the stew with each step of browning the vegetables and the meat. Toasted cumin and coriander add their warm spices to the tomato-based broth, which gets a kick from the addition of lemon zest and olives just before serving. I serve this with pearl-sized balls of Israeli couscous, larger than the standard North African dried semolina granules, which you boil in salted water and drain, just like pasta. Pass the Harissa (recipe follows), a spicy red pepper condiment you can whip up in the food processor.

Makes 6 servings

....

1¼ TEASPOON WHOLE CUMIN SEEDS

1½ TEASPOONS WHOLE CORIANDER SEEDS

1 TO 1½ POUNDS STEW BEEF, CUT INTO 1-INCH CUBES

KOSHER SALT

4 TABLESPOONS EXTRA-VIRGIN OLIVE OIL, DIVIDED

1 MEDIUM ONION, THINLY SLICED

1 RED, ORANGE, OR YELLOW BELL PEPPER, THINLY SLICED

½ TEASPOON RED PEPPER FLAKES

1 TABLESPOON TOMATO PASTE

¼ TEASPOON TURMERIC

1 (28-OUNCE) CAN WHOLE PEELED TOMATOES

1 TABLESPOON RED WINE VINEGAR

1 CUP DRIED CHICKPEAS, SOAKED FOR 8 TO 12 HOURS OR 1 (15-OUNCE) CAN GARBANZO BEANS, DRAINED AND RINSED

¼ TEASPOON BLACK PEPPER

4 OUNCES BRINED GREEN OLIVES, SUCH AS MAN-ZANILLA OR PICHOLINE, PITTED (ABOUT 1 CUP)

1 TABLESPOON LEMON ZEST

MORE CHOICE CUTS:
Baby Meatballs (page 82) are a fun substitution for the stew beef, and in combination with canned chickpeas, they make the quickest stew possible that simmers for 25 to 30 minutes.

Heat a dry small skillet over medium heat. Add the cumin seeds and stand by while they become fragrant and darken in color, about 1 minute. Quickly remove them from the pan and grind to a powder in a spice grinder or using a mortar and pestle. Repeat with the coriander seeds, toasting them until fragrant and darkened in color, about 1 minute. Grind them to a powder and mix with the cumin in a small bowl. Set it aside.

Season the meat liberally with the kosher salt. Heat 2 tablespoons of the olive oil in a Dutch oven over medium-high heat. Working in batches so that you don't overcrowd the pan and steam the meat, cook the beef cubes, turning 2 to 3 times until well browned, about 10 minutes per batch. Transfer the meat to a dinner plate and set it aside.

Add the remaining 2 tablespoons olive oil to the pan and cook the onion and pepper, stirring often, until they are wilted and beginning to brown, about 6 minutes. Stir in the reserved cumin and coriander, and pepper flakes, and cook until fragrant, about 2 minutes. Add the tomato paste and cook until it darkens in color and sticks to the bottom of the pot, about 3 minutes more.

Pour in 1½ cups of water and scrape the bottom of the pot clean. Add the reserved beef, turmeric, tomatoes with their liquid, vinegar, chickpeas (only if using dried), and the pepper. Bring to a simmer, cover, and cook until the beef is fork tender and you can mash the chickpeas with a fork, 1½ to 1¾ hours.

Stir the olives and lemon zest (and the chickpeas, if using canned) into the stew, and taste for salt. Serve in shallow bowls with the harissa, if desired.

HARISSA

This piquant red pepper sauce is not only a great stew garnish, it's also a lively spread for sandwiches and, for spice-lovers, a dip for Finger Steaks (page 183) or Beef Tongue Fritters (page 121). Store it in the refrigerator for up to one week.

Makes 1 cup
....

1 CUP PACKED ROASTED RED PEPPERS FROM A JAR

3 GARLIC CLOVES, PEELED

2 TABLESPOONS APPLE CIDER VINEGAR

¼ CUP EXTRA-VIRGIN OLIVE OIL

1½ TABLESPOONS RED PEPPER FLAKES

1 TEASPOON SALT

1 TEASPOON CARAWAY SEEDS

¾ TEASPOON GROUND CUMIN

⅛ TEASPOON SUGAR

Combine the peppers, garlic, vinegar, olive oil, pepper flakes, salt, caraway seeds, cumin, and sugar in the bowl of a food processor. Purée, pausing to scrape down the sides as necessary, until it is very smooth. Transfer the harissa into a bowl and store covered in the refrigerator until ready to use.

TWO-BEAN CHILI COLORADO

I learned about the magic of toasting dried chile peppers from the market women in Oaxaca City while eating more than my share of enchiladas. The heat of a dry skillet deepens and enlivens the flavors of the ancho chile peppers before they are soaked in water and puréed with stock. That purée is the backbone of this chili, which is also simmered with beer and black and pinto beans. (If using dried beans, you'll need to soak them eight to twelve hours in advance.) No slap-dash, tomato-heavy chili, this is worth making and waiting for, and the perfect game night fare for friends. As often as I can, I make a double batch of this chili to whip out the Chili Colorado Casserole variation to serve ten or more people at a potluck.

Makes 6 to 8 servings

....

12 WHOLE DRIED ANCHO CHILE PEPPERS, STEMMED AND SEEDED (SOURCES, PAGE 272)

1 WHITE ONION, PEELED

8 GARLIC CLOVES, UNPEELED

1 TABLESPOON VEGETABLE OIL

2 TO 2½ POUNDS STEW BEEF, CUT INTO ½-INCH CUBES

1 TABLESPOON GROUND CUMIN

2½ TEASPOONS SALT

1½ TEASPOONS DRIED OREGANO, PREFERABLY MEXICAN (SOURCES, PAGE 272)

¼ TEASPOON GROUND ALLSPICE

¼ TEASPOON CAYENNE

1 HEAPING TABLESPOON TOMATO PASTE

3 CUPS LOW-SALT BEEF STOCK (SHORT ORDER STOCK, PAGE 226; ROASTED BEEF STOCK, PAGE 228) OR WATER

1 (12-OUNCE) BOTTLE DARK BEER

½ CUP DRIED BLACK BEANS, SOAKED FOR 8 TO 12 HOURS OR 1 (15-OUNCE) CAN BLACK BEANS, DRAINED AND RINSED

½ CUP DRIED PINTO BEANS, SOAKED FOR 8 TO 12 HOURS OR 1 (15-OUNCE) CAN PINTO BEANS, DRAINED AND RINSED

2 TABLESPOONS MASA HARINA OR 2 CORN TORTILLAS, TORN INTO BITE-SIZED PIECES

2 OUNCES QUESO FRESCO OR FETA, CRUMBLED (ABOUT ½ CUP)

½ CUP LIGHTLY PACKED CHOPPED FRESH CILANTRO

Bring a teakettle of water to a boil over high heat. Heat a dry medium skillet over medium heat. Open the chiles flat and toast them in the hot skillet on each side 2 or 3 at a time. Use tongs to press them on the pan's hot surface until they lighten in color, about 30 seconds. Work quickly to avoid burning them. Turn and toast the other side. Put the toasted chiles into a bowl, submerge them in the boiling water, and soak for 20 minutes.

Meanwhile, slice the onion in half, chop half and set it aside. Put the other onion half cut side down onto the same dry skillet used to toast the chiles and leave it to lightly scorch over medium heat, about 5 minutes At the same time, put the unpeeled garlic cloves into the skillet and cook until they soften and blacken in spots.

Peel the garlic and transfer it to a blender. Add the scorched onion and the chiles along with ¾ cup of their soaking liquid. Purée until very smooth and set the chile sauce aside.

Heat the oil in a heavy-bottomed stockpot over medium-high heat. Add the reserved chopped onion and cook until it turns translucent, about 3 minutes. Add the beef, cumin, salt, oregano, allspice, and cayenne and cook until the beef is no longer pink and the liquid evaporates. Pour the reserved chile sauce into the pot and simmer the sauce until its red color deepens from brick red to red-brown, about 5 minutes. Add the tomato paste, stock, beer, and the drained and rinsed soaked black and pinto beans, if using dried. Partially cover, bring it to a simmer, and cook over low heat until the beef and beans are tender to the bite, 1 to 1¼ hours.

Taste for salt and cayenne, and add the masa harina. (If using canned beans, add them now.) Continue to simmer uncovered, stirring, until thickened, 10 to 15 minutes more. Serve the chili in deep bowls topped with the crumbled cheese and cilantro.

VARIATION: CHILI COLORADO CASSEROLE

Heat a small skillet over medium-low heat. Warm 15 6-inch tortillas one at a time in the skillet on both sides, about 15 seconds per side. Wrap the warmed tortillas in a kitchen towel to keep them pliable. Cut the tortillas in half. Whisk 1 cup sour cream with 3 or 4 tablespoons of water to thin it until it drizzles off a spoon. Grate 3 cups Monterey Jack cheese.

Preheat the oven to 375°F. Ladle about ½ cup of the sauce from the Two-Bean Chili Colorado into a 13 x 9-inch baking dish and spread it to cover the bottom. Make a single layer of tortillas over the sauce, fitting them as best you can, and top with half of the chili, 1 cup of the grated cheese, and drizzle with ¼ cup of the sour cream. Repeat the layers of tortillas, chili, cheese, and sour cream. Top with the remaining tortillas and grated cheese. Bake immediately to prevent the tortillas from getting too soft until the cheese is bubbling, 20 to 25 minutes. Keep warm in a low oven until ready to serve in slices drizzled with the remaining sour cream and the crumbled queso freso and cilantro, if desired.

GLOBAL BEEF CUISINE

The picture-perfect mountain valley where I live is a full day's drive from the Thai restaurants, gyro stands, and sushi bars I adore. As a result, I've become more of a culinary globe trotter in my own kitchen than I ever was as a city dweller.

What I've discovered is that many of the world's cuisines offer a model for eating less beef. When I make a stir-fry like Flying Greens with Beef in Oyster Sauce (page 145) with heaps of bok choy and slivers of steak, everything is in proportion. When I skewer kebabs with more vegetables than beef for Turkish Yogurt Kebabs with Grilled Summer Vegetables (page 138), a little meat goes a long way. Add a heap of steamed rice, pickled vegetables, or sliced fresh vegetables, and everyone is gratified to be eating food this is so colorful and energizing.

Asian cooking, from places including Laos, Vietnam, Korea, China, and Japan, inspired most of the recipes in this chapter. Beef, which in some places was not part of the tradition, is treated like a condiment and viewed as a luxury. In combination with the stellar flavors and textural contrast of fresh vegetables, herbs, and rice, beef is a supporting player.

My armchair traveling also touched down in other parts of the world, including Africa and South America. I returned from my research forays with recipes like Ethiopian Steak "Tartare" with Gingered Collard Greens (page 152) and Baked Argentinian Empanadas (page 159). What they all have in common is the judicious use of meat, especially the less butter-knife tender, leanest cuts that cooks here find hard to put to good use.

These recipes are designed to make global cooking accessible, especially for people who have never cooked these cuisines at home. The ingredient lists will appear long, but once you turn on the heat, most of these recipes come together before your eyes. The work is front-loaded, most of it chopping and measuring—all of which you can prepare an hour or up to two days in advance. (I wash and cut all the meat and vegetables, then store them in separate containers for a 10-minute weeknight dinner.) There are two learning recipes in this chapter, one for grilling meat on sticks (Rice Noodle Bowl with Lemongrass Beef, page 135)—a universal favorite way to serve beef—and one for stir-frying (Flying Greens with Beef in Oyster Sauce, page 145).

You may be unfamiliar with fish sauce, tamarind, or lemongrass, but even if you've never used them before, they are widely available nationwide. My own supermarket in the rural West was my litmus test. If I couldn't find an ingredient there, I made substitutions, listed it as optional, or suggested an alternative.

There are recipes for every season—from a mid-winter Tamarind Beef Satay with Indonesian Salad (page 140), a tropical fruit salad, to a summertime Laotian Beef Salad with Sticky Rice (page 146). Abounding in fresh herbs, salad greens, and seasonal produce, these are refreshing alternatives to grilling a steak. Many have become my go-to recipes, and I return to them for the excitement and sense of well-being they bring into my every day. When I sit down to eat with my family, I don't for a moment lament the lack of take-out options outside my door.

Quick-Cooked Choice Cuts

My principle is to use the most economical cut for the job, tougher cuts for the smallest slivers to moderately tender cuts for kebabs. Most of the recipes in this chapter rely on the cuts from the round primal, which are ultra-lean (especially grassfed) and tasty. They are also conveniently boneless, which eases the jobs of slicing, cubing, and chopping that most of the recipes request.

You'll want your knives at their sharpest to slice neatly and safely through the meat (Chopping and Mincing, page 47). It's also helpful if the meat is partially frozen to a popsicle-like consistency. If your meat is not frozen, pop it into the freezer for about twenty minutes. Once nice and firm, it won't wobble while you make those fine slices. If your meat is already frozen, catch it when it hasn't fully defrosted.

BOTTOM ROUND STEAK is the very lean, boneless cut from the large muscle of the outside round on the hindquarter. Slice it into slivers or chop, and be prepared for some chewiness.

EYE ROUND STEAK is crosscut from the tapered whole eye round muscle from the round, or hindquarters, found between the inside and outside round. Light-colored, lean, with a mild flavor and some chew, slice it very thin or chop it very fine.

HEART is a muscle in constant motion, fine-grained and the color of sun-baked brick. One of the leanest cuts, it needs to be cooked very quickly for the best eating. Slice it into wide strips for grilling or thin strips for stir-frying.

LEFTOVER STEAK OR ROAST BEEF is put to excellent use in many of the recipes. Instead of adding it as directed in each recipe, toss it in at the very end so that it has just enough time to warm up without cooking it any more.

SHOULDER TENDER, aka teres major, is an exceptionally tender, small tapered cut from the chuck. It should not be confused with mock tender, which is tough. Use it whenever only the most tender beef will do.

SIRLOIN TIP ROAST, aka round tip roast, is a boneless cut from the large muscle between the sirloin, or hip, and the round, or hindquarter. It is lean, fairly tender, economical, and extremely versatile for kebabs, satays, or stir-fries.

SKIRT STEAK is a long strip of boneless muscle from the diaphragm with an open, fibrous texture, and a papery membrane that needs to be peeled off before cooking (Trimming, page 51). Inside or outside steak are both great for quick cooking.

TOP BLADE STEAK, aka flatiron, is a boneless steak from the chuck, or shoulder, that has become a popular restaurant item. It's also a tender choice for kebabs, satay, and other quick-cooked meats.

TOP ROUND ROAST OR STEAK is a lean boneless cut from the most tender part of the round, or hindquarter. Once chopped, it brings great texture and excellent flavor to any quick-cooked dish.

TOP SIRLOIN ROAST OR STEAK is a boneless and fairly tender cut from the sirloin, or hip section. Popular as a steak, it is also great sliced for satay and cubed for kebabs.

TRI-TIP ROAST OR STEAK is a triangular-shaped roast cut from the outer hip or bottom sirloin. An overall great grilling cut, it has an irregular shape that cooks more evenly when cut into large chunks.

RICE NOODLE BOWL

with Lemongrass Beef

Skewers of lemongrass-marinated grilled beef top a bowl filled to the brim with lettuce leaves, rice noodles, copious fresh herbs, carrots, and cucumbers. The chile-laced dressing of fish sauce and lime juice called *nuoc cham* marries it all together. This one-bowl meal, based on Vietnamese *bun*, is one of the most light and satisfying last-minute dishes I know.

Makes 4 servings

....

¼ CUP FISH SAUCE

¼ CUP LIME JUICE

3 TABLESPOONS SUGAR

1 GARLIC CLOVE, MINCED

1 SERRANO PEPPER, STEMMED AND VERY THINLY SLICED INTO ROUNDS

1 POUND SIRLOIN TIP STEAK, CUT INTO 1-INCH CUBES

1 STALK LEMONGRASS, VERY FINELY CHOPPED OR 2 TABLESPOONS LEMONGRASS PURÉE (SOLD IN A TUBE)

1 SHALLOT, FINELY CHOPPED

1 (6- TO 8-OUNCE) PACKAGE DRIED RICE VERMICELLI NOODLES (MAI FUN)

6 LARGE GREEN OR RED LEAF LETTUCE LEAVES, TORN

1 CUP LIGHTLY PACKED FRESH CILANTRO LEAVES

1 CUP LIGHTLY PACKED FRESH THAI BASIL OR MINT LEAVES

1 LARGE CARROT, PEELED AND CUT INTO MATCHSTICKS

1 MEDIUM CUCUMBER, PEELED, CUT IN HALF LENGTHWISE, AND THINLY SLICED

Prepare the dressing by mixing the fish sauce, lime juice, sugar, garlic, and pepper with ½ cup water. Stir until the sugar dissolves. Put the beef cubes in a glass or ceramic bowl, toss with the lemongrass and shallot and splash in ¼ cup of the dressing. Marinate the beef for 25 to 30 minutes at room temperature.

Bring a large pot of water to a boil. Submerge the rice noodles into the water and simmer until tender to the bite, about 3 minutes. Drain the noodles in a colander, rinse with cold running water, and toss to drain them well.

Prepare a hot gas or charcoal grill, broiler, or grill pan on the stovetop. Thread the beef cubes onto 4 skewers, about 8 pieces per skewer, and discard the marinade. Position the skewers over the hottest part of the grill and cook, turning 2 to 3 times, for a total of 4½ to 5 minutes for medium rare.

Divide the lettuce, cilantro, and basil among 4 large serving bowls. Layer the greens with a quarter of the noodles along with the carrot, cucumber, and a skewer of the beef. Pour over the dressing to taste when ready to eat.

> **MORE CHOICE CUTS:**
> Top sirloin steak is always a good marinating and grilling option.
> Leftover grilled steak or roast beef are shortcuts for this summery noodle bowl. Just slice and toss with the marinade before assembling.

JAMAICAN JERKED TRI-TIP

with Coconut-Scallion Rice

Slathering meat with a wet rub is typical of Caribbean countries and goes by the curious name of "jerk." Jerk spice mixture combines chiles with spices and showcases the Jamaican pepper we know as allspice. This small tropical brown berry is redolent of clove, nutmeg, cinnamon, and ginger, flavors we associate with apple pie. This savory preparation matches allspice with tri-tip, a hearty beef cut that loves an assertive rub. Grassfed tri-tip is a small roast that cooks more uniformly when cut into serving pieces beforehand. The rub calls for jalapeño in place of the traditional blazing hot scotch bonnet chile, because it serves up plenty of heat for everyone I know. The Coconut-Scallion Rice (recipe follows) is a soothing, mildly sweet complement to the fiery beef.

Makes 6 servings

....

5 SCALLIONS, TRIMMED

2 MEDIUM JALAPEÑO PEPPERS, SEEDED IF YOU PREFER MILDER HEAT

3 GARLIC CLOVES, PEELED

1 TABLESPOON CHOPPED FRESH THYME OR 1 TEASPOON DRIED

2 TABLESPOONS PACKED DARK BROWN SUGAR

1 TABLESPOON GROUND ALLSPICE

1½ TEASPOONS GROUND GINGER

¾ TEASPOON BLACK PEPPER

½ TEASPOON GROUND NUTMEG

1 TABLESPOON KOSHER SALT

2 TABLESPOONS FRESHLY SQUEEZED LIME JUICE

1 TABLESPOON VEGETABLE OIL

1 (2- TO 2½-POUND) TRI-TIP ROAST

MORE CHOICE CUTS:

Sirloin tip roast or steak, aka round tip, is a boneless and lean cut, often overlooked for grilling.

Heart, sliced into 1-inch side strips, loves this strong jerk rub.

Separate the white part of the scallions from the green (reserve the green part if making the Coconut-Scallion Rice). Purée the white parts of the scallions, jalapeños, garlic, and thyme in a food processor, scraping down the sides once or twice to make a smooth paste. Add the brown sugar, allspice, ginger, pepper, nutmeg, salt, lime juice, and oil and pulse once or twice to blend. Let the jerk paste stand for about 10 minutes to let the flavors develop. You can prepare this up to 2 days in advance.

Starting from the tip, slice the trip-tip against the grain into large chunks about 4 inches long and 2 inches wide and thick, making them as uniform as you can from this irregular cut. Nestle the beef in a bowl, spoon the jerk paste over it, and turn to coat each piece. Let the meat marinate for at least 30 minutes at room temperature or in the refrigerator for up to 24 hours.

Prepare a gas or charcoal grill for medium-high heat (375° to 425°F), scrape the grate clean, and oil it lightly. Grill the beef over the hottest part of the grill for 4 to 4½ minutes with the cover closed, then use tongs to flip and grill the other side for another 4 to 4½ minutes for medium rare. For medium, slide the beef to the coolest part of the grill, cover and cook for 2 to 5 minutes longer.

COCONUT-SCALLION RICE

Makes 6 servings

....

1 (14-OUNCE) CAN REGULAR OR LIGHT COCONUT
    MILK
1½ CUPS SHORT- OR LONG-GRAIN WHITE RICE
1 TABLESPOON PACKED LIGHT BROWN SUGAR
¾ TEASPOON SALT
1 (1-INCH) CINNAMON STICK
5 SCALLIONS, GREEN PARTS ONLY (RESERVED
    FROM THE JERK SPICE RUB), VERY THINLY
    SLICED

Bring the coconut milk and ¾ cup water to a boil in a medium saucepan over medium-high heat. Add the rice, brown sugar, salt, and cinnamon stick, stir once, and cover the pan. Reduce the heat to low and simmer until all the coconut milk is absorbed and the rice is tender to the bite, 20 to 22 minutes. Discard the cinnamon stick and stir in the scallions just before serving.

TURKISH YOGURT KEBABS WITH GRILLED SUMMER VEGETABLES

Grilled meats slicked with yogurt are a specialty of the Turks. They understand how the thick, cultured marinade transports flavors into the beef while tenderizing it a bit. It also keeps the beef moist while grilling to make an aromatic cloak.

I use these extra-special kebabs as an excuse to create a Turkish-inspired feast, including a bevy of vegetables, rice pilaf, and pita breads, all displayed on my favorite platters. The accompanying vegetable kebabs, an assortment of eggplant, peppers, zucchini, and cherry tomatoes, make easy end-of-summer party fare when these crops are at their best. After grilling, I use a fork to push all of the vegetables into one big platter and serve the beef kebabs on their skewers. The lemon juice squeezed over the grilled meat makes the whole meal sing.

Makes 6 servings

....

¾ CUP PLAIN WHOLE YOGURT, PREFERABLY GREEK-STYLE*

5 TABLESPOONS EXTRA-VIRGIN OLIVE OIL, DIVIDED

3 GARLIC CLOVES, MINCED

1 TABLESPOON GRATED ONION

1 TABLESPOON LEMON ZEST

2 TEASPOONS CHOPPED FRESH THYME LEAVES OR ½ TEASPOON DRIED

2 TEASPOONS SALT, DIVIDED

2 TO 2½ POUNDS TOP SIRLOIN ROAST OR STEAKS, CUT INTO 1½-INCH CUBES

1 SMALL GLOBE EGGPLANT, CUT INTO 1½-INCH CHUNKS

1 LARGE SWEET ONION, PEELED AND CUT INTO WEDGES

2 POBLANO OR BELL PEPPERS, SEEDED AND CUT INTO ROUGHLY 1½-INCH PIECES

2 MEDIUM ZUCCHINI, CUT INTO 1-INCH ROUNDS OR HALF MOONS

1 POUND CHERRY TOMATOES

1 TEASPOON SWEET PAPRIKA

1 LEMON, QUARTERED

To make the marinade, whisk the yogurt, 3 tablespoons of the olive oil, garlic, onion, lemon zest, thyme, and 1 teaspoon of the salt in a medium mixing bowl until smooth. Thread the beef onto wooden or metal skewers leaving space between the cubes to make 6 beef kebabs. Lay them on a platter. Reserve ⅓ of the marinade for the eggplant and spread the remaining marinade over the beef kebabs. Turn them to coat completely, cover, and marinate for at least 1 hour at room temperature or up to 12 hours in the refrigerator.

Toss the eggplant cubes with the reserved marinade and thread them onto the skewers leaving a little space between them for even cooking. Toss the onion, peppers, zucchini, and tomatoes in a large mixing bowl with the remaining 2 tablespoons olive oil, the remaining 1 teaspoon salt, and paprika. Thread the vegetables in an alternating pattern onto skewers.

Prepare a charcoal or gas grill for high heat (425° to 475°F), scrape the grate clean, and oil it lightly. Put the beef and eggplant kebabs over the hottest part of the grill and the vegetable kebabs over medium heat. Cook the beef, turning 2 to 3 times, for a total of 7½ to 8 minutes for medium rare. The yogurt marinade will dry up and turn faintly brown. Cook the eggplant, turning 2 to 3 times, until they soften and turn translucent, for about 9 minutes. Slide them to the cooler part of the grill if they begin to char. Cook the vegetables until their skins wrinkle and char in spots, turning 2 to 3 times for about 12 minutes. Once you've removed the meat, shift the mixed vegetable skewers to the hotter part of the grill if necessary to brown them well. Serve the vegetables on or off the skewers and squeeze the lemon juice over the beef kebabs before serving.

NOTE: Greek-style yogurt is thicker and makes a marinade that will adhere better to the meat. To thicken standard yogurt, strain it through a cheesecloth-lined colander and let it drip in the refrigerator for at least 1 hour or up to 12 hours overnight. It will lose volume, so start with a scant 1 cup to end up with ¾ cup thickened yogurt. Discard the strained liquid.

MORE CHOICE CUTS:

Top round roast or steak, less expensive than top sirloin, is still tender enough for kebabs.

Sirloin tip roast or steak, aka round tip roast or steak, is equally enticing and boneless for easy cubing.

TAMARIND BEEF SATAY

with Indonesian Salad (*Rujak*)

Tamarind is an intoxicating sour and sweet fruit from Indonesia where satay is the go-to snack on a stick. It is incredible with beef, so I created a tamarind marinade that lacquers thin beef strips to grill or broil. Satay makes a wonderful appetizer; to fill it out for a main dish, I accompany it with another Indonesian favorite, a fruit salad called *Rujak* (recipe follows), which has as many renditions as pasta salad does in this country. My version is a beautiful chopped salad of cucumbers, jicama, pineapple, and mango that's crunchy, juicy, sweet, and tart. Served along with Sticky Rice (page 147) or steamed rice, it turns satay into a tantalizing meal, just the thing to wake up your taste buds in the middle of winter.

Makes 4 servings as a main dish;

8 as an appetizer

....

3 TABLESPOONS TAMARIND PASTE* (SOURCES, PAGE 272)

3 TABLESPOONS HONEY

1 TABLESPOON FISH SAUCE

½ TEASPOON CHILE SAUCE, SUCH AS SAMBAL OELEK

⅛ TEASPOON SALT

½ CUP UNSALTED DRY ROASTED PEANUTS

1 TO 1½ POUNDS TOP SIRLOIN STEAK, SLICED INTO ¼-INCH-THICK STRIPS

Mix the tamarind paste, honey, fish sauce, chile sauce, and salt in a medium-sized bowl. Pound the peanuts in a mortar and pestle or in a heavy-duty plastic bag with a rolling pin to the texture of fine breadcrumbs and stir into the tamarind sauce. Put the beef strips in the bowl, toss to coat, and marinate for about 15 minutes at room temperature or up to 12 hours refrigerated.

Preheat a charcoal or gas grill for high heat (425°F to 475°F), scraping the grate clean and oiling it lightly, or preheat the broiler. Thread the slices onto wooden or metal skewers, stitching the beef on and then stretching it along the skewer so that it looks like a miniature banner. Thread any short strips onto the same skewer.

Grill or broil the skewers for 1½ to 2 minutes per side and serve the satay warm or at room temperature accompanied by the fruit salad, if desired.

NOTE: Tamarind is available from Asian grocery markets in several different forms. Tamarind paste is the easiest form that can be used straight from the jar. If your tamarind is labeled concentrate, use only 1 tablespoon and mix it with 2 tablespoons water. If you have a block of tamarind, chop about ½ cup of it, use a fork to mash it with 6 tablespoons of boiling water, and let it soften for about 5 minutes. Use a fine-meshed strainer to extract 3 tablespoons of pulp, pressing on the mixture firmly with a spoon.

INDONESIAN SALAD (*RUJAK*)

Makes 4 servings

....

1 SHALLOT, FINELY CHOPPED

2 TABLESPOONS LIME JUICE

1 TABLESPOON SUGAR

1 TABLESPOON SOY SAUCE

1 TEASPOON PEANUT OIL OR VEGETABLE OIL

¼ TEASPOON CHILE SAUCE, SUCH AS SAMBAL OELEK

2 MEDIUM CUCUMBERS, PEELED, SEEDED AND CUT INTO
   1-INCH CHUNKS

2 CUPS PINEAPPLE, CUT INTO 1-INCH CHUNKS OR 1 (20-
   OUNCE) CAN PINEAPPLE CHUNKS, DRAINED

1 SMALL JICAMA, PEELED AND CUT INTO MATCHSTICKS

1 FIRM-RIPE MANGO, PEELED AND CUT INTO 1-INCH CHUNKS

1 RED CHILE PEPPER, SEEDED AND THINGLY SLICED INTO
   ROUNDS, OPTIONAL

SALT TO TASTE

Make the dressing by whisking the shallot, lime juice, sugar,
soy sauce, oil, and chile sauce in a bowl. Combine the cucumbers, pineapple, jicama, mango, and chile pepper, if using, in a
large mixing bowl. Add the dressing and salt and toss well.
Taste for salt and let it sit at room temperature to develop the
flavors while you grill or broil the beef satay.

MORE CHOICE CUTS:

Top blade steak, aka flatiron, is one of the remarkably tender cuts from
the chuck, just perfect for high-heat cooking and eating off a stick.

Top round steak is a somewhat chewier option with standout flavors
for this satay.

MIXED GRILL CHIMICHURRI

Chimichurri is a garlicky green herb sauce, akin to pesto, that is spectacular with beef. Parsley, that most undervalued herb, gets a chance to star in combination with cilantro, oregano, red pepper flakes, and a bracing splash of red wine vinegar. Made famous by the Argentinian *perillas* (grill restaurants), chimichurri is bold enough to use as a marinade or serve as a sauce. In this recipe, I use it for both purposes, since it's hard to get enough.

I'm hoping that the chimichurri will lure you into trying beef heart, a cut I've come to love grilled. It has a firm texture and concentrated beefiness and cooks in a flash—just like other lean meats. Grilled and accompanied with sirloin steak, chorizo, corn on the cob, and tomatoes, it makes fabulous party food for adventuresome friends. Mix it up as much as you like with other offal, including kidneys, or beef ribs and sausages—or stick with steak—plus as many late-summer vegetables as you can squeeze onto the grill.

Makes 8 to 10 servings

....

CHIMICHURRI:

2 GARLIC CLOVES, PEELED

1 MEDIUM ONION, CHOPPED

4 CUPS LIGHTLY PACKED FRESH PARSLEY LEAVES

2 CUPS LIGHTLY PACKED FRESH CILANTRO LEAVES

1 TABLESPOON KOSHER SALT

¼ CUP RED WINE VINEGAR

2 TEASPOONS DRIED OREGANO

1 TEASPOON RED PEPPER FLAKES

¾ CUP EXTRA-VIRGIN OLIVE OIL

MIXED GRILL:

1 BEEF HEART (ABOUT 2 POUNDS), SLICED INTO 1-INCH WIDE STRIPS

2 TOP SIRLOIN STEAKS (ABOUT 1½ POUNDS), 1 TO 1¼ INCHES THICK

12 OUNCES CHORIZO LINKS (PAGE 263)

6 TO 8 EARS CORN ON THE COB, HUSKED AND SILKED

4 TO 6 LARGE TOMATOES, THICKLY SLICED

To make the chimichurri, bring a teakettle of water to a boil. Put the garlic, onion, parsley, and cilantro into a food processor and purée, scraping down the sides as necessary, until it is finely chopped. Put the salt in a separate medium mixing bowl, add ¼ cup of the boiling water, and stir to dissolve it. Add the vinegar, oregano, pepper flakes, and the puréed herbs and stir until well blended. Add the olive oil, stir again, and let it sit at room temperature for about 10 minutes to develop the flavors. Taste for salt. If it zings in your mouth like a strong vinaigrette, it's just right. This will make 1¾ cups.

Put the beef heart and steak in a shallow dish just large enough to contain them. Add about ¾ cup of the chimichurri to coat them well. Cover and reserve the rest of the chimichurri for serving. Marinate the beef for at least 3 hours and up to 24 hours in the refrigerator.

Preheat a charcoal or gas grill for high heat (425° to 475°F), scrape the grate clean, and oil it lightly. Lift the pieces of beef heart and steak from the chimichurri marinade and discard the marinade. Grill the heart and steak over the hottest part of the grill. Cook the heart strips for 2½ to 3 minutes per side, watching the thinner ones. Cook the steak for 3½ to 4 minutes per side for medium rare. (For medium, slide the steak to the coolest part of the grill, close the lid, and cook for 1 to 3 minutes longer.) At the same time, grill the sausages where they'll fit, turning them 3 to 4 times, until they are nicely browned all over, 7 to 8 minutes. Meanwhile, space the corn around the edges of the grill—or once you've removed all the meats—turning every few minutes until lightly browned and tender to the bite, about 12 minutes.

Slice the steak ¼ inch thick against the grain, and cut the sausages into 2-inch serving pieces. Arrange the beef heart, steak, and sausages on a serving platter. Cut each corn cob into three pieces and arrange the corn and tomatoes on a separate platter. Spoon some of the reserved chimichurri over them, passing the rest at the table.

MORE CHOICE CUTS:

Tri-tip roast from grassfed beef is typically too small to serve a crowd, but this combination fills out the menu.

Hanger steak is another excellent grilling cut with substantial flavor and texture.

KOREAN BARBECUE

The classic Korean barbecue called *galbi* typically features grilled beef short rib meat marinated in a soy sauce and sesame oil marinade, sprinkled with toasted sesame seeds. Since the bone-in, thinly sliced short ribs called flanken-style or Korean can be hard to find, I substituted skirt steak. Like the ribs, it's got great chew and beefy character and loves a good, long marinade. Served with steamed rice, kimchee, and gochujang, Korean hot sauce (Sources, page 270), this meal lets everyone assemble it to their own tastes.

Makes 4 servings as an entree;

8 servings as an appetizer

....

¼ CUP APPLE CIDER

½ CUP SOY SAUCE

6 SCALLIONS, WHITE AND GREEN PARTS, TRIMMED
    AND VERY THINLY SLICED

3 GARLIC CLOVES, MINCED

3 TABLESPOONS PACKED LIGHT BROWN SUGAR

2 TABLESPOONS TOASTED SESAME OIL

2 TABLESPOONS CHINESE RICE WINE OR DRY
    SHERRY

¼ TEASPOON BLACK PEPPER

1½ POUNDS SKIRT STEAK, SLICED INTO 4-INCH
    LONG PIECES

2 TABLESPOONS TOASTED SESAME SEEDS*

¾ TEASPOON SALT

Whisk the cider, soy sauce, scallions, garlic, brown sugar, sesame oil, rice wine, and pepper together in a bowl. Add the beef and marinate it for 3 to 12 hours in the refrigerator.

Preheat a charcoal or gas grill for high heat (425° to 475°F), scrape the grate clean, and oil it lightly. Mix the sesame seeds with the salt and set it aside. Drain the beef, put it on a dinner plate, and discard the marinade.

Grill the beef over the hottest part of the grill until burnished brown, 2½ to 3 minutes per side. Because it is so thin, it will cook to medium. Sprinkle the beef with the reserved sesame seed mixture before serving warm or at room temperature.

NOTE: Sesame seeds are sold toasted, which are more expensive, and untoasted. To toast your own, heat a dry skillet over medium heat. Add the sesame seeds, reduce the heat to low, and stand by. As they start to snap, slide the pan back and forth across the burner every 30 seconds until most of the seeds are golden brown, 2 to 2½ minutes. Pour the seeds into a bowl to cool.

MORE CHOICE CUTS:
Flank steak is another boneless option to marinate and quick-grill.

Flanken-style short ribs are thin, crosscut shortribs, the standard for Korean barbecue; use 2 pounds to yield enough meat per serving.

DELI-STYLE SALAMI (PAGE 258) AND
GRASSFED BEEF TERRINE WITH CRACKERBREADS (PAGE 260)

BONELESS OXTAIL AND BUCKWHEAT CRÊPE PURSES WITH
CHIVE-HORSERADISH CREAM (PAGE 248)

DELUXE PIMENTO CHEESEBURGERS (PAGE 74) WITH
WHOLE-WHEAT HAMBURGER BUNS AND LARDO KETCHUP (PAGE 72)

GRASSFED TOP BLADE STEAK WITH
ARUGULA SALAD AND SCORCHED CROUTONS (PAGE 168)

TAMARIND BEEF SATAY WITH INDONESIAN SALAD (*RUJAK*) (PAGE 140)

HERBES DE PROVENCE ROAST WITH FIG-RED ONION MARMALADE (PAGE 215)

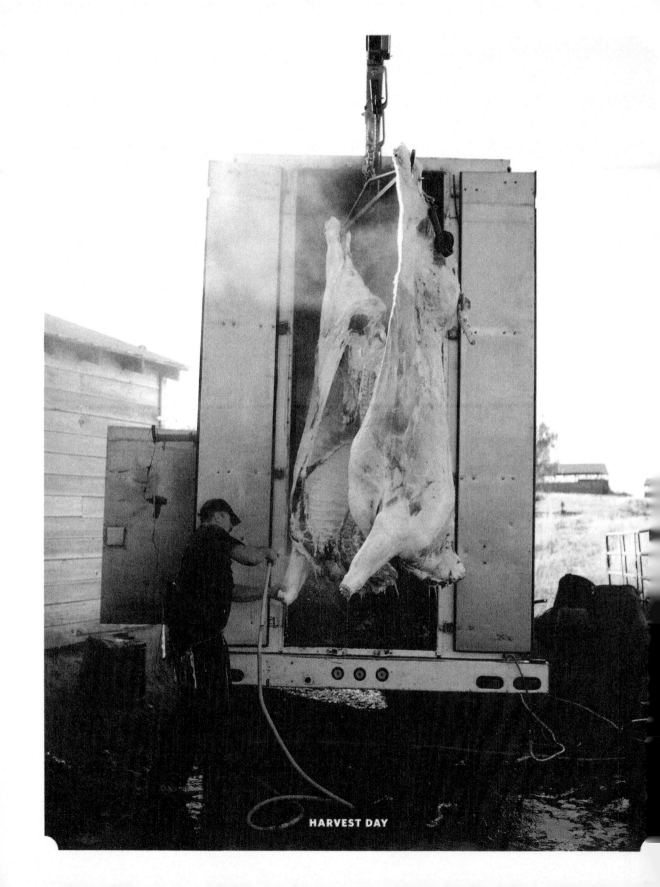

HARVEST DAY

KEVIN SILVEIRA, OWNER OF VALLEY MEAT SERVICES

SKILLET STEAK PEPERONATA (PAGE 196)

WINTER MINESTRONE (PAGE 236) AND OLIVE OIL BREADSTICKS (PAGE 178)

INDIAN-SPICED STUFFED PEPPERS (PAGE 98)

ROLLED CRANBERRY-GLAZED BEEF BRISKET (PAGE 107)

TOMATO-BRAISED BEEF CHEEKS WITH WILTED SPINACH AND OVEN POLENTA (PAGE 113)

AROMATIC EGGPLANT-BEEF TIMBALE (PAGE 157)

FLYING GREENS WITH BEEF
IN OYSTER SAUCE

The legend of flying greens in Thailand involves shooting flames, smoking oil, and greens on fire. This recipe is not nearly as wild as that, but it still involves quick cooking over high heat—two of the basic principles of stir-frying. Bok choy is crisp and tender and the leaves and stems cook at different times, so be sure to keep them separate. Combined with lean round steak and glossed with sauce, this easy stir-fry is one I enjoy with steamed short- or long-grained brown rice.

Makes 4 servings

....

1 OUNCE DRIED SHIITAKE MUSHROOMS

2 TEASPOONS CORNSTARCH

1 TABLESPOON SOY SAUCE

1¾ TEASPOONS RICE WINE VINEGAR

¼ CUP OYSTER SAUCE

1 TABLESPOON PEANUT OIL OR VEGETABLE OIL

2 GARLIC CLOVES, MINCED

1-INCH PIECE GINGER, PEELED AND VERY FINELY CHOPPED (1 TABLESPOON)

¾ TO 1 POUND TOP ROUND STEAK, SLICED INTO ¼ X ¼-INCH STRIPS ABOUT 2 INCHES LONG

1½ POUNDS BOK CHOY, STEMS AND LEAVES SEPARATED AND CHOPPED (ABOUT 6 CUPS TOTAL)

2 DRIED WHOLE RED CHILE PEPPERS, OPTIONAL

Bring a teakettle of water to a boil. Put the dried mushrooms in a small bowl, cover them with boiling water, and let them soak for 15 minutes. Drain the mushrooms, reserving ¼ cup of the soaking liquid. Discard the tough stems from the mushrooms, slice the caps very thin, and set them aside. Whisk the cornstarch with the soy sauce, vinegar, oyster sauce, and the reserved mushroom soaking liquid in a small bowl.

Heat the oil in a wok or large skillet over high heat. Add the garlic and ginger and stir-fry for 30 seconds. Add the beef and stir-fry just until it is no longer pink. Push it to the outer perimeters of the pan and add the stems of the bok choy to the center where the heat is concentrated. Stir continuously until the bok choy is crisp-tender, about 3 minutes. Add the bok choy leaves, reserved mushroom caps, and chiles, if using, and stir for 1 minute. Add the soy sauce mixture and stir until the sauce is bubbling and slicks the greens and beef well. Serve immediately.

> **MORE CHOICE CUTS:**
> Eye round is another good and economy-minded choice for this stir-fry.
> Top sirloin steak is a standard for stir-fry.

LAOTIAN BEEF SALAD

with Sticky Rice

Served at room temperature, Laotian Beef Salad makes a lively light supper for the hottest months. Based on a Southeast Asian favorite called "waterfall beef" that's similar to *larb*, this dish is fresh with herbs and the deep, nutty taste of toasted rice. While it can be served raw, I prefer to quick-cook cubes of tender top blade steak, aka flatiron, and use its juices to flavor the dressing and wilt the herbs. I serve it over a bed of baby Asian greens including mizuna and baby bok choy along with Sticky Rice (recipe follows). Substitute red or green leaf lettuce and steamed jasmine rice, if you like.

Makes 4 servings

....

¼ CUP STICKY RICE OR JASMINE RICE

¾ TO 1 POUND TOP BLADE STEAK, CUT INTO ¼-INCH
    CUBES (CHOPPING AND MINCING, PAGE 47)

½ TEASPOON SALT

1 TABLESPOON PEANUT OIL OR VEGETABLE OIL

1 LARGE SHALLOT, PEELED AND THINLY SLICED

1-INCH PIECE PEELED AND VERY FINELY CHOPPED
    FRESH GALANGAL OR GINGER (1 TABLESPOON)

1 TABLESPOON LIME JUICE

1 TABLESPOON FISH SAUCE

1 RED CHILE PEPPER, VERY FINELY CHOPPED,
    SEEDED IF YOU PREFER MILDER HEAT

6 SCALLIONS, BOTH WHITE AND GREEN PARTS,
    TRIMMED AND VERY THINLY SLICED

1 CUP LIGHTLY PACKED COARSELY CHOPPED FRESH
    CILANTRO

½ CUP LIGHTLY PACKED COARSELY CHOPPED
    FRESH MINT LEAVES

Heat a dry skillet over medium heat. Add the rice and toast, shaking the pan now and then, until the grains turn golden and wisps of smoke appear, about 10 minutes. Transfer to a spice grinder, blender, or mortar and pestle and crush it to a fine powder.

Put the beef in a small bowl and toss well with the salt. Heat the oil in a wok or large skillet over high heat. When it smokes, stir-fry the meat just until it is no longer pink and releases its juices, about 1 minute. Immediately remove the pan from the heat and splash in 1 tablespoon of water to make a small amount of stock.

Make the dressing by combining the shallot, galangal, lime juice, and fish sauce in a small mixing bowl. Add the warm beef with all of the liquid in the bowl and toss. Add the reserved toasted rice and toss along with the chile pepper, scallions, cilantro, and mint and taste for seasoning. Serve it with the sticky rice, if desired.

MORE CHOICE CUTS:

Shoulder tender, aka teres major, is another cut from the chuck that suits this quick-cooking method well.

Tenderloin, in small quantities, gets put to good use here when tenderness is paramount.

STICKY RICE

This long-grained white rice is often labeled "sweet rice" or "glutinous rice" and turns out just as the name says. My kids cannot get enough of it. Steamed, not boiled, it requires at least a one-hour soak. Bamboo baskets are traditional, but I use my trusty stainless steel pot with a steamer insert and wrap the rice in a dampened cloth napkin. It works great every time and holds for hours when kept moist and warm. It is a delight to eat with stir-fries as well as other sticky foods, like Ginger-Glazed Short Ribs (page 244).

Makes 4 servings

....

2 CUPS THAI STICKY RICE (*KOW NEOW*) (SOURCES, PAGE 272)

Put the rice in a bowl, cover by 2 to 3 inches with 100°F water (as warm as bath water you'd want to step into), and soak it for 1 to 2 hours. Alternatively, soak the rice for 4 to 8 hours in room temperature water. When it's done soaking it will crumble like chalk in your mouth when you chew a few grains. Drain the rice well.

Fill a pot with a steamer basket insert with about 3 inches of water, and make sure that the rice will not be in contact with the water while it steams. Rinse a cloth napkin or cheesecloth in water, squeeze it out, and use it to line the steamer basket. Put the rice into the napkin or cheesecloth and wrap it over the rice to cover it. Cover and bring the water to a boil over medium-high heat. Reduce the heat to low and steam the rice for 20 minutes. Keep your face away from the steam as you lift the lid and use a spatula to flip the bundle of rice over. Steam for another 10 minutes. Flip the rice again and peek inside the cloth. The rice will be translucent and glossy. Keep the rice wrapped in the cloth, either in the steamer with the heat off or in a serving bowl to keep it moist, until ready to serve.

DRY-FRIED BEEF WITH CRISPY KOHLRABI AND CARROTS

This is not your typical saucy stir-fry, but an arresting mix of chewy, browned slivers of beef and crunchy vegetables. It's all based on a unique cooking technique called dry-frying, used by Sichuan cooks, that I learned from Fuschia Dunlop's *Land of Plenty*. It takes a bit longer than the classic stir-frying method but still relies on high heat and quick action, so be sure to have your ingredients ready to go before turning on the heat and your hood fan.

Kohlrabi, also called cabbage turnip, is a mild bulb that deserves more attention; use peeled broccoli stems, asparagus, or snow peas in its place. Sichuan peppercorn, a tiny and prickly red-brown berry, is less spicy than effervescent in your mouth and creates a tingling sensation that adds to this stir-fry's appeal. Serve it with cooling Quick-Pickled Cucumber Salad (page 77) and steamed white rice.

Makes 4 servings

....

1 POUND TOP ROUND STEAK, VERY THINLY SLICED AGAINST THE GRAIN ¼ INCH THICK

¼ TEASPOON SALT

4 TABLESPOONS PEANUT OIL OR VEGETABLE OIL, DIVIDED

3 MEDIUM CARROTS, PEELED AND CUT INTO MATCHSTICKS

1 LARGE KOHLRABI BULB (ABOUT 8 OUNCES), PEELED AND CUT INTO MATCHSTICKS

2-INCH PIECE GINGER, PEELED, SLICED VERY THIN, AND CUT INTO FINE STRIPS, DIVIDED

6 SCALLIONS, TRIMMED WITH WHITE PARTS CUT INTO MATCHSTICKS AND GREEN PARTS FINELY CHOPPED

2 TABLESPOONS SOY SAUCE

1 TABLESPOON HOISIN SAUCE

1 TABLESPOON CHINESE RICE WINE OR DRY SHERRY

1 TABLESPOON ORANGE ZEST

¾ TEASPOON TOASTED SESAME OIL

½ TEASPOON TOASTED AND GROUND SICHUAN PEPPER, OPTIONAL* (SOURCES, PAGE 272)

Season the beef with the salt. Heat 3 tablespoons of the oil in a wok or large skillet over high heat. When smoking, add the beef and stir until the beef is no longer pink. Spread the beef out into a single layer and let it cook until the juices have nearly evaporated, about 4 minutes. When the oil is clear once again, stir the beef strips leisurely, until they sizzle and turn mahogany brown, an additional 3 to 3½ minutes. Transfer the beef to a bowl.

Heat the remaining 1 tablespoon of oil over high heat. Add the carrots and kohlrabi and cook, stirring constantly, until they start to become limp but remain crisp, about 4 minutes. They will pick up color from the beef. Add them to the bowl with the beef.

Add the ginger and the white parts of the scallions and cook, stirring, for 30 seconds. Add the soy sauce, hoisin sauce, rice wine, and orange zest and stir-fry until fragrant. Add the beef and vegetables back into the pan along with the sesame oil and stir until hot. Serve immediately, sprinkled with the chopped scallion greens and Sichuan pepper, if using.

NOTE: Toast Sichuan peppercorns as you do any whole spice: heat a small dry skillet over medium-low heat and stand by so it doesn't burn. Swirl the pan on the burner to roll the spices around a few times until they become fragrant and your kitchen smells like incense.

MORE CHOICE CUTS:

Sirloin tip steak, aka round tip steak is another more tender option for dry-frying.

Top sirloin steak is a ready stand-in for any stir fry.

TACOS

with Avocado-Tomatillo Salsa

Traveling back to Oregon from Seattle on a Tuesday, my husband, Benjamin, and I pulled into a taco stand in central Washington. We had only ten dollars in cash and with that we ate our fill of tacos filled with the seared beef called *carne asada*. There is no secret marinade or ingredient for the habit-forming tacos sold at roadside stands and food carts: the beef is diced very fine, salted, and then browned on a griddle with onions and cilantro. You get a heaping tablespoon of scrumptious beef on top of two soft corn tortillas and a wedge of lime. It's up to you to flavor it with a great salsa like this smooth and tart Avocado-Tomatillo Salsa (recipe follows). Be sure to offer bowls full of radishes, cucumbers, and pickled carrots to fill out the meal, which is especially easy and family-friendly for weeknights on the run.

Just before cooking, put the beef in a medium mixing bowl, sprinkle on the salt and toss to distribute it. Heat the oil in a large skillet over high heat. When it shimmers, add the beef, stir once, and let it cook without stirring until the liquid evaporates and the beef sears and browns, about 4 minutes. Add the onion and cook, stirring occasionally, just until it begins to brown, about 3 minutes. Remove the skillet from the heat, stir in the cilantro, and distribute the beef among the tortillas to serve with a squeeze of lime, sour cream, and the salsa, if desired.

Makes 4 servings

....

12 OUNCES TOP ROUND STEAK, CUT INTO ⅛-INCH
  CUBES (CHOPPING AND MINCING, PAGE 47)

1 TEASPOON SALT

2 TEASPOONS VEGETABLE OIL

1 WHITE ONION, VERY FINELY CHOPPED

½ CUP LIGHTLY PACKED FINELY CHOPPED FRESH
  CILANTRO

12 CORN TORTILLAS, PREFERABLY FRESHLY MADE

LIME WEDGES, FOR SERVING

SOUR CREAM, FOR SERVING

MORE CHOICE CUTS:

Tongue is a standard filling for tacos, simmered in water with a clove of garlic and an onion for 3½ to 4 hours until you can pierce it easily with a skewer, peeled, and diced to use in place of steak.

Top sirloin steak is a natural for tacos.

AVOCADO-TOMATILLO SALSA

Avocados aren't just for making guacamole, and this smooth and creamy quick-cooked salsa makes two avocados go far. It involves briefly steaming the tomatillos and jalapeños before puréeing them with the avocados.

Makes 2 cups

....

6 TOMATILLOS, HUSKS REMOVED AND RINSED

1 JALAPEÑO PEPPER, SEEDED IF YOU PREFER MILDER HEAT

2 RIPE AVOCADOS

1 GARLIC CLOVE, PEELED

¼ CUP LIGHTLY PACKED CHOPPED FRESH CILANTRO

½ TEASPOON SALT

Fill a medium saucepan with about 2 inches of water and place the pan over high heat to bring the water to a boil. Add the tomatillos and jalapeño, reduce the heat to low, and steam until the tomatillos turn pale and soft, about 7 minutes.

Transfer the tomatillos and jalapeño with ¼ cup of the cooking liquid into a food processor or blender. Pit and peel the avocado and add it along with the garlic, cilantro, and salt. Purée until the salsa is very smooth and thick but pourable. Pour it into a small serving bowl and let it cool to room temperature before serving. Best eaten the day it is made, it will store in the refrigerator for up to 2 days.

ETHIOPIAN STEAK "TARTARE"

with Gingered Collard Greens

Called *kitfo*, the tender, lean beef spiced with cardamom and cayenne-spiked butter is a specialty of this east African country. I adore cardamom, but not raw meat. Instead of dressing the chopped beef with the hot spiced butter the traditional way (which you can do if you like), I opted to sauté it to rare and pair it with quick-cooked collard greens or kale to make a transporting supper.

Makes 4 servings

....

1 TABLESPOON VEGETABLE OIL

3 TABLESPOONS UNSALTED BUTTER, DIVIDED

2 GARLIC CLOVES, PEELED AND VERY THINLY SLICED

1-INCH PIECE GINGER, PEELED AND VERY FINELY CHOPPED (1 TABLESPOON)

1 MEDIUM ONION, THINLY SLICED

1 POUND COLLARD GREENS OR KALE, TOUGH STEMS REMOVED AND ROUGHLY CHOPPED

1 TEASPOON SALT, DIVIDED

½ TEASPOON GROUND CARDAMOM

¼ TEASPOON GROUND TURMERIC

¼ TEASPOON CAYENNE

1 POUND SHOULDER TENDER, CUT INTO ½-INCH CUBES

Heat the oil and melt 1 tablespoon of the butter in a large skillet over medium-high heat. When the butter foams, add the garlic, ginger, and onion. Cook, stirring occasionally, until they are fragrant and translucent but not browned, about 2 minutes. Add the collard greens with ¼ teaspoon salt. Cook, stirring now and then, until the greens darken in color but retain some crispness, 7 to 8 minutes. Transfer them to a platter and cover to keep warm. (If the greens release excess liquid, drain them before putting them on the platter.)

Melt the remaining 2 tablespoons butter in the pan over high heat. When it foams, add the cardamom, turmeric, and cayenne and cook, stirring, until fragrant, about 30 seconds. Add the beef and the remaining ¼ teaspoon salt and cook, stirring, just until the meat is no longer pink, about 2 minutes. Spoon the beef and all of the butter over the greens, and serve immediately.

> **MORE CHOICE CUTS:**
> Top blade steak, aka flatiron, is another exceptionally tender cut from the chuck so long as you trim away the band of sinew while cubing it.
> Tenderloin tails, saved from your own tenderloin trimming or from an accommodating butcher, are another option for this dish that calls for a very tender cut.

THAI RED CURRY WITH ROASTED PEANUTS

This nearly instant Thai curry dish is what I make when I need to put together a meal while twenty-minute jasmine rice is steaming. I adapted this recipe from Judy Bastyra's *Thai: The Essence of Thai Cooking*, and it couldn't be simpler. Slivers of beef cook quickly in a sauce rich with coconut milk, peanuts, and prepared Thai red curry paste. I find the bottom round steak cut from a rump roast to offer a nice chew, but if you want tenderness, choose one of the other suggested cuts instead.

Makes 4 servings

....

¾ CUP ROASTED PEANUTS

1 (14-OUNCE) CAN COCONUT MILK

1 TABLESPOON RED CURRY PASTE (SOURCES, PAGE 272)

2 TABLESPOONS FISH SAUCE

1 TABLESPOON PACKED LIGHT BROWN SUGAR

1 POUND BOTTOM ROUND STEAK, SLICED INTO ¼ x ¼-INCH STRIPS ABOUT 2 INCHES LONG

1 TABLESPOON LIME ZEST

1 TABLESPOON LIME JUICE

12 FRESH BASIL LEAVES, SLICED INTO FINE RIBBONS, OPTIONAL

Put the peanuts into a heavy-duty resealable plastic bag and pulverize with a meat mallet or heavy rolling pin until they are like coarse breadcrumbs. Set them aside.

Bring 1 cup of the coconut milk to a boil in a medium saucepan over medium heat and stir until the cream separates and looks curdled. Whisk in the red curry paste and cook until it darkens in color, stirring often, about 5 minutes. Stir in the remaining coconut milk, the fish sauce, and brown sugar and stir until it is very smooth. Add the beef, the reserved peanuts, lime zest, and lime juice and simmer over low heat until the beef is just cooked through and the sauce is thick, 8 to 10 minutes. Serve sprinkled with the basil, if using.

MORE CHOICE CUTS:

Sirloin tip steak, aka round tip steak, is another cut from the round that is lean and tender.

Top round steak is a great choice for this quick-simmered dish.

JAPANESE SURF AND TURF STEW

(*Nikujaga*)

This Japanese beef-potato stew contains what in our country is a paltry, laughable, why-bother quantity of meat for four. Simmered in a pleasingly sweet soy sauce broth, just eight ounces of beef becomes a bowl of satisfaction and comfort. A home-style favorite in Japan, this twenty-minute stew is served with rice. Try it over soba noodles or on its own and put some wasabi on the table for those who are partial to its heady kick.

The broth's backbone is dashi, the Japanese seaweed and fish stock used to make miso soup. Here, I employ instant dashi stock, available in supermarkets, which gives this one-pot dish hints of both land and sea.

Serves 4

....

3 TABLESPOONS SOY SAUCE

3 TABLESPOONS MIRIN OR RICE WINE

2 TABLESPOONS SUGAR

1 TEASPOON INSTANT DASHI STOCK, OPTIONAL (SOURCES, PAGE 272)

8 OUNCES TOP SIRLOIN STEAK, CUT INTO STRIPS 1-INCH WIDE AND ½ INCH THICK

1 MEDIUM ONION, THINLY SLICED

3 MEDIUM CARROTS, PEELED AND CUT INTO ½-INCH-THICK ROUNDS

1 POUND SMALL RED POTATOES (ABOUT 4), CUT INTO ROUNDS ½ INCH THICK

2 SCALLIONS, WHITE AND GREEN PARTS, TRIMMED AND VERY THINLY SLICED

1 TEASPOON DARK SESAME OIL

Bring 2 cups of water to a simmer in a large saucepan over medium heat. Add the soy sauce, mirin, sugar, and dashi stock, if using, and stir until the sugar dissolves. Add the beef and skim any foam that rises to the surface. Add the onion, carrots, and potatoes. Cover the pan and simmer until the potatoes and carrots are fork tender, 15 to 20 minutes. Add the scallions and sesame oil just before serving.

MORE CHOICE CUTS:

Top blade steak, aka flatiron, and shoulder tender, aka teres major, are more tender options for this light and tasty stew.

Ground beef, the leaner the better, can be stirred into the simmering broth so that it breaks into crumbles.

ROASTED TOMATILLO POSOLE

with Cilantro Cream

While posole is typically a long-simmered stew, this version is quick. It's made with tomatillos, a warm-weather crop that grows surprisingly well in our alpine climate. I roast them to a near char to deepen their flavors, then purée them to make a lively base for this stovetop stew. Chock full of hominy—whole preserved corn kernels—and beef cubes, its tartness is rounded out with the garnish of cilantro-sour cream. I eat a bowlful with a spoon in one hand and a warm rolled corn tortilla in the other for dipping.

Makes 4 servings

....

12 OUNCES TOMATILLOS, HUSKED

1 SMALL WHITE ONION, CHOPPED

3 GARLIC CLOVES, PEELED

1 TO 2 JALAPEÑOS, SEEDED IF YOU PREFER
MILDER HEAT

1 TABLESPOON SUGAR

1½ TEASPOONS SALT

1 TABLESPOON VEGETABLE OIL

1 POUND TOP ROUND STEAK, CUT INTO ½-INCH
CUBES

2 CUPS LOW-SALT BEEF STOCK (SHORT ORDER
STOCK, PAGE 226; ROASTED BEEF STOCK,
PAGE 228) OR WATER

1 (29-OUNCE) CAN YELLOW OR WHITE HOMINY,
DRAINED

½ CUP SOUR CREAM

½ CUP LIGHTLY PACKED FINELY CHOPPED FRESH
CILANTRO

6 SCALLIONS, WHITE AND GREEN PARTS, TRIMMED
AND THINLY SLICED

Preheat the broiler with the oven rack in the highest position. Arrange the tomatillos in a single layer on a rimmed baking sheet. Broil them until they blister and char, about 5 minutes. They'll release a lot of juice. Turn them over using tongs and broil the second side. Purée the tomatillos and all of their juices with the onion, garlic, jalapeños, sugar, and salt in a blender until smooth.

Heat the oil in a large saucepan over medium-high heat. Add the tomatillo sauce all at once, being careful to avoid splatters. Once it boils, reduce the heat to low and simmer the sauce until it thickens and its color darkens a shade or two, stirring occasionally, about 10 minutes. Add the beef, stock water, and hominy, and simmer gently until the beef is cooked through, 10 to 12 minutes. Taste for salt and simmer for 5 to 10 minutes longer if you'd like it a bit thicker.

Mix the sour cream with the cilantro in a small bowl. Swirl it into individual serving bowls of posole along with a generous sprinkling of the scallions.

> **MORE CHOICE CUTS:**
> Top sirloin and sirloin tip, aka round tip, are lean and tender steaks suitable for quick simmering.

BOBOTIE

"You have to include bobotie," said my cookbook-collecting friend, Judy Amster, though I'd never heard of it. Considered the national dish of South Africa, it's a classic of curried beef baked in a savory custard. I'm always drawn to dishes that give leftover roast beef new life, and now that I've tasted it, I can't quite get enough. The combination of beef with curry, dried apricots, and toasted almonds is a great alternative to roast beef hash. You have the option here to begin with uncooked beef, and this is an especially good use for any of the least tender, lean, but still tasty cuts from the round. It reheats well, and I eat it for brunch on a wintery day. For authenticity, serve it with rice and your favorite chutney.

Makes 6 servings

....

2 ½-INCH SLICES FIRM WHITE BREAD

1¼ CUPS WHOLE MILK, DIVIDED

2 TABLESPOONS UNSALTED BUTTER

2 MEDIUM ONIONS, CHOPPED

2 GARLIC CLOVES, MINCED

1 TABLESPOON MILD CURRY POWDER

1½ POUNDS BOTTOM ROUND ROAST, FINELY
    CHOPPED (CHOPPING AND MINCING,
    PAGE 47)

2 TEASPOONS SALT, DIVIDED

½ TEASPOON BLACK PEPPER

2 OUNCES DRIED APRICOTS, CHOPPED (ABOUT
    ⅓ CUP)

1 TABLESPOON LEMON ZEST

2 EGGS

1 EGG YOLK

PINCH OF GROUND NUTMEG

2 OUNCES SLICED ALMONDS (ABOUT ⅔ CUP)

Preheat the oven to 350°F and lightly grease an 8- or 9-inch square baking dish or pie plate and set it aside.

Trim the crust from the bread, tear it into bite-sized pieces, and soak it in ¼ cup of the milk until saturated, about 10 minutes. Meanwhile, melt the butter in a large skillet over medium heat. Add the onions and cook, stirring occasionally, until they turn caramel colored, about 8 minutes.

Add the garlic and curry powder and cook until it is aromatic, about 1 minute. Add the beef, 1¾ teaspoons of the salt, and the pepper and cook, stirring once or twice, until the beef is no longer pink. Remove the pan from the heat and stir in the soaked bread, apricots, and lemon zest. Taste for curry powder and salt. Let it cool slightly then beat 1 of the eggs and stir it in until everything is well blended. Spoon the beef mixture into the prepared baking dish.

Prepare the custard topping by whisking the remaining 1 cup milk with the remaining egg, egg yolk, the remaining ¼ teaspoon salt, and nutmeg. Pour it over the beef mixture and sprinkle on the almonds. Bake it until the custard is just set and the top is golden brown, 45 to 50 minutes.

MORE CHOICE CUTS:

Top round, sirloin tip, and eye round, which are more tender than bottom round, can be left more coarsely chopped.

Ground beef can replace the hand-chopped beef if you choose extra lean.

Leftover steak or roast, trimmed and chopped, shortens the cooking time and slips right into the mixture once the onions and curry powder are cooked.

AROMATIC EGGPLANT-BEEF TIMBALE

This layered rice, eggplant, beef, and tomato dish is a stunning make-ahead party dish. Beneath the rosette of fresh tomatoes and sandwiched between eggplant slices, chopped lean beef is seasoned with cinnamon and allspice—a spice combination as old as civilization. Inspired by May Bsisu's recipe in *The Arab Table*, this version takes less work than lasagna, and you can prepare the eggplant and the beef one day in advance. It presents with the stature of a layer cake and serves up neatly in scoops from the platter, a standout with a crunchy Romaine salad.

Makes 8 to 10 servings

....

2 MEDIUM EGGPLANTS (ABOUT 2 POUNDS), SLICED INTO ½-INCH-THICK ROUNDS

2¾ TEASPOONS SALT, DIVIDED

1½ CUPS BASMATI OR LONG-GRAIN WHITE RICE

3 TABLESPOONS OLIVE OIL, PLUS ADDITIONAL ½ CUP FOR BRUSHING THE EGGPLANT

1 MEDIUM ONION, FINELY CHOPPED

1 POUND TOP ROUND STEAK, COARSELY CHOPPED (CHOPPING AND MINCING, PAGE 47)

1½ TEASPOONS GROUND CINNAMON

¾ TEASPOON GROUND ALLSPICE

¼ TEASPOON BLACK PEPPER

2½ CUPS LOW-SALT BEEF STOCK (SHORT ORDER STOCK, PAGE 226; ROASTED BEEF STOCK, PAGE 228) OR WATER, DIVIDED

1 POUND FIRM, RIPE TOMATOES (ABOUT 2), SLICED ½ INCH THICK

¼ TEASPOON SAFFRON THREADS

1 TABLESPOON PINE NUTS, LIGHTLY TOASTED IN A DRY SKILLET, OPTIONAL

MORE CHOICE CUTS

Stew beef, trimmed of any fat and chopped as directed, is put to new use in this baked dish.

Ground beef, 90 to 95 percent lean, is a convenient substitute for the top round steak.

CONTINUES ▶

Place a large wire rack in a rimmed baking sheet. Arrange the eggplant slices on the rack in a single layer and sprinkle them with 1 teaspoon of the salt to expel some of their liquid. Let them drain for about 30 minutes.

Meanwhile, soak the rice in warm water to cover for 30 minutes, drain it well, and set it aside.

Heat the 3 tablespoons of the oil in a large skillet over medium-high heat. Add the onion, chopped beef, cinnamon, allspice, ¾ teaspoon of the salt, and pepper. Cook, stirring occasionally, until the beef begins to brown, about 10 minutes. Add ½ cup of the stock, reduce the heat to low, and cook until the liquid reduces to a film, about 5 minutes.

Meanwhile, preheat the broiler. Pat the eggplant slices dry, brush them on both sides with the remaining oil, and broil them on the baking sheet in a single layer until they are nicely browned, about 5 minutes per side.

Preheat the oven to 350°F. Lightly grease the bottom of a round, tall-sided 8-cup oven-safe baking dish, such as a soufflé dish. Arrange the tomato slices in an overlapping layer over the bottom. Use half of the eggplant to make a layer of overlapping slices and top with all of the beef mixture. Make another layer with all of the remaining eggplant. Top with the reserved rice.

Combine the remaining 2 cups stock with the saffron and the remaining 1 teaspoon salt in a saucepan and bring it to a boil over high heat. Pour it over the rice immediately. It will trickle through the layers. Cover the baking dish tightly with a lid or aluminum foil and bake immediately until the liquid is nearly absorbed and the rice is tender, 65 to 75 minutes. If the rice in the very center is not quite tender, gently stir the rice layer and bake for 15 minutes more.

Let the timbale cool covered for 10 minutes. Invert a large plate over the dish and grip tightly with both hands to flip it over. Slowly lift off the baking dish. Scatter the pine nuts over the top, if using, and serve in generous scoops.

BAKED ARGENTINIAN EMPANADAS

There are many reasons to love this hand pie: within the cracker-crisp crust is a beguiling beef and potato filling spiced with *pimentón* and cumin. It's no wonder empanadas are a staple of Argentina (and many other Latin and South American countries, in infinite variations). I've kept this close to the classic with smoked paprika and chopped olives that bring excitement to lean beef and diced potato. I love the texture from the hand-chopped beef in these hand pies, which can be a great way to use up a small amount of leftover steak or roast beef. Make these ahead, freeze, and then bake, for either a grab-and-go soccer night supper or first-rate appetizers at your next party.

The Hot Water Pie Dough (recipe follows) is exceptionally user-friendly, but you can substitute frozen puff pastry for convenience, following the method described in the variation.

Makes 18 4 x 2-inch hand pies

....

1½ POUNDS PIE DOUGH, SUCH AS HOT WATER PIE DOUGH (RECIPE FOLLOWS)

1 SMALL RED POTATO (ABOUT 5 OUNCES), PEELED AND CUT INTO ½-INCH CUBES

1 TABLESPOON VEGETABLE OIL

1 MEDIUM ONION, FINELY CHOPPED

2 GARLIC CLOVES, MINCED

8 OUNCES TOP SIRLOIN STEAK, FINELY CHOPPED (CHOPPING AND MINCING, PAGE 47)

2 TEASPOONS SMOKED PAPRIKA, SUCH AS PIMENTÓN DE LA VERA (SOURCES, PAGE 272)

2 TEASPOONS GROUND CUMIN

½ TEASPOON SALT

⅛ TEASPOON RED PEPPER FLAKES

6 TABLESPOONS UNSALTED BUTTER, CUT INTO CUBES

½ CUP PITTED KALAMATA OLIVES, COARSELY CHOPPED

¼ CUP LIGHTLY PACKED CHOPPED FRESH PARSLEY

1 EGG, BEATEN

CONTINUES ▶

Make the pie dough (opposite page) and chill it for at least 30 minutes. Put the potato in a small saucepan and cover it with water. Bring it to a boil over high heat, then reduce the heat to low and simmer until it is fork tender, about 6 minutes. Drain well, cover, and set it aside.

Heat the oil in large skillet over medium-high heat. Add the onion and garlic and cook, stirring, until the onion turns translucent, about 3 minutes. Add the beef, paprika, cumin, salt, and pepper flakes and cook until the meat browns, about 8 minutes. Splash in ¼ cup of water and stir in the butter to make a light gravy. Stir in the olives, parsley, and the reserved potato and taste for salt. Transfer the beef mixture to a bowl and chill while you roll out the dough. (You can also store the beef mixture overnight in the refrigerator.)

Dust the counter lightly with flour and have 2 ungreased baking sheets on hand. Divide the dough into 2 pieces and keep 1 wrapped while you work with the other. Roll out the dough very thin—go for ⅛ inch thick. If the dough cracks, let it sit at room temperature for a few minutes to warm up. Use a cutter, plate, jar, or plastic lid about 4 inches in diameter to cut circles of dough and put them in a single layer on the baking sheets. Repeat with the second piece of dough. Collect the scraps of dough and re-roll to make about 18 circles.

Preheat the oven to 375°F. Put the egg in a small bowl and use a pastry brush to moisten the edges of each circle. Put 1 generous tablespoon of the meat filling in the center of each round, fold the dough over to make a semicircle, and press with your fingers to seal them well. Crimp the edges with your fingers to make a scalloped edge or press with the tines of a fork. Brush them with the egg wash. Space the finished empanadas on one of the ungreased baking sheets and bake until they are golden brown, 16 to 18 minutes. (If freezing the empanadas, do not brush the outside with the egg wash. Crowd them onto a baking sheet, freeze them until firm, and repackage them into resealable freezer bags. Bake them directly from the freezer on ungreased baking sheets—brushing them with egg wash for a more golden crust, if you like—for 22 to 25 minutes.)

VARIATION: Thaw 1 pound frozen puff pastry at room temperature for 40 minutes. Roll out each puff pastry sheet into a 13-inch square ⅛ inch thick. Cut, fill, seal, and brush with egg wash as directed. Bake in a preheated 400°F oven until golden brown, 16 to 18 minutes.

MORE CHOICE CUTS:

Bottom round steak, or cube steak, which gives you a head start on hand chopping, both bring great flavor to these and other hand pies. Ground beef is the typical cut found in pastry filling; be sure to use extra-lean.

HOT WATER PIE DOUGH

What a surprise to stir hot water into flour and make a dough that's as easy as the homemade play dough I make for my kids. You'll need to muscle this dough around when rolling, but miraculously, it never gets tough. It bakes into a crust that's sturdy enough to hold in your hand yet delightfully light and tender. Use this dough to make authentic Baked Argentinian Empanadas (page 159) or any other hand pie, also known as pasties or turnovers, with a filling of leftover pot roast or stew.

Makes 1½ pounds dough, enough for 18 medium-sized empanadas or hand pies

....

½ CUP WATER

¼ CUP MILK

¾ TEASPOON SALT

6 OUNCES (12 TABLESPOONS) LARD OR VEGETABLE
    SHORTENING

3 CUPS (13½ OUNCES) ALL-PURPOSE FLOUR

Put the water, milk, and salt in a saucepan, stir to dissolve the salt, and bring it to a boil over medium-high heat. Add the lard and whisk until it melts and becomes frothy. Remove it from the heat and let it cool slightly. Put the flour into a large mixing bowl or the bowl of a stand mixer.

To mix the dough by hand, pour in the warm liquid and use a rubber spatula to mix vigorously to make a rough dough. Turn the dough onto a lightly floured countertop and knead it about 12 times until the dough is supple and fairly smooth. It will have a crinkly surface.

To mix the dough in a stand mixer, put the flour into the mixing bowl and attach the paddle. Pour in the warm liquid and stir on low speed until it collects into a dough. Mix for 1 minute more to knead it. Turn the dough onto a lightly floured countertop. It will be fairly smooth and soft.

Shape the dough into a disk, wrap it in plastic, and chill it for at least 30 minutes before rolling.

CHAPTER 7

STEAKS DONE RIGHT

J ust cut it all up into rib steaks and T-bones," a customer once told my butcher, Kevin Silveira, voicing a common belief that a cow is a series of steaks from head to haunch. If that were the case, I'd likely never have come back to beef, since it was steak that had turned me into a vegetarian as a teenager. Toward the end of my first summer as a cow-pooling customer, T-bones were some of the few cuts left in my deep freezer. Since I had a deck with a new grill, I lifted out the frosty package. Two ruby-colored steaks coupled in the package fit in my outstretched palm. I'd give it a shot and make a steak dinner for two.

One moonless night seven years later, when we had become a family of four, I was grilling two more T-bones. It was a January night, the temperature was in the teens, and I'd forgotten my flashlight indoors, but when I poked the steaks' centers with my finger I could tell just by touch that they were ready. As I rushed inside, it dawned on me how fond I'd grown of steak and how comfortable I was cooking it—under any conditions, apparently. Steak anchored a meal that everyone at our table gladly devoured, and it was a welcome accompaniment to anything else I served—from tossed salad and corn on the cob to roasted potatoes and steamed broccoli. On the busiest nights, steak was a quick, no-mess meal I could conjure from scratch in ten minutes or less.

This chapter revels in steak. By definition, this is any thin, flat-sided cut of meat. Some of the steaks you'll find in this chapter are the steakhouse specimens, those prized cross-sections from the tender middle that go by the names of rib-eye, strip loin, Porterhouse, tenderloin, or dozens of other aliases (beauty steak is my favorite). Along with these classic cuts, there are new steaks to try out, known in the restaurant world as flatiron (top blade steak) and culotte (top sirloin cap), which are as tasty as the spendiest steaks. Another group classified as bistro steaks, including flank, skirt, and bavette, or sirloin flap, is collected here. Coarser and chewier, they are naturally thin muscles with great character and an open grain for drinking up marinades.

Grilling is a steak's best friend, and there are plenty of recipes to keep your interest, if you're already comfortable with flame and char (within reason). If you're a novice like I was, or have doubts about grilling grassfed steaks, read through Grassfed Top Blade Steak with Arugula Salad and Scorched Croutons (page 168). This learning recipe will guide you through grilling steaks to whatever doneness you desire, a method you'll use to make Coriander-Rubbed Sirloin with Pita Bread Salad (page 172) and Tequila-Lime Skirt Steak Fajitas with Roasted Corn Salsa (page 174), just two of the grilled steak recipes in this chapter.

Other recipes bring steak indoors, where a sear in a hot skillet gives them the crust that elevates beef from good to great. From Bistro Steak with Herb Aïoli and Oven Steak Fries (page 186) to Martini Steak Sandwich with Green Olive Tapenade (page 192), you'll experience variations on searing methods—the ones restaurants use—

and learn to trust yourself to turn those burners up high. The bonus of these skillet techniques is that you'll have a foundation to make pan sauces for superlative meals, such as Filet Mignon in Brandy Sauce with Mixed Mushroom Sauté (page 189). Other recipes demonstrate how steak can become a comfort-food skillet supper, like Steaks Smothered in Bacon-Stout Sauce (page 184), Chicken Fried Steak with Buttermilk Gravy (page 182), and Skillet Steak Peperonata (page 196).

You'll notice that there are no fourteen-ounce single-serving Porterhouse steaks on this menu. These recipes bring beef portions down to scale and demonstrate two ways to serve less steak— by portioning steaks *before* cooking or slicing them afterwards. Recipes like T-bone Steak with Fennel-Radicchio Relish and Olive Oil Flatbreads (page 176) feed six with less than two pounds of steak. The one pound of beef called for in Steak Stroganoff (page 191) is enough for four.

The seasonal side dishes accompanying the recipes slant away from the steak and potatoes of yesterday to the farmer's market produce of today. From grilled romaine for a rib steak (page 170) to Chard-Gorgonzola Gratin for strip loin steak (page 195) and herb sauces (page 166) for any of them, this is steak for everyone to get excited about.

Choice Cuts for Steak

Due to their prevalence and popularity, steaks have the most nicknames of all the beef cuts. Along with the classic steaks from the rib and loin, there are also newer choices from the chuck, or shoulder, and the flank, or underbelly. Bone-in or boneless, these are marbled, lean cuts. However, grassfed steaks tend to be less marbled, leaner, and smaller than conventional beef cuts. As a rule, you'll encounter more of these steaks in the supermarket, especially the less common ones, during the summer grilling months when demand is high.

BAVETTE, see Sirloin flap steak.

CHUCK-EYE STEAK is a boneless and tender cut from the first cut off the chuck, or shoulder. The main muscle running through the center is a continuation of the rib-eye muscle. It is a well-marbled bargain steak for the grill or skillet.

COULOTTE, see Top sirloin steak.

FLANK STEAK is a thin abdominal muscle from the bottom sirloin with thick meat fibers running in the same direction. Boneless, lean, and full-flavored, it was the original London Broil— cooked quickly with high heat and thinly sliced against the grain. The flank makes a good candidate for stuffing (page 180) and lends itself well to braising (chapter 5, page 100).

FLATIRON, see Top blade steak.

HANGER STEAK, aka hanging tender or onglet, is a boneless cut from the diaphragm. There is only one on every beef. Hanger steak has a stronger taste (some describe as gamey) and a firm texture that lends itself well to marinating. Considered one of the bistro steaks (it is a popular cut in France), it has a band of connective tissue running down the center that can be removed before or after cooking to yield two slender steaks.

PORTERHOUSE is the same cut as a T-bone, a crosscut from the loin section, but contains a larger portion of tenderloin than T-bone and is generally a very thick cut.

RIB STEAK is a bone-in cut from the tender rib section. The muscle tapers toward the chuck, so a larger rib-eye muscle indicates that it was cut toward the loin primal. This is the most marbled of all the premium steaks and many consider its flavor superior to all other steaks. A bone-in rib steak can be called a cowboy steak; boneless it is a rib-eye or Delmonico steak.

SHOULDER TENDER, aka teres major, is a small, boneless, and tender cut from the chuck, or shoulder. Slender and tapered like the tenderloin, it can be roasted whole or cut into medallions for any high-heat cooking method. (Not to be confused with the chuck tender, aka mock tender, which is very tough.)

SIRLOIN FLAP STEAK, aka bavette, is a boneless cut from the bottom sirloin adjacent to the flank with a long even grain, similar to flank steak, but slightly thicker. It is categorized as a bistro steak, one of the less expensive and chewier steaks gaining popularity.

SIRLOIN TIP STEAK, aka round tip steak, is a relatively tender, boneless cut that comes the the knuckle muscle located between the sirloin, or hip, and the round, or hindquarter. It is a suitable substitute for top sirloin steak, especially if you find center cut or side tip steaks, or top round steak.

SKIRT STEAK is a long strip of boneless muscle from the diaphragm that gained popularity as the fajita steak. It has an open, fibrous texture, and a papery membrane that needs to be peeled off before cooking (Trimming, page 51). Similar to the flank steak in texture, skirt steak is typically grilled, but it has a wonderful fall-apart quality when braised. The outside skirt steak is less common than inside skirt, but can be treated in exactly the same manner.

STRIP LOIN STEAK, aka top loin steak, is a bone-in steak cut from the loin once the whole tenderloin muscle has been removed. The premier steakhouse cut, it is known as shell steak, New York Strip, and Kansas City strip. When the whole strip loin muscle is removed from the backbone, it can be cut into boneless steaks.

T-BONE STEAK is a bone-in cross cut from the loin, the premium middle section of beef. The tenderloin muscle sits on one side of the bone and the strip loin muscle on the other. T-bone steaks typically contain a smaller tenderloin eye than Porterhouse steaks, but otherwise differ in name only.

TENDERLOIN STEAK, aka filet mignon, is a cross cut of the long, boneless tenderloin muscle that yields small, rounded steaks also called medallions or tournedos.

TERES MAJOR, see Shoulder tender.

TOP BLADE STEAK, aka flatiron, is one of the newer steaks from the chuck, or shoulder, found to be only second to the tenderloin in tenderness. Depending on how it was butchered, blade steaks may have a line of gristle running through the center, which you can either cut out to make two long, skinny steaks before cooking, or remove it afterwards. It's becoming more common to find top blade roast, a thin, flat steak with the gristle already removed. If you buy a whole top blade roast, you can butterfly it (page 46), trimming off the gristle to make two flatiron steaks.

TOP ROUND STEAK is a lean, boneless steak from the inside of the round. Less popular than any of the other steaks listed here, it is a good value with great flavor and is most tender when cooked to medium rare.

TOP SIRLOIN STEAK is any boneless, lean steak cut from the sirloin, the large, well-muscled hip area. More economical than strip loin steak or rib steak, sirloin steak is renowned for its excellent flavors. It's a hearty and versatile cut that takes well to rubs and marinades. The top sirloin cap, aka culotte, is a flap of muscle covering the sirloin that is sometimes separated and cut into steaks.

TRI-TIP STEAK is a boneless steak cut from the triangular trip-tip roast that comes from the bottom sirloin. It is a griller's favorite for robust rubs or marinades.

HERB SAUCE FOR STEAK

Chimichurri (page 142) is a popular herb sauce for steak, but it's not the only one to enjoy. Improvise with all kinds of tender, leafy herbs, such as cilantro, mint, basil, Italian parsley, and oregano to make up your own fresh salsa verde for steak. Use what's in season, what you have, and whatever suits your mood. I like the texture best when I hand chop the herbs. Cut a clove of garlic into thin slices, sprinkle with a pinch of coarse salt, and using the side of a chef's knife blade, smear it into a paste. Coarsely chop a generous handful of herbs and stir them into the garlic in a bowl, then drizzle in enough olive oil to make it saucy. Add a splash of sherry vinegar, lemon juice, or capers for punch, add red pepper flakes to taste, and season it well with salt. Let it stand at room temperature for at least 30 minutes to bloom. With a well-grilled steak and fresh herbs, you cannot go wrong.

FLAVORED BUTTER COINS

Butterfat is a wonderful medium to deliver complementary flavors to a steak. Mix any of these flavored butters, roll into a log, chill, and slice ½ inch thick. As soon as a steak comes off the grill or out of the skillet or oven, top it with a coin of butter, which will melt and mingle with the meat juices to create its own sauce. Swirl the butter disks into reduced wine, beer, spirits, or beef stock to enrich a pan sauce such as Filet Mignon in Brandy Sauce (page 189). You can also press a coin into the center of a hamburger when forming patties, whisk a few coins into a stew to give it body and gloss, or butter a baguette for a roast beef sandwich.

All of the flavored butter variations below call for ¼ pound (½ cup or 1 stick) of unsalted butter at room temperature. Mix the butter with the other ingredients listed for each butter flavor in a small bowl, smashing the mixture with a fork until smooth and blended, and add a generous pinch of salt to taste. Transfer to a ramekin to chill or use plastic wrap to roll it into a log and chill it well for slicing round "coins."

Garlic-Balsamic Butter: Mince 2 garlic cloves and combine with 2 teaspoons of good-quality balsamic vinegar.

Caramelized Shallot Butter: Finely chop 2 shallots and cook in 1 teaspoon of vegetable oil over medium heat, stirring often, until they brown, about 10 minutes. Cool to room temperature.

Green Butter: Blanch ⅓ cup very finely chopped tender herbs or greens, such as basil, tarragon, or chives in boiling salted water for 30 seconds, which will keep them bright green. Drain well and cool to room temperature.

GRILLED TOP BLADE STEAK WITH ARUGULA SALAD AND SCORCHED CROUTONS

When I crave a steak and a salad, this is what I envision: a small but exquisite piece of grilled beef with a heap of peppery greens and grilled croutons—all drizzled with dressing and meat juices.

Also known as flatiron, top blade steak is a new favorite on restaurant menus because this steak is the second most tender cut of all. It's a thin cut, about one inch thick, and has no bones to get in the way of a great steak experience. I treat it to nothing more than coarse sea salt to form a crispy crust over the high heat of the grill or a grill pan. Prewashed baby salad mix, as long as it's very fresh, makes a fine substitute for the custom blend of arugula and herbs.

Makes 4 servings

....

2 TOP-BLADE STEAKS (ABOUT 1½ POUNDS), 1 TO 1¼ INCHES THICK

KOSHER SALT

2 THICK SLICES ARTISAN BREAD, CRUSTS REMOVED AND TORN INTO
    RAGGED 1½-INCH PIECES

2 TABLESPOONS EXTRA-VIRGIN OLIVE OIL, DIVIDED

1 TEASPOON SHERRY OR RED WINE VINEGAR

5 OUNCES BABY ARUGULA (ABOUT 6 CUPS)

1 CUP LIGHTLY PACKED FRESH HERB LEAVES, SUCH AS BASIL, PARSLEY,
    DILL, CHIVES, CHERVIL, TARRAGON, MINT, OR A COMBINATION

FINISHING SALT, SUCH AS COARSE SEA SALT OR FLAKE SALT (SOURCES,
    PAGE 272)

FRESHLY GROUND BLACK PEPPER

Pat the steaks dry with a paper towel and season liberally with the kosher salt. Toss the bread with 1 tablespoon of the olive oil and set it aside.

Preheat a charcoal or gas grill for high heat (425° to 475°F), scrape the grate clean, and oil it lightly. Cook the steaks on the hottest part of the grill until seared, 3 to 3½ minutes. Use tongs to flip them and sear the second side for another 3 to 3½ minutes for medium rare. (To cook the steaks medium or beyond, slide them over to the coolest part of the grill and close the cover, then cook for 1 to 4 minutes more.)

Grill the reserved bread croutons while the steaks rest, turning them 2 to 3 times, until they are tinged with brown.

For indoor cooking, heat a grill pan over medium-high heat and preheat the broiler. Lay the steaks in the pan and cook without moving them for 3½ to 4 minutes. Use tongs to flip them and sear the second side for an additional 3½ to 4 minutes for medium rare. (To cook the steaks further, slide the pan off the burner but leave the steaks in the pan for 1 to 3 minutes more.) Meanwhile, toast the croutons under the broiler, keeping a sharp eye on them and turning them once, until golden brown.

Transfer the steaks to a cutting board. While they rest, make the salad dressing by whisking the vinegar with the remaining 1 tablespoon olive oil in a small bowl. Put the arugula and herbs in a salad bowl and toss with the dressing. Slice the steak against the grain into ½-inch-thick slices and put 4 to 5 slices on each plate. Pile a portion of the salad on top of each serving and balance a few croutons on top. Drizzle any meat juices from the cutting board over it all and sprinkle to taste with the finishing salt and black pepper.

MORE CHOICE CUTS:

Rib-eye and any of the other exceptional grilling steaks, including strip loin and top sirloin, will do quite well here.

Chuck-eye steak is fattier but tender enough to grill.

RIB-EYE STEAKS AND GRILLED ROMAINE

with Hot Tomato Vinaigrette

The rib-eye is the king of steaks, the most desired for its balance of tenderness, taste, and marbling. To honor it, I keep the seasonings simple with a hit of paprika, and serve it sliced over a wedge of grilled romaine with a bright-tasting tomato vinaigrette. While many enjoy eating a steak off the bone, the boneless rib steak, called rib-eye, is the same cut of meat more readily sliced for serving.

Makes 4 servings

....

1¼ TEASPOONS KOSHER SALT

¾ TEASPOON SMOKED PAPRIKA, SUCH AS PIMENTÓN DE LA VERA (SOURCES, PAGE 272)

¼ TEASPOON BLACK PEPPER

2 RIB-EYE STEAKS (ABOUT 1½ POUNDS), 1 TO 1¼ INCHES THICK

1 HEAD ROMAINE LETTUCE

½ CUP EXTRA-VIRGIN OLIVE OIL

1 SMALL GARLIC CLOVE, MINCED

1 LARGE RIPE TOMATO, CHOPPED

2 TABLESPOONS FRESHLY SQUEEZED LEMON JUICE

⅛ TEASPOON SALT

MORE CHOICE CUTS:

Strip loin steak is another premium steak that's available bone-in or boneless.

Top sirloin, bavette, or hanger are chewier but great-tasting alternative boneless cuts.

Mix the kosher salt, paprika, and pepper together in a small bowl. Pat the steaks dry and season them on both sides with the salt blend.

Slice the romaine in half lengthwise, wash it by swishing each half in a large bowl of cool water to rinse out the dirt between the leaves. Place the halves cut side down in a large colander to drain.

Combine the olive oil with the garlic and tomato in a small saucepan and cook over low heat until the oil shimmers and the garlic smells fragrant. Remove the pan from the heat to a warm spot while you prepare a charcoal or gas grill for high heat (425° to 475°F). Scrape the grate clean and oil it lightly.

Use a pastry brush to lightly coat the romaine halves with some of the tomato oil and place them cut side down on the outer edges of the grill. Grill the romaine until the cut sides are burnished with grill marks and the outer leaves are wilted. Cut out the core, slice each half into quarters, and set it aside.

Grill the steaks over the hottest part of the grill for 3 to 3½ minutes, then use tongs to flip them and grill for 3 to 3½ minutes on the second side for medium rare. (To cook the steaks medium or beyond, slide them over to the coolest part of the grill and close the cover, then cook for 1 to 4 minutes more.)

Transfer the steaks to a cutting board. While they rest, make the tomato vinaigrette by whisking the lemon juice and salt into the reserved tomato oil. Slice the steaks against the grain ½ inch thick. Place a wedge of romaine and 4 to 5 slices of steak on each plate and spoon the tomato vinaigrette over all.

HAWAIIAN-STYLE TERIYAKI

Sink your teeth into this teriyaki using shoulder tender, aka teres major, a chuck cut nearly as tender as tenderloin at a fraction of the cost. Cut into nuggets, the beef gets three applications of the sweet and salty sauce: first as a marinade, then brushed on after grilling, and finally as a thickened dipping sauce at the table for those who can't get enough of it.

To serve this Hawaiian style, mound bowls with steamed rice, add handfuls of finely shredded green cabbage and a few chopped scallions, and top with the teriyaki-bathed beef. If you're feeding big eaters, double the quantity of beef for the same amount of marinade.

Makes 4 servings

....

½ CUP LOW-SALT SOY SAUCE

5 TABLESPOONS SUGAR

1-INCH PIECE GINGER, PEELED AND VERY FINELY
    CHOPPED (1 TABLESPOON)

1 GARLIC CLOVE, MINCED

1 POUND SHOULDER TENDER, CUT INTO 8 PIECES

2 TABLESPOONS CORNSTARCH

Put the soy sauce and ½ cup water in a measuring cup and stir in the sugar until it dissolves. Add the ginger and garlic. Put the meat in a medium bowl, pour the sauce over it, and marinate for at least 30 minutes and up to 2 hours while you preheat a charcoal or gas grill to medium-high heat (375° to 425°F). Scrape the grate clean and oil it lightly.

Use tongs to hold back the meat in the bowl as you pour the marinade into a small saucepan. Bring the marinade to a simmer over low heat. Whisk the cornstarch with 1 tablespoon of water and whisk into the marinade. Boil until thickened, about 1 minute. Remove from the heat and set it aside.

Grill the beef over the hottest part of the grill for 2 to 2½ minutes then use tongs to flip it and cook on the second side for 2 to 2½ minutes more for medium rare. Since the sizes and shapes vary, you may need to cook thicker pieces 1 to 3 minutes longer. Drizzle the beef with the reserved teriyaki sauce and serve the extra in a small bowl.

MORE CHOICE CUTS:
Tri-tip and hanger steak, with a coarser texture and more chew, will also please teriyaki steak fans as will easy-to-find sirloin.

Tenderloin tails (the tips of whole tenderloin roasts) make to-die-for teriyaki. Save them if you trim your own tenderloin or find an accommodating butcher to sell them to you for a relative bargain.

CORIANDER-RUBBED SIRLOIN

with Pita Bread Salad (*Fattoush*)

Treated to a Middle Eastern-inspired dry rub, a sirloin steak is ready for the grill. Sirloin steaks, generally sold boneless, are renowned for delivering on flavor, but they can vary in tenderness. Look for or request a center-cut sirloin or top sirloin cap (sometimes sold as culotte), which are single muscle cuts and the most tender and marbled. The accompanying salad is a pita bread salad called *fattoush* (recipe follows), a mix of summertime vegetables, parsley, and mint tossed with toasted pita bread, and an exotic spice called sumac.

Toast the coriander seeds by heating them in a dry small skillet over medium heat. Stand by while it becomes fragrant and darkens in color, about 1 minute. Quickly remove them from the heat and grind to a powder in a spice grinder or with a mortar and pestle. Combine the toasted coriander, caraway, paprika, and kosher salt and mix well. Pat the steaks dry, rub them on both sides with the coriander mixture, and let them sit at room temperature for 30 minutes.

Prepare a charcoal or gas grill for high heat (425° to 475°F), scrape the grate clean, and oil it lightly. Cook the steaks on the hottest part of the grill until seared, 3 to 3½ minutes. Use tongs to flip them and grill the second side for another 3 to 3½ minutes for medium rare. (To cook the steaks medium or beyond, slide them over to the coolest part of the grill and close the cover, then cook for 1 to 4 minutes more.) Let the steaks rest 10 minutes before slicing ½ inch thick against the grain to serve alongside the Pit Bread Salad, if desired.

Makes 4 servings

....

1 TABLESPOON WHOLE CORIANDER SEEDS

1 TEASPOON GROUND CARAWAY

½ TEASPOON SWEET PAPRIKA

1½ TEASPOONS KOSHER SALT

2 TOP SIRLOIN STEAKS (ABOUT 1½ POUNDS), 1 TO 1¼ INCHES THICK

MORE CHOICE CUTS:

Top round steak, rubbed and grilled to medium rare, may surprise those who don't think of it as a grilling steak.

T-bone steak and bone-in strip loin steak are both excellent options for simple seasoning and quick grilling.

PITA BREAD SALAD (*FATTOUSH*)

Makes 4 servings

....

2 (6-INCH) ROUNDS PITA BREAD

2 MEDIUM CUCUMBERS, PEELED

3 MEDIUM RIPE TOMATOES, CHOPPED

¼ TEASPOON SALT

3 TABLESPOONS EXTRA-VIRGIN OLIVE OIL

1 TABLESPOON RED WINE VINEGAR

¼ CUP CHOPPED FRESH MINT

¼ CUP LIGHTLY PACKED CHOPPED FRESH PARSLEY

4 OUNCES FETA CHEESE, CRUMBLED (ABOUT 1 CUP)

3 TABLESPOONS TOASTED SESAME SEEDS (PAGE 144)

1½ TEASPOONS CRUSHED SUMAC, OPTIONAL (SOURCES, PAGE 272)

MIXED SALAD GREENS, FOR SERVING, OPTIONAL

Preheat the oven to 350°F. Cut the pita bread into 1-inch squares, arrange them in a single layer on a baking sheet, and toast them in the oven until crisp, about 12 minutes. Slice the cucumbers in half lengthwise, use a teaspoon to scrape out the seeds, and slice them into ½-inch-thick crescents.

Toss the cucumbers, tomatoes, and salt with the oil and vinegar in a large salad bowl. Add the mint, parsley, feta, sesame seeds, and sumac, if using, toss again and taste for seasoning. Toss the salad with the pita bread immediately to soften it or 20 minutes before serving if you like it crisper. Serve the bread salad on a bed of mixed salad greens, if desired.

TEQUILA-LIME SKIRT STEAK FAJITAS

with Roasted Corn Salsa

Skirt steak is the original fajita steak. Nearly a yard long and narrow, like a belt, the fibers of the meat are so coarse, the steak looks woven. This quality lets the marinade do its work, and at less than a half inch thick, skirt steak cooks in a flash. A single steak can feed a crop of friends when wrapped in soft corn tortillas, topped with onion, cabbage, and cilantro to taste, and Roasted Corn Salsa (recipe follows), served alongside bowls full of chopped fresh radishes, cucumbers, and pickled jalapeños.

Makes 6 servings

....

1 SKIRT STEAK (ABOUT 1½ POUNDS)

4 GARLIC CLOVES, PEELED

¾ TEASPOON KOSHER SALT

¼ CUP TEQUILA

2 TABLESPOONS FRESHLY SQUEEZED LIME JUICE

FOR SERVING:

1 DOZEN FRESH CORN OR FLOUR TORTILLAS

1 SMALL WHITE ONION, FINELY CHOPPED

1 CUP SHREDDED GREEN CABBAGE

1 BUNCH FRESH CILANTRO, COARSELY CHOPPED

Use a thin-bladed knife, such as a boning knife, to remove any thin, papery membrane from the steak (Trimming, page 51) and cut it in half. Make a garlic paste by slicing the garlic and sprinkling on the kosher salt. Use the side of a chef's knife to smash the garlic into a coarse paste. Rub the meat with the garlic paste and lay it in a shallow glass or ceramic dish. Pour in the tequila and lime juice, cover, and marinate it in the refrigerator for at least 3 hours and up to 12 for the most prominent flavor and any tenderizing effects.

Drain the steak from the marinade, pat it dry with paper towels, and discard the excess marinade. Prepare a charcoal or gas grill for high heat (425° to 475°F), scrape the grate clean, and oil it lightly.

When the grill is hot, lay the steaks on the grate and cook for 2½ to 3 minutes. Use tongs to flip them and cook for an additional 2½ to 3 minutes. Because it is thin, it will cook to medium. Slice the steaks against the grain into very thin strips. Pile the meat onto a platter to serve warm or at room temperature along with the tortillas and bowls of the onion, cabbage, cilantro, and the Roasted Corn Salsa, if desired.

MORE CHOICE CUTS:
Flank steak has a thick grain similar to skirt steak, and is just as amenable to marinating.
   Sirloin flap steak, aka bavette, is another good griller to be served thinly sliced.

ROASTED CORN SALSA

This chunky salsa makes use of the Mexican technique of dry roasting on the stovetop to cook the corn. The brief scorching adds a nice smoky flavor to this quick-cook salsa, ideal for late summer when both corn and tomatoes are at their peak.

Makes 2 cups

....

2 EARS FRESH CORN, SHUCKED AND SILKED OR
    1½ CUPS FROZEN CORN

2 GARLIC CLOVES, UNPEELED

1 SMALL JALAPEÑO

2 MEDIUM, RIPE TOMATOES, CHOPPED

6 SCALLIONS, WHITE AND GREEN PARTS TRIMMED
    AND THINLY SLICED

1 TABLESPOON LIGHTLY PACKED CHOPPED FRESH
    CILANTRO

2 TEASPOONS LIME JUICE

½ TEASPOON SALT

Hold the corn upright in a large mixing bowl and use a chef's knife to slice off the kernels. (If using frozen corn, cook it directly from the freezer.)

Heat a large, dry cast-iron skillet over medium-high heat. Add the garlic cloves and jalapeño and let them cook undisturbed until tinged with black, turning them 2 to 3 times. Transfer the garlic and jalapeño to a cutting board, and add the corn to the pan. Cook, stirring frequently, until the kernels are speckled brown and fragrant.

Transfer the corn to a medium mixing bowl. Peel the garlic and chop it finely. Seed the jalapeño if you prefer milder heat and chop it finely. Gently toss them with the corn. Add the tomatoes, scallions, cilantro, lime juice, and salt and toss well. Taste the salsa for lime juice and salt and serve it at room temperature with the fajitas.

T-BONE STEAK

with Fennel-Radicchio Relish and Olive Oil Flatbreads

A big grilled steak adorned with a crunchy and shredded vegetable salad is one of my ultimate no-fuss summer meals. Toss sweet fennel and bitter radicchio with a lemony anchovy dressing while the steaks rest. Fold slices of steak and the relish into grilled flatbread, and you create *piadina*, an Italian-inspired grilled flatbread sandwich. Prepare the Olive Oil Flatbreads in advance (recipe follows) or use store bought.

Makes 6 servings

....

1 SMALL RED ONION, VERY THINLY SLICED

⅛ TEASPOON ANCHOVY PASTE

1 TABLESPOON LEMON ZEST

2 TABLESPOONS FRESHLY SQUEEZED LEMON JUICE

½ TEASPOON SALT

¼ CUP WALNUT OIL

2 TABLESPOONS EXTRA-VIRGIN OLIVE OIL

1 FENNEL BULB

1 HEAD RADICCHIO OR SMALL ROMAINE, FINELY
   SLICED INTO RIBBONS

2 T-BONE STEAKS (ABOUT 2 POUNDS), 1 TO 1¼
   INCHES THICK

KOSHER SALT

½ CUP TOASTED WALNUT PIECES

2 OUNCES RICOTTA SALATA OR FETA CHEESE,
   CRUMBLED (ABOUT ½ CUP)

6 FLATBREADS, EITHER OLIVE OIL FLATBREADS
   (RECIPE FOLLOWS) OR STORE BOUGHT,
   OPTIONAL

Put the onion in a small bowl, cover with cool water, and let it soak for 5 minutes to mellow its bite. Drain it well, put it into a large mixing bowl, and set it aside.

Make the dressing by whisking the anchovy paste, lemon zest, lemon juice, and salt with the walnut oil and olive oil. Set it aside to let the flavors develop.

Trim the fronds from the fennel stems. Chop ½ cup of the fronds for the salad and save the rest for another use or discard them. Trim the stems from the fennel bulb, cut it in half, core it, and slice it as thin as you can using a sharp chef's knife or a mandoline. Toss the chopped fennel fronds and fennel bulb into the bowl with the onion. Add the radicchio or romaine and toss well. Keep the salad chilled while you grill the steaks.

Pat the steaks dry, season them liberally with the kosher salt, and let them sit at room temperature while you prepare a charcoal or gas grill for high heat (425° to 475°F), scrape the grate clean, and oil it lightly. Grill the steaks for 3½ to 4 minutes per side for medium rare. (To cook the steaks further, slide them to the coolest part of the grill and close the cover, then cook them for 1 to 4 minutes more.) Let the steaks rest 10 minutes while you finish the relish and grill the flatbreads as directed on page 178, if using.

Toss the fennel mixture with just enough of the reserved dressing to coat it lightly. Add the walnuts and cheese and toss again. Taste it for salt and lemon juice. To serve the steaks, slice them perpendicular to the bone ¼ inch thick. Alternatively, cut out the bone (Boning, page 46), toss it to your dog, and slice each meat section separately, trimming excess fat, if you like. Put 3 to 4 slices of steak on each plate along with the relish and any reserved dressing to drizzle directly onto the steaks. Serve with the flatbreads, if desired, to make *piadina*.

MORE CHOICE CUTS:

Rib steak is another premium grilling steak, called **rib-eye** when boneless.

Strip loin steak, from the same tender midsection as the T-bone (or Porterhouse), is a narrower steak with meat on only one side of the bone.

This quick, tender, easy-to-handle dough is the one I use to make flatbreads for grilled Italian steak sandwiches called *piadina* and snappy breadsticks for soup (Variation, page 178). It spins together in short order in a food processor and can also be mixed and kneaded in a stand mixer. It is a very sticky dough that bakes into crispy breads. After it rises for forty-five minutes, you can shape it into the form you like and bake it—or try your hand at grilling flatbreads to make *piadina*, a great party trick.

Makes 8 round 7-inch-wide flatbreads

....

3½ CUPS (15¾ OUNCES) ALL-PURPOSE FLOUR

2¼ TEASPOONS INSTANT OR ACTIVE DRY YEAST

1¾ TEASPOONS SALT

1¼ CUPS WARM WATER (75° TO 80°F)

6 TABLESPOONS EXTRA-VIRGIN OLIVE OIL, PLUS
　　ADDITIONAL IF BAKING

To make the dough in a food processor, put the flour, yeast, and salt in the processor bowl fitted with the plastic dough blade. Attach the cover and turn it on for 5 seconds. Put the water and oil in a measuring cup and pour it through the feed tube with the machine running. A ball of dough will form and slap around the bowl. Let the dough spin around 10 times to knead it before stopping the machine. The dough will feel warm, soft, and tacky. Collect any bits of dough from around the bowl and attach them to the ball. Replace the cover on the food processor bowl, slip in the feed tube pusher and let the dough rise for 45 minutes to 1 hour. It will look pillowy, nearly doubling in volume.

To make the dough in a stand mixer, combine

CONTINUES ▶

the flour, yeast, and salt in the mixing bowl and stir to blend with a rubber spatula. Add the water and olive oil and stir to make a rough dough. Attach the dough hook and knead the dough on medium speed until it is so elastic that strands of dough pull away from the sides of the bowl, 7 to 8 minutes. Scrape down the dough, cover the bowl, and let the dough rise at room temperature for 45 minutes to 1 hour. It will look pillowy, nearly doubling in volume.

To shape the flatbreads, turn the dough out onto a lightly floured countertop. Use a bench knife or chef's knife to cut it into 8 pieces and flour your hands. Working with each piece of dough, use a rolling pin or your hands to pat and stretch it into rounds roughly 7 inches wide and ⅛ inch thick. The rustic shape is part of its charm, so don't worry about making them perfect. Dust them with flour and stack them between with layers of parchment or waxed paper. Let them rest and rise slightly while the oven or grill preheats.

To bake the flatbreads, preheat the oven to 450°F. Lightly oil two baking sheets and put 2 of the flatbreads onto each one, spaced 2 inches apart. Bake until they bubble, crisp, and brown in spots, 7 to 8 minutes. Repeat with the remaining flatbreads and serve them warm.

To grill the flatbreads, thoroughly scrape and oil the grate of a preheated hot grill to keep the breads from sticking. Lay the flatbreads two at a time onto the hottest part of the grill and cook until they get grill marks on the bottom, then use tongs to flip them and grill until they are puffed and lightly charred, 2 to 2½ minutes per side. Repeat with the remaining flatbreads and serve warm.

VARIATION: OLIVE OIL BREADSTICKS

Mix, knead, and let the dough rise as directed. Lightly flour the countertop. Scrape the dough from the bowl onto the flour. Use your hands to press it into a rectangle, 12 inches by 6 inches, with the long side facing you.

Preheat the oven to 425°F. Pour 1 tablespoon of extra-virgin olive oil onto each of 2 baking sheets and use your hands to spread it around. Spread the oil left on your hands all over the dough. After wiping your hands dry, sprinkle the dough with coarse salt. (If you'd like to add sesame seeds, poppy seeds, or red pepper flakes, sprinkle them on now and lightly press them into the dough. Some of them will fall off during shaping, but that's okay.)

Use a pizza cutter or chef's knife to slice the dough along the long edge ½-inch wide to make 24 strips. Cut the strips in half to make 48 pieces. Stretch the dough by grasping each strip by the ends and lifting it up as if you're holding a piece of string. Gently bounce the strip of dough until it stretches to the length of your sheet pan. If you like, twist the breadsticks as you lengthen them for show. The breadsticks will be as thin as drinking straws. Place the first 24 breadsticks ¼ inch apart on one of the oiled baking sheets.

Bake until they are toasted brown and crisp, 12 to 13 minutes. Repeat with the second baking sheet. Store them for 1 day at room temperature or in the freezer for up to 1 month.

OLIVE OIL-POACHED STEAKS WITH THYME

Unusual as it may seem, poaching beef in olive oil might be the ideal grassfed cooking method. Heated in a low oven, the olive oil cooks the steaks tenderly, preserves all their moisture, and keeps them warm for ages. (It turns out that submerging cooked steaks in butter or oil is a technique used in fine dining, and we all know how juicy those steaks are.) An instant-read thermometer is an important tool for gauging doneness in this recipe, but if you catch the steaks just before they lose their rosy blush, they'll be medium rare.

I've adapted this recipe from *The Herbal Kitchen* by Jerry Traunfeld, the chef who taught me all I know about cooking with fresh herbs. In place of tenderloin, I poached chuck-eye steak in thyme- and garlic-infused olive oil. (Substitute fresh rosemary, oregano, savory, or a combination.) The chuck-eye steak is just one cut away from a rib-eye, nicely marbled and tender at the center with a border of fattier rib cap meat. It emerges from the olive oil with an earthy-colored exterior and pink center. It's the perfect occasion for pulling out your exotic sea salts, the flakier and crunchier the better.

This simple technique uses a fair amount of olive oil, so don't use extra-virgin. While the steaks sit in their golden bath after cooking, I steal some of the oil to make the Mixed Mushroom Sauté (page 190) and sautéed asparagus. Or, serve this with a prepared Chard-Gorgonzola Gratin (page 195) that bakes within twenty minutes once the steaks are cooked and wait, warm and patient.

Makes 4 to 6 servings

....

4 CHUCK-EYE STEAKS (ABOUT 2½ POUNDS),
    1 TO 1¼ INCHES THICK

4 GARLIC CLOVES, PEELED

3 SPRIGS FRESH THYME

2½ TO 3 CUPS OLIVE OIL

FINISHING SALT, SUCH AS COARSE SEA SALT OR
    FLAKE SALT (SOURCES, PAGE 272)

Preheat the oven to 250°F. Place the steaks in a baking dish just large enough to hold them in a single layer without touching one another or the sides of the dish. Insert the garlic and thyme into the spaces between the steaks and pour in enough oil so that they are completely covered.

Bake the steaks for a total of 35 to 40 minutes; after the first 20 minutes, turn them over to bake for about 15 minutes more before monitoring their temperature with an instant-read thermometer. When the beef is still pink and reaches 125° to 130°F, check the temperature frequently. When the beef is between 132° to 135°F for medium rare, immediately remove the dish from the oven. (Or, leave the steaks for a few more minutes to reach 138° to 140°F for medium.) Since the steaks will not continue cooking, you can hold them in the warm oil until you're ready to serve. Use tongs to lift the steaks from the oil, slice them ½ inch thick, and serve with finger pinches of the salt to taste. Let the oil cool before discarding it.

> **MORE CHOICE CUTS:**
> Rib-eye steaks, the pricier version of the chuck-eye steak, luxuriates in the olive oil treatment.
> Top-blade steak, aka flatiron, is only second to the tenderloin in tenderness and a natural fit for this unique technique.

FLANK STEAK SPIRALS WITH SPINACH, FIGS, AND FONTINA

and Port Sauce

Grilled, roasted—or even braised—this stuffed flank steak slices into beautiful spirals of savory green filling with melted cheese. Preparing it involves butterflying a flank steak, making a five-minute filling, and rolling it into a roast—all of which can be accomplished one day in advance. Transformed, this thin steak is company fare to serve with Oven Polenta (page 114) or Butternut Squash Bread Pudding (page 206)—side dishes with great holding power.

Makes 4 servings

....

6 DRIED FIGS, STEMMED AND THINLY SLICED

½ CUP RUBY PORT

1 TABLESPOON EXTRA-VIRGIN OLIVE OIL, PLUS ADDITIONAL FOR PREPARING MEAT

1 SHALLOT, FINELY CHOPPED

12 OUNCES FRESH BABY SPINACH OR 1 (10-OUNCE) BAG FROZEN SPINACH, THAWED AND DRAINED

¼ TEASPOON SALT

⅛ TEASPOON BLACK PEPPER

1 TEASPOON SHERRY VINEGAR OR RED WINE VINEGAR

⅓ CUP PINE NUTS, TOASTED

2 OUNCES FONTINA OR MOZZARELLA CHEESE, CUT INTO ¼-INCH CUBES (ABOUT ¼ CUP)

1 FLANK STEAK (1 TO 1½ POUNDS)

KOSHER SALT

FRESHLY GROUND BLACK PEPPER

3 TABLESPOONS SALTED BUTTER, CHILLED AND CUT INTO ½-INCH CUBES

Cover the figs with the port in a wide and shallow glass bowl, heat in the microwave until warm, and let steep for at least 30 minutes.

Heat 1 tablespoon of the olive oil in a large skillet over medium-high heat and cook the shallot until fragrant, about 1 minute. Add the spinach all at once along with the salt, and let it steam and compress into the skillet. Use tongs to turn the spinach and cook until it wilts. Season it with pepper, stir in the vinegar, and cook for 1 minute more.

Drain the spinach well in a fine-meshed strainer and transfer it to a medium mixing bowl. Drain the figs, reserving the port, and add them to the spinach along with the pine nuts and Fontina. Use the tongs to mix all the ingredients evenly, taste for salt, and put in the refrigerator to chill for at least 20 minutes.

Trim any silverskin from the flank steak (Trimming, page 51) and butterfly it (Butterflying, page 46). Alternatively, if the flank steak is less than 1 inch thick, pound it with a meat mallet to ½ inch thick. With the long side running parallel to the counter, use a fork to spread the spinach filling to within 2 inches of the far edge and 1 inch from the sides. Starting from the edge closest to you, roll the meat tightly over the filling like a cinnamon roll. Tie the roll in 5 to 6 places with butcher's twine, secure with silicone bands, or use three short wooden skewers to stitch the end closed. If any bits of filling spill out, just tuck them back in the ends. Transfer the steak to a baking sheet, rub it with olive oil, and season it with the kosher salt and pepper.

To grill the flank steak, prepare a charcoal or gas grill for medium heat (350° to 375°F), scrape the grate clean, and oil it lightly. Put the flank steak top side down over the coolest part of the grill. Close the cover and grill until an internal-read ther-mometer reaches 125°F, 20 to 30 minutes. For all-over browning, turn the steak roll 2 to 3 times. Alternatively, roast the steak roll in a preheated 375°F oven until an internal-read thermometer reaches 125°F, 20 to 30 minutes.

Let it rest for 10 minutes. Meanwhile, make the port sauce by bringing the reserved port to a simmer in a small saucepan. Cook for 2 minutes until the port is syrupy, then reduce the heat to low. Whisk in the cold butter one piece at a time until the sauce is thickened and season it to taste with salt and pepper. To serve, snip the ties from the steak and discard them. Use a sharp, long-bladed knife to slice the flank steak into ½-inch-thick slices and drizzle each piece with the port sauce.

VARIATION:
BRAISED FLANK STEAK

Prepare the flank steak as instructed up the point of cooking. Heat 1 tablespoon olive oil in a medium skillet with a tight-fitting lid over medium-high heat. Transfer the steak to the skillet and brown it well on 2 sides, about 5 minutes per side. Add the reserved port plus ½ cup low-salt beef stock (Short Order Stock, page 226; Roasted Beef Stock, page 228) or water. Cover, reduce the heat to low, and simmer until you can pry the meat fibers apart at one end easily with a fork, 1¼ to 1½ hours. Transfer the steak to a platter and tent with aluminum foil to keep warm. Raise the heat and bring the liquids to a boil. Simmer until they are reduced to ½ cup, about 7 minutes. Strain, if desired, whisk in the butter, and taste for salt before serving over ½-inch-thick slices of steak.

CHICKEN FRIED STEAK

with Buttermilk Gravy

Chicken fried steak is the recipe every ranch wife makes with the tough, cheap steaks from the bottom round. To get this one right, I consulted several local cooks and applied everything I'd ever learned about fried chicken. It turns out that seasoning the meat well and careful frying are the keys to success. Unlike chicken, these less tender beef cuts need a good hammering with a meat mallet to become more tender (one veteran told me, "Pound the hell out of it!"), or you can use mechanically tenderized steaks labeled "cubed" or "Swiss." My favorite cut is top round, which is more naturally tender and only needs a few blows to pound it thin. I also break from tradition by using buttermilk in the milk gravy because I love the tang it layers onto perfectly crisp, deep-fried grassfed beef. Substitute whole milk if you prefer it. Complete with baked potatoes and steamed broccoli, this is an honest, old-fashioned meal.

Makes 4 servings

....

2 TOP ROUND STEAKS (ABOUT 1¼ POUNDS), 1 TO
    1¼ INCHES THICK

¾ CUP ALL-PURPOSE FLOUR

1¼ TEASPOONS SALT

½ TEASPOON BLACK PEPPER

2 EGGS, BEATEN WITH 1 TABLESPOON WATER

1½ CUPS COARSE, DRY BREADCRUMBS

VEGETABLE OIL FOR DEEP-FRYING

BUTTERMILK GRAVY:

2 TABLESPOONS UNSALTED BUTTER

2 TABLESPOONS ALL-PURPOSE FLOUR

1½ CUPS BUTTERMILK

½ TEASPOON SALT

⅛ TEASPOON CAYENNE

Cut each steak in half and work with 1 piece at a time. Put the meat into a gallon-size resealable heavy-duty plastic bag but don't seal the bag. Pound the steak with a meat mallet or heavy rolling pin until it is an even ¼ to ⅓inch thick. Remove the steak and re-use the bag to pound the remaining steak.

Whisk the flour with the salt and pepper in a wide, shallow bowl. Put the eggs and breadcrumbs into separate shallow dishes. Dredge each steak through the flour and shake off the excess, dip it into the eggs, letting the excess drip off, and press it into the breadcrumbs to coat the steak completely. Put the breaded steaks onto a large plate. To set the breading, refrigerate the steaks uncovered for at least 20 minutes and up to 12 hours.

To make the gravy, heat the butter in a small saucepan over medium heat until it foams. Whisk in the flour and cook over medium heat until it is golden and smells nutty, about 2 minutes. Whisk in the buttermilk and bring to a boil. Reduce the heat to low and simmer, stirring often, until the gravy is smooth and as thick as heavy cream, 7 to 8 minutes. Season it with the salt and cayenne, taste for seasoning, cover, and keep it warm over low heat.

When you're ready to fry the steaks, pour oil to a depth of about two inches into a deep skillet fitted with a deep-fry thermometer and place over medium-high heat. If you own a splatter screen, have it on hand. Lay a wire rack in a rimmed baking sheet and preheat the oven to 250°F. When the oil registers 350°F or sizzles immediately when you sprinkle in a wisp of flour, add 2 of the steaks. Fry until they are deep golden brown, use tongs to flip them, taking care not to splash the oil, for a total of 4 to 5 minutes. Transfer the steaks to the prepared wire rack and keep them warm, uncovered, in the oven. Check that the oil temperature recovers to 350°F before frying the remaining steaks. Serve them as soon as possible with the buttermilk gravy.

MORE CHOICE CUTS:
Cube steak (mechanically tenderized bottom round steak) saves the work of pounding and is the traditional choice for chicken fried steak.

Sirloin tip steak, aka round tip steak, is lean and fairly tender, like top round steak.

VARIATION: FINGER STEAKS

For kids or to serve as an appetizer, slice the steaks into strips 1-inch wide and 3 inches long. Dredge in flour, dip into the egg, and coat the meat with the breadcrumbs as directed. Fry the finger steaks in small batches until they are golden brown, sprinkle them with coarse salt, and serve with Tangy Barbecue Sauce (page 223), Herb Aïoli (page 187), or ginger sauce (page 244) for dipping.

STEAKS SMOTHERED IN BACON-STOUT SAUCE

The Italians have perfected turning less popular steaks into wonderful dinners. Pounded thin and dredged in seasoned flour, then fried and paired with a simple sauce, any inexpensive, boneless steak, such as this uncelebrated sirloin tip steak (aka round tip steak), gets to shine. This dark beer sauce is from Adele Nash, a young grassfed beef rancher and professional cook who helped me test recipes for this book. Salty from the bacon, sweet from the onion, and laced with a mild bitterness from the beer, this sauce begs for a side of mashed potatoes. Flour dredging and quick frying is a good general method to use with any of the less tender steaks. For a simpler treatment prepare these crispy cutlets the way I had them in Mexico where they're called *Milanesas*: with a dollop of fresh salsa in place of the sauce and accompanied by refried beans and rice.

Makes 4 servings

....

SAUCE:

8 OUNCES BACON (ABOUT 6 SLICES), FINELY CHOPPED

2 MEDIUM ONIONS, FINELY CHOPPED

2 TABLESPOONS ALL-PURPOSE FLOUR

¾ CUP STOUT OR OTHER DARK BEER

¾ CUP MILK

¼ TEASPOON SALT

½ TEASPOON BLACK PEPPER

STEAKS:

2 SIRLOIN TIP STEAKS (ABOUT 1½ POUNDS), 1 TO 1¼ INCHES THICK

½ CUP ALL-PURPOSE FLOUR

1 TEASPOON SALT

¼ TEASPOON BLACK PEPPER

2 TABLESPOONS VEGETABLE OIL

2 TABLESPOONS SALTED BUTTER

To make the sauce, preheat a medium skillet over medium heat. Add the bacon and cook, stirring occasionally, until the fat melts and the bacon begins to brown, about 6 minutes. Add the onions and cook, stirring frequently, until they turn caramel colored, about 8 minutes. Add the flour, stir until it thickens into a paste and cook for 1 minute more to remove any starchy flavor. Add the beer and milk, whisk to make a thick sauce and bring it to a simmer. Season the sauce with salt and pepper and taste for seasoning. Cover the pan and keep it over low heat while you prepare the steaks.

Working with 1 steak at a time, put it into a gallon-size resealable heavy-duty plastic bag but do not seal the bag. Pound the steak with a meat mallet or heavy rolling pin until the steak is an even ¼ inch thick. Remove the steak and re-use the bag to pound the remaining steak.

Mix the flour with the salt and pepper in a wide, shallow dish. Dredge the steaks in the flour to coat them well, and gently shake off the excess. Line a rimmed baking sheet with a wire rack and preheat the oven to 250°F. Heat the oil and butter in a large skillet over medium-high heat. Cook the steaks 1 at a time until golden brown, 1½ to 2 minutes per side. Put them on the rack and keep warm in the oven. Repeat with the remaining steaks.

Slip the steaks into the sauce and cover them with it. Serve them immediately, or to hold them, turn off the heat and cover the pan to keep them warm until you're ready to serve.

MORE CHOICE CUTS:
Eye round and top round steaks are two more super-lean steaks that perform best with a super-quick sauté.

BISTRO STEAK WITH HERB AÏOLI

and Oven Steak Fries

When the weather is too inclement to grill, try this high-heat, two-part restaurant technique for steaks. First, you sear the steak on the stovetop then finish cooking in a hot oven. You get a perfectly juicy steak with a beautiful crust. Try a popular bistro steak like hanger, with its coarser texture and satisfying chew. Aïoli (*ay-oh-lee*), the silken homemade garlicky mayonnaise (recipe follows) is a tasty counterpoint for the steak and is great for dipping fries like the Oven Steak Fries (recipe follows). Be sure to start preparing the fries one hour in advance so they'll be crisp when the steaks are ready to serve.

Makes 4 servings
....

1 HANGER STEAK (ABOUT 2 POUNDS)

1 LARGE GARLIC CLOVE, PEELED AND CUT IN HALF

KOSHER SALT

FRESHLY GROUND BLACK PEPPER

1 TEASPOON VEGETABLE OIL

1 TEASPOON BUTTER

1 CUP HERB AÏOLI (RECIPE FOLLOWS)

Divide the steak along the line of gristle running through the center, trim it off, and cut each of the long pieces in half to make 4 serving pieces. Pat them dry, rub with the cut side of the garlic, and season both sides liberally with the kosher salt and pepper.

Preheat the oven to 475°F and place a large oven-safe skillet over medium-high heat. Add the oil and butter to the pan. When the butter foams, add the steaks and cook to sear the outside for 2 minutes. Use tongs to flip them and sear the second side for 2 minutes more. Put the skillet into the hot oven and roast the steaks 4½ to 5 minutes for medium rare. (To cook the steak further, turn off the oven and leave the steaks inside for 1 to 3 minutes more.) Serve the steaks drizzled with the pan juices, a dollop of the aïoli right alongside it, and a heap of the fries, if desired.

> **MORE CHOICE CUTS:**
> Rib-eye, the boneless, well-marbled steak of restaurant fame, can be treated to this skillet-sear and oven-finish method to achieve a crispy, browned crust when cooked to order—preferably medium rare.
>
> Top sirloin steak is another good searing steak with a robust flavor and nice chew.

HERB AÏOLI

Homemade mayonnaise is an affordable luxury that takes minutes to make by hand and less if you own an immersion blender. Use it liberally with steaks and on hamburgers or for a dipping sauce for fried foods, such as Finger Steaks (page 183).

Makes 1 cup
....

1 EGG YOLK MIXED WITH 1 TABLESPOON WATER*

1 GARLIC CLOVE, MINCED

1 TEASPOON LEMON JUICE

⅛ TEASPOON SALT

¾ CUP VEGETABLE OIL

2 TEASPOONS FINELY CHOPPED FRESH TARRAGON

1 TEASPOON FINELY CHOPPED FRESH CHIVES

1 TEASPOON LIGHTLY PACKED FINELY CHOPPED
FRESH PARSLEY

To make the aïoli by hand, whisk the yolk, garlic, lemon juice, and salt in a medium mixing bowl until it is frothy and light in color. Wrap a damp kitchen towel around the base of the bowl to stabilize it and put the oil into a measuring cup with a spout. While whisking, trickle the oil down the sides of the bowl allowing time for it to be incorporated. Continue whisking and drizzling until the yolk mixture begins to develop a thicker consistency like yogurt. At this stage, you can increase the flow of oil, pulling back if the mixture begins to look curdled, until all of the oil is used.

To make the aïoli with an immersion blender, put the yolk, garlic, lemon juice, salt, and the oil into the tall canister. Insert the wand all the way to the bottom. Turn the blender on and gradually withdraw the wand until the mixture is thick and smooth, within 1 minute.

Taste the mayonnaise for lemon juice and salt. Add the tarragon, chives, and parsley and stir to blend. Store the aïoli in the refrigerator until ready to use, up to 3 days.

VARIATIONS:

Stir in any of the following ingredients, alone or in combination, into your aïoli to make it more like remoulade or tartar sauce:

½ teaspoon anchovy paste

2 teaspoons capers, rinsed

2 tablespoons finely chopped dill pickles

1 teaspoon Dijon mustard

½ cup cooked and smashed chickpeas

NOTE: If consuming raw eggs is a concern for you (because you are feeding small children, are pregnant or elderly, or have an immune system disorder), simply whisk the garlic and herbs with 1 cup of your favorite jarred mayonnaise. Include as many of the ingredients in the variations as you like.

CONTINUES

OVEN STEAK FRIES

Now that I make French fries in the oven instead of the deep fryer—a production that took up the stovetop and dominated my attention—they are no longer only for special occasions. These golden, hand-cut fries turn out extra-crisp every time, and their hand-cut irregularities are part of their appeal. I use a speedy boiling water rinse to remove some of the excess starch for better crunch. Beef suet and duck fat make dynamite fries, but olive oil is excellent, too.

Makes 4 servings

....

2 POUNDS YUKON GOLD POTATOES (ABOUT 6 MEDIUM), WELL-SCRUBBED

2 TABLESPOONS MELTED BEEF SUET, DUCK FAT, OR EXTRA-VIRGIN OLIVE OIL

1 TEASPOON COARSE SEA SALT

Slice 1 of the potatoes in half the long way. Turn the halves cut side down, side by side on the cutting board and cut them lengthwise into ⅜-inch-thick slices. Repeat with the remaining potatoes. (You can prepare the potatoes up to 1 day in advance and hold them submerged in cool water in the refrigerator to prevent browning.)

Bring 2 quarts of water to a boil over high heat in a stockpot. When the water comes to a boil, add the potatoes, and boil for 1 minute. Drain the potatoes well and put them back in the pot uncovered over low heat to steam dry for 5 minutes.

Preheat the oven to 475°F. Toss the potatoes with the suet so that they are glossy all over. Add the salt, toss them again and spread them out in a single layer on the baking sheet. Roast the potatoes, turning them 2 to 3 times, until they are deep golden brown, 25 to 30 minutes.

FILET MIGNON IN BRANDY SAUCE

with Mixed Mushroom Sauté

Here is a steak from classic French cuisine to add to your bag of steak tricks. It sounds luxurious, but it's actually a quick meal of sautéed steaks and an easy pan sauce. If you don't have a supply of Frozen Stock Cubes (page 230) to finish the brandy sauce, use a store-bought demi-glace base, or skip that step and just swirl in the butter. The accompanying Mixed Mushroom Sauté (recipe follows) will more than make up for it.

Makes 4 servings

....

4 TENDERLOIN STEAKS (ABOUT 1½ POUNDS),
   1¼ TO 1½ INCHES THICK

KOSHER SALT

FRESHLY GROUND BLACK PEPPER

1 TABLESPOON VEGETABLE OIL

3 TABLESPOONS UNSALTED BUTTER, CHILLED AND
   DIVIDED

2 SHALLOTS, FINELY CHOPPED

¼ CUP BRANDY

2 TABLESPOONS FROZEN STOCK CUBES (PAGE 230)
   OR DEMI-GLACE, OPTIONAL

Pat the steaks dry and season both sides liberally with the kosher salt and pepper. Heat the oil and 1 tablespoon of the butter in a large skillet over medium-high heat. When the butter foams, add the steaks and cook without moving them until well browned, 3 to 3½ minutes. Use tongs to flip them and brown the second side, 3 to 3½ minutes more for medium rare. (For medium, reduce the heat to low and cook for 1 to 4 minutes more.) Transfer the steaks to a dinner plate and cover them with aluminum foil to keep them warm.

Add the shallots to the pan and cook over medium-high heat, stirring, for 30 seconds until fragrant. Remove the pan from the heat while you add the brandy to prevent a flare up. Reduce the heat to low and stir with a wooden spoon to scrape all the browned bits from the pan. Simmer the brandy for 30 seconds to reduce it slightly, add the stock cubes, if using, and cook until they melt.

Remove the pan from the heat, add the remaining 2 tablespoons butter, and whisk to make a smooth sauce. Add any of the meat juices from the resting steaks. Put 1 steak on each plate, spoon the sauce over it, and serve with a portion of the Mushroom Sauté, if desired.

MORE CHOICE CUTS:

Shoulder tender, aka teres major, if you can find this newly touted chuck cut, is wonderfully tender, too. Tapered like the tenderloin, it can be crosscut into round steak medallions for a quick sauté.

Chuck-eye steak, another boneless cut from the chuck, contains a round rib-eye muscle you can cut out to make a nicely marbled medallion (page 49).

CONTINUES ▶

MIXED MUSHROOM SAUTÉ

Makes 4 servings

....

1 TABLESPOON EXTRA-VIRGIN OLIVE OIL

1 TABLESPOON UNSALTED BUTTER

1½ POUNDS FRESH MIXED MUSHROOMS, SUCH AS
    CREMINI, PORTABELLA, WHITE BUTTON, AND
    SHIITAKE, THINLY SLICED*

2 GARLIC CLOVES, MINCED

½ TEASPOON SALT

2 TABLESPOONS LIGHTLY PACKED CHOPPED FRESH
    PARSLEY

⅛ TEASPOON BLACK PEPPER

2 TABLESPOONS HEAVY CREAM, OPTIONAL

Place a large skillet over medium heat with the oil and butter. When the butter foams, add the mushrooms, garlic, and salt. Like sponges, the mushrooms will immediately absorb all the fat in the pan. Stir the mushrooms until they start to release their moisture and shrink, about 2 minutes. Increase the heat to medium-high so that you hear a steady sizzle. In about 5 minutes, the liquid will evaporate and the mushrooms will begin to brown. Cook them, stirring only occasionally, until many are tinged with color, about 3 minutes more. Turn off the heat, toss the mushrooms with the parsley, pepper, and the cream, if using, and taste for salt.

NOTE: No matter if the mushrooms are wild or commercially grown, I *always* wash the dirt from them that a brush just cannot remove. Just before cooking, fill a big bowl with cool water, swish the mushrooms around like a washing machine agitator, and lift them out to drain in a colander. Use them promptly.

STEAK STROGANOFF

It feels like a magic trick to make a meal for four from a single premium steak like strip loin. Once you sear the steak to rare (don't worry if you like it cooked further, the steak will cook again in the sauce), you slice it into strips to heat in the creamy sauce. Serve this Russian-born dish the all-American way, over boiled egg noodles. Since it's rich, I prefer it over a heap of steamed greens.

Makes 4 servings
....

1 BONELESS STRIP LOIN STEAK (8 TO 12 OUNCES),
    1 TO 1¼ INCHES THICK

KOSHER SALT

FRESHLY GROUND BLACK PEPPER

2 TABLESPOONS BUTTER, DIVIDED

1 SMALL ONION, THINLY SLICED

8 OUNCES MUSHROOMS, SLICED

¼ TEASPOON SALT

2 TABLESPOONS DRY SHERRY

½ CUP HEAVY CREAM

½ CUP SOUR CREAM

1 TEASPOON DIJON MUSTARD

1 TABLESPOON FRESH CHOPPED DILL OR
    1½ TEASPOONS DRIED

Pat the steak dry and season it liberally with the kosher salt and pepper on both sides. Melt 1 table-spoon of the butter in a large skillet over high heat. When it foams, add the steak and cook without disturbing for 2½ to 3 minutes. Turn and sear on the other side for an additional 2½ to 3 minutes. Transfer it to a cutting board to rest.

Lower the heat to medium, add the remaining 1 tablespoon butter, and cook the onion, stirring, until it turns translucent, about 3 minutes. Add the mushrooms and salt, and cook, stirring occasionally, until they release their juices. Add the sherry and cook until most of the liquid evaporates, about 8 minutes. Add the cream and simmer until bubbling and thick, about 5 minutes. Reduce the heat to low, whisk in the sour cream and mustard, and taste for salt and pepper.

Slice the steak against the grain into ¼-inch-thick strips. It will be rare. Stir the strips into the sauce to rewarm, and, if you prefer the steak more done, cook it in the sauce over low heat for 2 to 3 minutes more. Stir in the dill just before serving.

MORE CHOICE CUTS:

Rib-eye is another deluxe steak option for this quick skillet supper.

Top round steak is very lean, and tender enough when cooked quickly and sliced thin.

MARTINI STEAK SANDWICH

with Green Olive Tapenade

I'm a fan of a gin martini with two olives. Juniper berries, the tiny fruits fermented into gin, are piney and tart, so I created a juniper berry-rubbed steak sandwich with vermouth pan sauce to serve on baguettes with the olive relish called tapenade.

This quick-sear technique is best for thin steaks like the now-popular sirloin flap often called by its French name, bavette. This high-heat technique nearly blackens the steak but leaves it perfectly pink inside. Turn on the fan hood before you begin searing the steaks.

Makes 4 servings

. . . .

TAPENADE:

1 GARLIC CLOVE, PEELED

2 ANCHOVIES, RINSED

2 TEASPOONS CAPERS, RINSED

4 OUNCES BRINED GREEN OLIVES, SUCH AS MAN-ZANILLA OR PICHOLINE, PITTED (ABOUT 1 CUP)

4 TABLESPOONS EXTRA-VIRGIN OLIVE OIL

1 TEASPOON LEMON ZEST

1 TABLESPOON LIGHTLY PACKED FINELY CHOPPED FRESH PARSLEY

STEAKS:

1 TABLESPOON WHOLE JUNIPER BERRIES

½ TEASPOON WHOLE GREEN OR BLACK PEPPER-CORNS

1 SIRLOIN FLAP STEAK AKA BAVATTE (ABOUT 1½ POUNDS), CUT INTO 4 SERVING PIECES

KOSHER SALT

1 TABLESPOON VEGETABLE OIL

½ CUP DRY VERMOUTH

1 TABLESPOON GIN, OPTIONAL

8 ½-INCH-THICK SLICES CRUSTY PEASANT-STYLE BREAD

To make the tapenade in a food processor, put the garlic, anchovies, capers, and olives in the processor bowl and pulse, pausing to scrape down the sides of the bowl, until evenly chopped. Alternatively, mince the ingredients using a sharp chef's knife and a steady rocking motion. Put the chopped olive mixture in a small bowl and stir in the olive oil, lemon zest, and parsley. The recipe makes about 1 cup and can be stored in the refrigerator for up to 2 weeks.

Crush the juniper berries and peppercorns in a mortar and pestle or spice grinder until they are as coarse as coffee grounds. Pat the steaks dry, season them liberally with the kosher salt, and sprinkle on the juniper berry rub, massaging it gently into the meat.

Place the oil in a large skillet over high heat. When it smokes, add the steaks and cook until well-browned, 2½ to 3 minutes. Use tongs to flip them and cook on the second side for an additional 2½ to 3 minutes for medium rare. (For medium, lower the heat to low and cook the steaks for 1 to 3 minutes more.) Transfer the steaks to rest on a cutting board while you make the sauce.

Reduce the heat to medium-low. Take the pan off the heat while you add the vermouth and gin, if using, to avoid a flare up. Set it back on the burner and simmer until a thin glaze of about 3 tablespoons of liquid remains in the pan, about 3 minutes.

Toast the bread slices and thinly slice the steak against the grain. For each sandwich, drizzle the vermouth sauce onto a slice of bread and generously layer on slices of steak. Spread the other slice of bread with about 1 tablespoon of the tapenade and press it down on top of the steak. Alternatively, serve slices of the steak with the vermouth sauce spooned on top, a generous dollop of tapenade, and the toasted bread on the side.

MORE CHOICE CUTS:

Flank steak and skirt steak, two other bistro-style steaks, stand up to this flash-in-the-pan method.

Top round steak is another steak best when quickly seared.

SALT-SEARED STEAK

with Chard-Gorgonzola Gratin

This recipe brings the steakhouse experience home with a well-crusted steak and dark leafy greens in a blue cheese gratin. The technique of searing on coarse sea salt, such as *sel gris*, is a novel one for indoor steak cookery. Salt can handle heat up to 1200°F and sprinkling it into a blazing hot cast-iron skillet produces a wonderfully seared and seasoned crust on the steak that's a deep rosy pink inside. The Chard-Gorgonzola Gratin (recipe follows) provides double duty as a side dish and a creamy sauce for the steak. You can prepare the gratin one day in advance to bake while the steaks are cooking and resting. If you like, serve the steaks with one of the Flavored Butter Coins (page 167) melted on top.

Makes 4 servings

....

2 TABLESPOONS COARSE SEA SALT

2 BONELESS STRIP LOIN STEAKS (ABOUT 1¼ POUNDS), 1 TO 1¼ INCHES THICK

FRESHLY GROUND BLACK PEPPER, FOR SERVING

Put the salt into a large dry cast-iron skillet, shake the pan and use your fingers to disperse it evenly. Place the skillet over medium-high heat and pat the steaks dry. When the salt crackles and snaps, after about 3 minutes, lay the steaks on top and cook without moving them for 3½ to 4 minutes. The salt will pop and crackle loudly, but it can withstand intense heat, so don't worry, it can't burn. Use tongs to flip the steaks and cook for 3½ to 4 minutes more for medium rare. (To cook to medium or beyond, slide the pan off the burner and leave the steaks in the pan to finish cooking with the residual heat, 1 to 3 minutes more.) Let the pan cool completely before discarding the salt.

Transfer the steaks to a cutting board to rest for 10 minutes. Brush any excess salt crystals from the steaks and sprinkle them with black pepper to taste. Slice them ½ inch thick against the grain and serve alongside the chard gratin, if desired.

> ### MORE CHOICE CUTS:
> Boneless, premium steaks, including rib-eye, strip loin, as well as the lesser known top-blade steak, aka flatiron, all revel in this simple salt treatment.
>
> Ground beef, formed into hamburger patties, gets a beautifully browned and tasty crust with this salt-searing technique.

CHARD-GORGONZOLA GRATIN

Using both the leaves and stems of the chard brings a depth of flavor and texture to this creamy baked side dish. Substitute one pound fresh or frozen spinach if desired (see Note).

Makes 4 to 6 servings

....

1 POUND FRESH CHARD, STEMS AND LEAVES
    SEPARATED*

4 TABLESPOONS UNSALTED BUTTER, DIVIDED

3 TABLESPOONS ALL-PURPOSE FLOUR

1½ CUPS MILK, DIVIDED

¼ TEASPOON SALT

¼ TEASPOON BLACK PEPPER

4 OUNCES GORGONZOLA OR GOOD-QUALITY BLUE
    CHEESE, CRUMBLED (ABOUT 1 CUP)

½ CUP COARSE, DRY BREADCRUMBS

NOTE: To substitute fresh spinach, cook it as directed for the chard, squeezing out as much of the moisture as possible before mixing it with the cream sauce. To substitute frozen, use a 10-ounce package frozen chopped spinach, thawed and squeezed dry.

Chop the chard stems into ½-inch-long pieces. Coarsely chop the leaves and set them aside. Bring a large pot of salted water to a boil over high heat. Add the chard stems and cook until they turn translucent and fork tender, about 5 minutes. Use a slotted spoon to transfer them to a colander to drain.

When the water comes back to a boil, plunge in the chard leaves. Cook for 2 minutes and transfer them to the bowl with the chard stems. Use the back of the spoon to press out as much of the water as you can.

Melt 2 tablespoons of the butter in a saucepan over medium heat. When it foams, add the flour and cook, stirring, until the flour paste is very smooth and smells nutty, about 2 minutes. Whisk in ½ cup of the milk. Use a heatproof spatula or wooden spoon to collect the flour from corners of the pan, then whisk until thick and smooth.

Add the remaining 1 cup of milk, salt, and pepper and whisk vigorously until the sauce boils and becomes as thick and smooth as heavy cream. Simmer the sauce for 1 minute. Remove the pan from the heat, whisk the blue cheese into the sauce until it is smooth again, and taste for salt. Add the chard to the cream sauce and stir until it is well blended. Spoon the chard mixture into a 9-inch square or round shallow baking dish. (You can prepare it in advance up to this point and store it overnight covered in the refrigerator.)

Preheat the oven to 400°F. Melt the remaining 2 tablespoons butter and mix it with the breadcrumbs in a small bowl with a fork until they are moistened. Spread the breadcrumbs over the chard in an even layer and tamp them down lightly. Bake the gratin uncovered until the cream sauce is bubbling and the breadcrumbs are golden brown, 12 to 15 minutes (or 20 to 25 minutes if chilled overnight).

SKILLET STEAK PEPERONATA

With an ample mix of sweet peppers, a single steak makes my kind of steak supper—fresh, light, and a little unexpected. Peperonata is a delectable Italian condiment that I married with steak for a taste that's reminiscent of a great pepper steak sandwich. Serve this colorful sauté with orzo, Oven Polenta (page 114), or spaghetti squash (page 91). You could go all the way and turn this into a submarine sandwich on a toasted roll or wrapped in Olive Oil Flatbreads (page 177). The recipe makes ample peperonata to load it up.

Makes 4 servings

....

3 TABLESPOONS EXTRA-VIRGIN OLIVE OIL, DIVIDED

1 RED ONION, THINLY SLICED

3 MEDIUM BELL PEPPERS (RED, YELLOW, ORANGE, OR A COMBINATION), CORED AND SLICED INTO THIN STRIPS

1 GARLIC CLOVE, MINCED

¾ TEASPOON SALT

½ TEASPOON SMOKED PAPRIKA, SUCH AS PIMENTÓN DE LA VERA (SOURCES, PAGE 272)

PINCH OF RED PEPPER FLAKES

½ CUP TOMATO SAUCE

2 TABLESPOONS LIGHTLY PACKED FINELY CHOPPED FRESH PARSLEY

1 TABLESPOON SHERRY VINEGAR OR RED WINE VINEGAR

1 TOP SIRLOIN STEAK (8 TO 12 OUNCES), 1 TO 1¼ INCHES THICK

KOSHER SALT

FRESHLY GROUND BLACK PEPPER

Heat 2 tablespoons of the oil in a large skillet over medium-high heat. Add the onion and peppers and cook, stirring occasionally, until they are limp and begin to brown, about 8 minutes.

Add the garlic, salt, paprika, and pepper flakes, and cook until it becomes fragrant, about 1 minute. Add the tomato sauce, parsley, and vinegar and cook until the sauce thickens to nearly a paste and the peppers are tender, about 10 minutes.

Preheat the oven to 250°F. Spoon the mixture into a bowl and keep it warm in the oven. Wipe out the skillet to cook the steak.

Pat the steak dry and season it liberally with the kosher salt and pepper. Heat the remaining 1 tablespoon of olive oil in the skillet over medium-high heat until it shimmers. Add the steak and brown it for 3 to 3½ minutes. Use tongs to flip it and brown the second side for an additional 3 to 3½ minutes for medium rare. (To cook to medium or beyond, slide the pan off the burner and leave the steaks in the pan to finish cooking with the residual heat, 1 to 3 minutes more.) Transfer the steak to a cutting board and let it rest. Slice it across the grain into ¼-inch strips. Serve slices topped with the peperonata or toss them with the pepper mix if serving with bread or as a topping.

> ### MORE CHOICE CUTS:
> Top round steak is wonderfully lean with excellent beefy flavors for this bold combination.
> Tri-tip steak has a pleasing coarse texture for this rustic steak supper.

WINNING ROASTS

A roast is a celebration. It is a Sunday supper or holiday dinner, an event that usually means you have a crowd to feed. Perhaps it is for this reason that I used to feel anxious about roasts. They were larger than any other piece of beef I'd ever cooked and each one was unique in shape. Nor could I peek to see what was happening deep inside: there's no fiddling with a roast, and the entire meal rested on it. But, after a year of regular roasting, I've learned that a good roast is simply a matter of preserving moisture within the meat. With just a few tools, my anxieties evaporated and I found roasts to be the most hands-off meats to cook. Once seasoned and in the oven at the appropriate temperature, they allowed me to mingle and enjoy the occasion—and always provided leftovers.

A roast is both a cooking method and a beef cut. Roasting is an ancient technique of cooking over an open flame. Modern ovens roast using dry radiant heat, typically 400°F and up for achieving a handsome crust on large, naturally tender and marbled cuts. But, dry-heat roasting can also occur at low temperatures—300°F and below. Called slow-roasting, it is useful and beneficial for the leanest large cuts, primarily from the round, or

hindquarter. (In fact, if you're ever uncertain how to cook any roast, slow-roasting is the way to go.)

These recipes create feasts for sharing—with enough for roast beef sandwiches the next day or for Bobotie (page 156), Baked Argentinian Empanadas (page 159), or Shepherd's Pie (page 86). Also, you can use leftover roast beef in many of the recipes in Chapter 6: Global Beef Cuisine.

In these pages you'll find a whole range of methods for cooking the largest beef cuts, from seared Grassfed 4-Bone Rib Roast on Hay and Herbs (page 204) to Smoked Brisket with Tangy Barbecue Sauce (page 222). There are roasts to cook with high heat, including Roast Beef Stuffed with Red Onions, Mushrooms, and Barley (page 210) and others that do best with slow-roasting to keep the meat juicy, such as Garlicky Roast Beef with Gravy and Yorkshire Pudding (page 212).

Roasts tend to be the priciest cuts, but they do not need to be. In this chapter, you'll find the most luxurious roasts, including standing rib roast and whole tenderloin mingling with sirloin tip roast, aka round tip roast, and eye round roast, two cuts that get short shrift. All of them offer the most relaxed way of entertaining I know.

Roasting Choice Cuts

Although the average thousand-pound steer has several good roasting cuts, you'd never glean it from the supermarket meat counter. Prime rib and tenderloin are the most celebrated and therefore the most expensive muscles, but there are many more economical options for both high-heat and slow-roasting. Grassfed roasts, which are significantly leaner inside and out and generally smaller by weight, will cook slightly faster than conventional beef roasts and appear more pink at your desired serving temperature. Keep a close eye on the clock, have your trusty thermometer on hand, and pull the roast from the oven eight to ten degrees lower than your desired finishing temperature (Timetable for Roasting, page 201).

BRISKET, the boneless, flat pectoral muscle is sold whole or in halves: the "flat" is the leanest and most uniform portion while the "point" or "nose" has a layer of fat running through the middle. Brisket is not a typical cut for dry-heat cooking, but like other cuts from the chuck, it gets quite tender when slow-roasted at or below 300°F for several hours. Renowned as the beef for barbecuing, it demands time for hot smoking or can be slow-roasted in the oven.

BOTTOM ROUND ROAST, aka rump roast, is a very lean, boneless rounded cut from the upper part of the outer leg or round. Slow-roasted to medium rare and sliced very thin—all the better if you have access to a meat slicer—it makes excellent deli-style roast beef.

CHUCK ROAST refers to several different cuts, all from the shoulder, usually relegated to braising, or moist-heat cooking. Like brisket, these tough cuts can also be cooked with dry heat at low temperatures and smoked. Chuck roasts are trickier to slice because of the confusion of muscles, but can be readily shredded for serving.

EYE ROUND ROAST is a long, nearly cylindrical single-muscle roast that resembles tenderloin in shape. Very lean, boneless, and modestly tender, it is lighter in color than the other muscles of the round (top round and bottom round) that surround it, and has a milder flavor, too. It makes a fine roast as long as it is slow-roasted and thinly sliced.

PRIME RIB is the common term for a rib roast with the back ribs removed. See Rib roast.

RIB ROAST is a large, lean roast with three to seven back bones attached, also known as a standing rib roast. A "first cut" rib roast contains the first four ribs from the loin end, is very uniform and has a large rib-eye muscle; the "second cut" sits closer to the chuck with more fat around the smaller rib-eye muscle. Both make exceptional roasts. Without the bones, a rib roast is called a rib-eye roast or prime rib. Supremely tender and flavorful, it's very versatile for the cook to roast fast or slow, to grill, or even to smoke.

SIRLOIN TIP ROAST, aka round tip roast, is a lean, boneless cut from below the hip joint where the loin and round primals meet, a muscle sometimes called the knuckle. It is an underrated roast well suited to high heat or low-heat roasting.

STRIP LOIN ROAST, aka top loin roast, is usually sliced into steaks. A whole boneless strip loin roast can be treated like a rib-eye roast, and is typically roasted or grill-roasted using high heat.

TENDERLOIN is a long, slender, tapering muscle running all along the spine, from the short loin to the sirloin. The most tender muscle on the cow, it is also called filet or filet mignon, and is a valuable, expensive roast. It is very lean, but is sometimes sold with a fatty strip of meat called the chain that should be trimmed before use as a roast. A whole tenderloin is a great butchering exercise that's manageable, albeit spendy, for a home cook (Trimming, page 51).

TOP SIRLOIN ROAST comes from the big top sirloin butt muscle, and is sometimes called American chateaubriand. Butchers usually slice it into thick top sirloin steaks, but they can just as easily cut a roast sized to suit, and the center cut is most prized. Modestly priced with great flavor, a whole roast sirloin can be grilled or roasted in the oven like a rib-eye roast.

TOP ROUND ROAST is a rounded, lean, boneless whole muscle with a thin cover of fat on some of it. This is the cut commonly used to make deli-style roast beef and is sadly underrated by home cooks. To make it as tender and juicy as possible, it is best cooked at low temperatures until medium rare and then thinly sliced.

TRI-TIP ROAST is a lean and boneless cut with a shape like a boomerang from the outer part of the sirloin, also called triangle tip. It is a small roast, averaging two to three pounds when grassfed, that is manageable to grill-roast whole. It is relatively tender and is praised for its standout flavor that stands up to potent rubs and grilling. It may be hard to find outside of the West.

How Would You Like Your Meat?

SERVING PREFERENCE	INTERNAL TEMPERATURE AFTER RESTING	INTERNAL TEMPERATURE TO REMOVE FROM OVEN*	APPEARANCE OF THE SLICED MEAT	TEXTURE OF THE SLICED MEAT
Very rare	125°F	115°F	Bright red to the outer edge and nearly raw in the center	Yielding to the touch and barely warm in the center
Rare	130°F	120°F	Cherry red to the outer edge with flowing bright red meat juices	Yielding to the touch and warm at the center
Medium-rare	135°F	125°F	Red to rose in the center with red meat juices	Springy to the touch and warm in the center
Medium	140°F	130°F	Pink in the center fading to brown toward the surface with pink meat juices	Taut but resilient to the touch and very warm in the center
Medium-well	145°F	135°F**	Traces of pale pink at the very center with browned meat juices	Firm to the touch and hot in the center
Well	155°F and above	140°F**	No trace of pink in the center with browned meat juices	Very firm to the touch and hot in the center

* This assumes a temperature rise of 8°F to 12°F during a 20 to 30 minute resting period.

** Serve end cuts from a roast or reduce the heat below 300°F for medium-well and well to maintain juiciness.

Timetable for Roasting

	ROASTING TEMPERATURE	RECOMMENDED BEEF CUTS	TIME PER POUND	INTERNAL TEMPERATURE TO REMOVE FROM OVEN	SERVING TEMPERATURE AFTER 20-30-MINUTE REST	SAMPLE RECIPE
HIGH-HEAT ROASTING	475°F to 500°F	Very tender, boneless, and small roasts, including tenderloin, shoulder tender, and tri-tip	8 to 10 minutes per pound	120°F for rare / 125°F for medium-rare / 130°F for medium	128°F to 132°F for rare / 133°F to 137°F for medium-rare / 138°F to 142°F for medium	Porcini-rubbed Tenderloin (page 207)
HIGH-HEAT ROASTING	350°F to 375°F	Tender and larger roasts (bone-in or boneless), including rib roast, strip loin, top sirloin, or the modestly tender sirloin tip	18 to 20 minutes per pound	120°F for rare / 125°F for medium-rare / 130°F for medium	128°F to 132°F for rare / 133°F to 137°F for medium-rare / 138°F to 142°F for medium	Roast Beef Stuffed with Red Onions, Mushrooms, and Barley (page 210)
SLOW ROASTING	275°F to 300°F	Any roast, but especially the less tender, lean roasts, including top round, eye round, and bottom round	26 to 28 minutes per pound	120°F for rare / 125°F for medium-rare / 130°F for medium	128°F to 132°F for rare / 133°F to 137°F for medium-rare / 138°F to 142°F for medium	Garlicky Roast Beef (page 212)
SLOW ROASTING	200°F to 250°F	Tough roasts, including chuck roast and brisket	1 to 2 hours per pound	185°F to 200°F	—	Mojo Beef (page 218)

Use this chart as a planning tool whenever you prepare a roast, but know the time per pound is only an estimate. Your oven, the raw meat's temperature, roast shape, and other variables will determine the actual cooking time. The utility of this chart is in calculating roughly how far in advance you'll want to season the roast, preheat the oven, and start roasting (with an allowance for resting time, page 203) to get dinner to the table on time. Note that most of the recipes instruct you to have the roast at room temperature one to two hours before roasting, which will only begin to take off the refrigerator's chill, but it's a start.

Roasts offer wiggle room because they stay warm for a long time (if you're concerned about rapid cooling, wrap the roast securely with aluminum foil and keep it near the stove or in a turned off oven—125°F or below—with the door left ajar). In the event the roast is running behind schedule, bear in mind that cooking accelerates as the internal temperature climbs, so the final fifteen minutes are crucial and the final ten to twenty-degree temperature rise is rapid. If you can't wait it out, increase the oven temperature by 25°F up to 50°F for fifteen minutes and babysit the roast so that you can pluck it from the oven the moment it's ready.

THE ESSENTIAL INTERNAL
READ THERMOMETER

Believe me, I've tried, but a finger jab to a roast can't tell you what's going on inside. For that insight, you need a thermometer probe inserted into the center of the roast to get an accurate temperature reading. An electronic thermometer with a leave-in probe continuously monitors the temperature and has an alarm and a timer to ease your mind. For more hands-on types, an instant-read thermometer—dial or digital—works, although you need to pull the roast out of the oven so that you don't lose oven heat while waiting for the temperature to register (they're not *that* instant). The Thermapen, which logs the temperature as fast as you can open an oven door, is the quickest probe thermometer around with an extra-large display for easy reading. I made the investment in this hundred-dollar gadget when my thirty-dollar digital died after only three months of use. But, any one of the affordable thermometers on the market will serve you well in mastering the art of roasting large meat cuts.

GIVE IT A REST

I once watched a three-pound roast beef I'd baked at 250°F surge from a perfect medium rare to medium well *after* I'd pulled it from the oven. I was crushed and bewildered: How could a relatively small roast cooked in a low oven increase *eight whole degrees*? From that point forward, I monitored every roast I cooked—no matter the size or the oven temperature—with my digital instant-read thermometer while it rested. I was repeatedly astounded by the capacity of beef to keep cooking long after it's removed from the heat source.

Many people resist the resting notion as foodie fussiness, but it's really the final cooking stage for meat. A short rest is good for any sized cut, but it's especially important for whole roasts. The larger the roast, the greater the temperature increase and the longer it takes for the heat to conduct through it. (Think of it like trying to bring a supertanker to a halt in the water.) Start carving a roast that hasn't rested and every slice will cook in the residual heat as fast as you can slice, turning gray-brown before it hits the serving platter. I've done it myself, and I nearly cried.

Expect temperature increases of a minimum of eight, ten, and even twelve degrees, when resting beef. This is the reason I alert you to remove your roast from the oven or grill ten degrees *below* the serving temperature you want. It's more conservative than other cookbooks, and you may worry that your roast will be underdone, but I've never seen this happen.

The other reason for resting is that it redistributes the juices that rush toward the meat's center during cooking. You witness this when you grill a hamburger and it puffs up in the middle. Roasts don't change shape, but the same effect is in action.

I think of the resting time as a convenient pause to finish pulling the rest of the meal together, to season the sauce just right, or maybe to take a breather. If you're worried about the roast growing cold, make it a blanket of aluminum foil and keep it away from drafts. In any case, roasted meats are not served piping hot. (That's what the gravies and sauces are for; make sure they're steaming when you serve them.)

After the twenty to twenty-five minutes of resting time, I make sure to use my sharpest knife to carve with ease through the meat and avoid squeezing out those precious juices that register in our taste sensors as pure succulence.

GRASSFED 4-BONE RIB ROAST ON HAY AND HERBS

with Butternut Squash Bread Pudding

A standing rib roast is a formidable cut, tall and armored in bone. Given its worth, roasting it can be intimidating. The irony of the big roasts is that they're nearly effortless to prepare, and it's best to do as little as possible to let the glory of the beef shine.

I became inspired by an intriguing yet simple method espoused by Iron Chef Vitaly Paley of Portland, one of the first big-name chefs that Carman Ranch won over to its grassed beef: roasting the beef on a bed of hay. It's playful and symbolic to cook the animal on its own (winter) feed. "It emphasizes the barnyard notes, in a good way," said Vitaly. He cooks meat on hay every chance he gets.

For all those without access to a feed store (though they're cropping up in urban areas), you can prepare an ample bed using only the onions and sprigs of fresh rosemary and thyme. All impart an herbaceous quality to the meat, and especially to the jus.

Make this two-stage roasting method a standard for any of the large, lean, and tender cuts from the rib and loin primals (The Tender Middle, page 54). Popped into a searing hot oven, the outside crust browns enticingly before the oven is turned down to complete the roasting process. If you like, bake the Butternut Squash Bread Pudding (recipe follows) alongside to serve with this phenomenal roast.

Makes 10 to 12 servings

....

1 (7- TO 8-POUND) 4-BONE RIB ROAST

KOSHER SALT

FRESHLY GROUND BLACK PEPPER

1 SMALL BUNCH HAY, OPTIONAL

2 LARGE ONIONS, ROUGHLY CHOPPED

4 BRANCHES FRESH ROSEMARY

6 LARGE SPRIGS OF THYME

6 BAY LEAVES

1½ CUPS LOW-SALT BEEF STOCK (SHORT ORDER STOCK, PAGE 226; ROASTED BEEF STOCK, PAGE 228) OR DRY WHITE WINE

3 TABLESPOONS FROZEN STOCK CUBES (PAGE 230), DEMI-GLACE, OR FLAVORED BUTTER COINS (PAGE 167), OPTIONAL

Up to 2 days in advance, put the rib roast on a baking sheet, season it generously with kosher salt and pepper, and store it uncovered in the refrigerator. Let it sit at room temperature for about 2 hours before roasting. Wash the hay, if using, in a large sinkful of water and let it drain in a colander.

Preheat the oven to 475°F. Cover the bottom of a roasting pan with the hay and arrange the onions, rosemary, thyme, and bay leaves on it to make a bed. Position the roast on the bed with the bone side down and the fat cap side up.

Roast the meat for 15 minutes. The fat cap on the meat will be walnut brown and sizzling. Lower the oven temperature to 375°F and continue roasting until an instant-read thermometer registers 115°F, about 45 minutes more for a total of 1 hour.

Remove the roast if you like it very rare, or check the temperature every 10 minutes and remove it as soon as the center of the roast reaches 120°F for rare or 125°F for medium rare (Timetable for Roasting, page 201). Transfer the roast to a cutting board,

tent it with aluminum foil, and let it rest for at least 30 minutes to reach the final serving temperature. (This is longer than some other resting times because the bones store a lot of heat, which takes longer to disperse evenly through the meat.)

To make the jus, add the stock to the bed of hay and herbs from the roasting pan to pick up some of the flavors and then strain it into a small saucepan. Bring the stock to a simmer and whisk in the stock cubes, if using, to enrich it. Spoon off any excess fat, taste the jus for salt, and keep it warm over low heat.

Use a thin-bladed, flexible knife, such as a boning knife, to remove the back ribs (Boning, page 46) and set them aside. Slice the meat against the grain into ½-inch-thick slices. Slice between the backbones and serve them to those who relish nibbling meat from the bone. Or, save them for another meal, such as Ginger-Glazed Short Ribs (page 244). Spoon the jus over the beef slices and serve with the Butternut Squash Bread Pudding, if desired.

MORE CHOICE CUTS:

Rib-eye roast, the boneless version of this same cut (sometimes referred to as prime rib), and boneless strip loin roast are two other top choices. Without bones, it will cook more quickly, so start checking the roast's temperature 30 minutes after turning down the heat to 375°F and monitor it regularly to reach your desired temperature according to the Timetable for Roasting on page 201.

Top sirloin roast, nicknamed "American chateaubriand" when center cut, is a more economical choice. Because it is boneless, it will need less time to cook; start checking the roast's temperature after 30 minutes of roasting and cook to your liking according to the Timetable for Roasting.

CONTINUES ▶

BUTTERNUT SQUASH BREAD PUDDING

This no-fuss sidedish can be prepared a day in advance (without the stock) and bakes alongside the standing rib roast (page 204), or all on its own. It also reheats well.

Makes 10 to 12 servings

....

10 (½-INCH) SLICES ARTISAN-STYLE MULTIGRAIN OR
    WHOLE-WHEAT BREAD (ABOUT 12 OUNCES)

2 MEDIUM SWEET ONIONS, SLICED

1½ POUNDS BUTTERNUT SQUASH, PEELED,
    SEEDED, AND CUT INTO 1-INCH CUBES (ABOUT
    5 CUPS)

¼ CUP EXTRA-VIRGIN OLIVE OIL

1 TABLESPOON CHOPPED FRESH SAGE OR
    1 TEASPOON DRIED

2 TEASPOONS CHOPPED FRESH THYME OR
    ½ TEASPOON DRIED

1¼ TEASPOONS SALT

¼ TEASPOON BLACK PEPPER

1 TABLESPOON UNSALTED BUTTER, SOFTENED

1½ CUPS GRATED GRUYÈRE OR SWISS CHEESE,
    DIVIDED

3½ CUPS LOW-SALT CHICKEN STOCK

Preheat the oven to 350°F. Tear the bread into roughly 1-inch pieces on a baking sheet and bake until crisp, stirring once, 10 to 12 minutes. Set it aside.

Raise the oven temperature to 400°F. Toss the onion slices and butternut squash with the olive oil, sage, thyme, salt, and pepper and arrange in a single layer on a sheet pan. Roast until the onions begin to brown and the squash is fork tender, 22 to 25 minutes.

Butter a 13 x 9-inch baking dish. Arrange half of the bread into a single, uneven layer in the bottom of the baking dish. Distribute half of the roasted onion and squash mixture over the bread. Sprinkle on half of the cheese. Repeat with a second layer of bread, the rest of the onions and squash, and top with the remaining cheese. (Store it covered in the refrigerator for up to 1 day.)

Pour in the chicken stock, pausing to let it seep into the bread and packing it down with a spoon, if necessary. Cover the dish with aluminum foil and place it on a baking sheet to catch drips.

To bake the bread pudding with the 4-Bone Rib Roast, put it on a rack below the roast into the 475°F oven. Bake covered for 15 minutes and remove the aluminum foil when you reduce the oven heat to 375°F as instructed in the 4-Bone Rib Roast recipe (page 204). Bake for another 35 to 40 minutes until bubbling, puffed, and deep golden brown. Recover with the foil to keep it warm. Once you remove the roast, you can turn off the oven and pop the bread pudding back in while the roast rests.

To bake the bread pudding on its own, preheat the oven to 375°F. Bake covered for 30 minutes, then remove the foil and continue baking until bubbling, puffed, and deep golden brown, 35 to 40 minutes more for a total of 65 to 70 minutes.

PORCINI-RUBBED TENDERLOIN

with Saba Sauce and Braised Lentils

Whenever I taste great grassfed beef, it brings to mind the earthy essence of wild mushrooms. My mushroom hunting skills are not up to the challenge of locating the king bolete mushrooms that pop up in the woods here in the spring. Luckily, my neighbor, farmer, and forager, Gene Theil, who is famous in Portland's restaurant world, sells them to me whenever I ask. I buy dried *boletus* related to the Italian porcini, and grind them to a powder in a spice grinder. You can also buy porcinis already ground. It's the simplest thing to mix the mushroom powder into a wet rub for a tenderloin (or any other roast, steak, or burger) that alchemizes in the oven to a gorgeously browned roast. A five-hundred-degree oven may seem daunting, but so long as you keep an eye on the clock and a reliable thermometer handy, it's a sure-fire way to get a great sear on one of the most tender cuts of all.

I serve this tenderloin with accompanying umami elements including a sweet-and-sour wine sauce made with saba, a syrup of reduced and aged winegrapes, similar to balsamic. The side dish of Braised Lentils (recipe follows), which smell amazing as they simmer, pulls the whole meal together.

Makes 8 servings

....

RUB:

¼ CUP PORCINI POWDER (SOURCES, PAGE 272)

2 TEASPOONS KOSHER SALT

¾ TEASPOON BLACK PEPPER

3 TABLESPOONS EXTRA-VIRGIN OLIVE OIL

1 (2½- TO 3-POUND) CENTER-CUT TENDERLOIN

SAUCE:

2 CUPS RED WINE

2 SHALLOTS, FINELY CHOPPED

3 TABLESPOONS SABA*

2 TABLESPOONS SALTED BUTTER, CUT INTO ½-INCH
    CUBES AND WELL CHILLED

CONTINUES

To make the rub, combine the porcini powder, kosher salt, and pepper together in a small bowl. Add the olive oil and stir to make a thick, gritty paste. Tie the tenderloin in 4 or 5 places using butcher's twine or silicone bands to support its shape to make nice, rounded serving slices. Put the tenderloin on a rack in a small roasting pan. Spread the porcini rub all over the roast and leave it at room temperature for 1 hour.

Meanwhile, start the sauce by bringing the wine and shallots to a boil in a small saucepan over medium-high heat. Reduce the heat to low to simmer steadily until the wine is reduced to roughly ½ cup, about 25 minutes, and set it aside.

Preheat the oven to 500°F.

Roast the tenderloin until an instant-read thermometer registers 115°F, 20 to 25 minutes. Remove the roast if you like it very rare, or check the temperature every 5 minutes and remove it as soon as the center of the roast reaches 120°F for rare or 125°F for medium rare (Timetable for Roasting, page 201). Transfer the tenderloin to a cutting board, tent with aluminum foil, and let it rest for at least 20 minutes to reach its final serving temperature while you finish the sauce.

To finish the sauce, add the saba to the reserved wine mixture over low heat. Whisk in the butter, a few cubes at a time, to make a sauce that barely coats the back of a spoon. Taste for salt and add a pinch if it needs it.

Slice the tenderloin into ½-inch-thick slices and spoon the sauce, including plenty of the shallots, over each serving alongside a portion of the Braised Lentils, if desired.

NOTE: In place of the saba, combine ¼ cup of good-quality balsamic vinegar and 1 tablespoon of sugar in a small saucepan. Bring it to a simmer over medium heat and cook until it is reduced to 3 tablespoons of syrup, about 3 minutes.

MORE CHOICE CUTS:

Rib-eye roast is a thicker cut that will take a bit longer to roast. After roasting at 500°F for 15 minutes, reduce the oven temperature to 350°F and monitor with an instant-read thermometer to reach the final temperature according to the Timetable for Roasting on page 201.

Top round roast, not a celebrated roast, gets an upgrade with this treatment. After roasting it at 500°F for 15 minutes, reduce the oven temperature to 300°F and monitor with an instant-read thermometer to reach the final temperature according to the Timetable for Roasting.

BRAISED LENTILS

This simple side dish is stirred on the stovetop like a risotto (only less constantly), along with wine and beef stock, in a recipe adapted from Judy Rodgers's *Zuni Cafe Cookbook*. Since the tenderloin roasts so quickly, you'll want to start the lentils after you rub the roast and while it waits to go into the oven. Once the lentils are tender, they will sit patiently and hold their shape while covered over low heat, so that you can devote all your attention to the precious tenderloin.

Because I live just to the south of the Palouse, one of the top lentil- and dry pea-growing regions of the world, I've been exposed to this legume's many colors, shapes, and sizes. I love the small, rounded green lentils de puy and the black lentil called beluga, both of which bring a nutty texture to complement an out-of-this-world tenderloin (page 207).

Makes 8 servings

....

3 TABLESPOONS EXTRA-VIRGIN OLIVE OIL

1 RED ONION, FINELY CHOPPED

1 CARROT, FINELY CHOPPED

1 CELERY STALK, FINELY CHOPPED

3 GARLIC CLOVES, MINCED

½ CUP RED WINE

1¾ CUPS DRY LENTILS, SUCH AS LENTILS DE PUY OR BLACK BELUGA, RINSED

1½ TEASPOONS SALT

½ TEASPOON BLACK PEPPER

2 BAY LEAVES

2½ CUPS LOW-SALT BEEF STOCK (SHORT ORDER STOCK, PAGE 226; ROASTED BEEF STOCK, PAGE 228) OR WATER, DIVIDED

Heat the olive oil in a large saucepan over medium heat. Add the onion, carrot, celery, and garlic and cook, stirring often, until the vegetables soften and turn translucent, about 5 minutes.

Add the wine and cook until it has nearly evaporated, about 5 minutes. Stir in the lentils, salt, pepper, and bay leaves. Add 1½ cups of the stock or water, reduce the heat to low, and simmer the lentils uncovered, stirring occasionally until the liquid has nearly been absorbed.

Add more of the stock or water in small doses, about ½ cup at a time, using just enough so that the lentils are tender and there is about 1 inch of liquid in the bottom of the pan, for a total of 40 to 45 minutes. Remove and discard bay leaves. Taste for salt and pepper and keep it covered over low heat until ready to serve.

ROAST BEEF STUFFED WITH RED ONIONS, MUSHROOMS, AND BARLEY

For a celebratory meal, a stuffed, rolled roast is an impressive offering that comes with a built-in side dish. It involves butterflying a roast (Butterflying, page 46) and preparing a whole grain stuffing (you'll need one cup of cooked barley, see note), both of which you can do one day in advance. A sirloin tip roast, aka round tip roast, is big, beefy, lean, and affordable. Once roasted, it looks as opulent as any large beef cut and slices neatly to reveal the stuffing inside. (I sometimes double the quantity of stuffing to make a bed for the slices of stuffed roast beef.)

Makes 8 servings

....

2 TABLESPOONS EXTRA-VIRGIN OLIVE OIL, PLUS ADDITIONAL FOR
    PREPARING ROAST

3 RED ONIONS, CHOPPED

8 OUNCES CREMINI MUSHROOMS, ROUGHLY CHOPPED

1½ TEASPOONS SALT

¼ TEASPOON BLACK PEPPER

2 TABLESPOONS BALSAMIC VINEGAR

2 TEASPOONS FINELY CHOPPED FRESH ROSEMARY, DIVIDED

1 CUP COOKED PEARLED BARLEY*

1 (3- TO 3½-POUND) SIRLOIN TIP ROAST

KOSHER SALT

FRESHLY GROUND BLACK PEPPER

2 GARLIC CLOVES, MINCED

Heat the olive oil in a medium skillet over medium-high heat. Add the onions and cook, stirring often, until they turn translucent, about 3 minutes. Add the mushrooms, salt, and pepper and cook, stirring occasionally, until the liquid evaporates, about 8 minutes.

Stir in the vinegar and 1½ teaspoons of the rosemary and cook until very fragrant, about 1 minute more. Remove the pan from the heat, stir in the barley, and set it aside to cool.

Butterfly the roast (Butterflying, page 46). Coat it with olive oil and season it liberally with the kosher salt and pepper on both sides. With the rough, butterflied side of the meat facing up, rub in the garlic and sprinkle on the remaining ½ teaspoon of rosemary.

Preheat the oven to 450°F and cut 3 (18-inch) lengths of butcher's twine or have large silicone bands on hand to roll and tie the roast once assembled. Spoon about two-thirds of the stuffing into the center of the roast and roll it up starting from one of the shorter ends. Tie the roast securely in the center and at each end. Use your hands to stuff the remaining filling into the ends. Put it into a roasting pan seam side down.

Roast the meat for 20 minutes to brown the outside, and reduce the oven temperature to 350°F. Continue roasting until an instant-read thermometer registers 120°F, 30 to 35 minutes more. Remove the roast if you like it rare, or check the temperature every 10 minutes and remove it as soon as the center of the roast reaches 125°F for medium rare (Timetable for Roasting, page 201). Transfer the meat to a cutting board, tent with aluminum foil, and let it rest for at least 20 minutes to reach its final serving temperature.

Strain the pan juices from the roasting pan into a measuring cup. To serve, snip the ties off the roast with a paring knife or kitchen shears and discard them. Use a sharp, long-bladed knife to slice the roast into ¼- to 1-inch-thick slices and serve them drizzled with the pan juices.

NOTE: To prepare the barley, bring 1 cup of water to a boil in a small saucepan over medium-high heat. Add ½ cup of pearled barley and ¼ teaspoon salt, reduce the heat to low, and simmer covered until tender to the bite, about 30 minutes. Drain the barley and set aside it aside to cool to room temperature before making the stuffing as directed.

MORE CHOICE CUTS:
Top sirloin roast is another less expensive option to stuff and roast.

Rib-eye roast is the premium boneless roasting cut well complemented by this stuffing.

GARLICKY ROAST BEEF

with Gravy and Yorkshire Pudding

Roasted garlic perfumes this roast, the pan gravy, and the kitchen, beckoning everyone to come enjoy an old-fashioned roast beef and gravy dinner. Lean roasts from the round, one of most challenging cuts to cook well, come out perfectly when baked in a three-hundred-degree oven, staying juicy within the garlic paste rub. Milk gravy is the standard in the rural West, though I use a different sauce-thickening technique where a paste of butter and flour, called *beurre manie* (*burr man-yay*), is whisked into the liquids. It makes a foolproof lump-free gravy instantly (enough for hot open-faced roast beef sandwiches the following day). While the meat rests, you have the perfect amount of time to bake the easy Yorkshire Pudding (recipe follows) for sopping up the gravy. Round out this English-inspired supper with a side dish of buttery green peas or green beans.

Makes 8 servings with leftovers

....

12 GARLIC CLOVES, PEELED

1½ TABLESPOONS KOSHER SALT

½ TEASPOON BLACK PEPPER

1 (3½- TO 4-POUND) TOP ROUND ROAST

GRAVY:

3 CUPS MILK

3 TABLESPOONS UNSALTED BUTTER, SOFTENED

3 TABLESPOONS ALL-PURPOSE FLOUR

Up to 24 hours in advance, smash the garlic with the kosher salt and pepper into a paste using a mortar and pestle, the flat side of a chef's knife blade, or a food processor. Rub the garlic paste all over the roast and put it on a rack in a metal roasting pan, fat side up. Refrigerate it until 1 hour before roasting.

Preheat the oven to 300°F. Roast until an internal-read thermometer reads 115°F, 1½ to 1¾ hours. Remove the roast if you like it very rare, or check the temperature every 10 minutes and remove it as soon as the center of the roast reaches 120°F for rare or 125°F for medium rare (Timetable for Roasting, page 201). (If you are making the Yorkshire Pudding, raise the oven temperature to 425°F once you've removed the roast and bake as directed on the next page.) Transfer the meat to a cutting board, tent it with aluminum foil, and let it rest for at least 20 minutes to reach its final serving temperature.

To make the gravy, remove the rack, pour the milk into the roasting pan, and bring it to a boil on the stovetop over medium heat. Use a wooden spoon to scrape up all the browned garlic bits. Use a fork to mash the butter and flour together in a small bowl until they are well blended. Whisk the butter mixture into the simmering liquid and cook until it thickens to coat the back of a spoon, about 3 minutes. Taste the gravy for salt and pepper, pour it into a small saucepan, and keep it warm over low heat.

Slice the roast ¼ inch thick with a sharp slicing knife and serve with the hot gravy.

YORKSHIRE PUDDING

These beloved little pastries are what I make when there's no time for dinner rolls. They're perfect for mopping up the meat juices and gravy with a roast, and are a convenience for the cook because they bake while the roast is resting. But I make them other times, too, because they're also the perfect size to plunk on top of the Salt-Seared Steak with Chard-Gorgonzola Gratin (page 194) or a slice of Pure Beef Meatloaf (page 78). More like popovers than "puddings," these don't demand a special baking pan to achieve their loft. A 12-cup muffin tin is all you need, plus a hot oven. Just be sure to mix up the batter at least 20 minutes in advance so that the flour has time to absorb the liquids and swell the starches.

Whisk the flour, salt, eggs, yolk, and milk together in a medium mixing bowl, beating vigorously to make a perfectly smooth batter. Pour the batter into a 2-cup or larger measuring cup with a spout and let it stand at room temperature for 20 minutes.

Preheat the oven to 425°F. Pour ½ teaspoon of the suet into each cup of a 12-cup muffin tin and put it in the oven to heat for 2 to 3 minutes. When you can hear the suet sizzling, take it out of the oven and pour in the batter, distributing it evenly to fill each cup about halfway. Put the muffin tin in the oven and keep the oven door sealed so that they rise in the intense heat. Bake the puddings until they are puffed and golden brown, 20 to 25 minutes.

Makes 12 servings

....

1 CUP (4½ OUNCES) ALL-PURPOSE FLOUR

½ TEASPOON SALT

2 EGGS

1 EGG YOLK

1 CUP MILK

2 TABLESPOONS MELTED BEEF SUET OR OLIVE OIL

MASHED POTATO MIX UP

Warm and pillowy mashed potatoes are the classic side dish for a roast (and steak, meatloaf, and so many other beef dishes). I veer toward the bevy of other fall and winter vegetables, and treat them in the same way: boiled in salted water, steam-dried, mashed, or puréed with softened butter, and seasoned to taste with salt and pepper. Like potatoes, these vegetables boil in twenty to twenty-five minutes if cut into roughly 2-inch chunks. When blending them with potatoes, it's best to cook each vegetable separately. Use an immersion blender, food processor, or food mill to get them perfectly smooth, and keep them warm covered in a bowl over simmering water.

CAULIFLOWER: Core a head of cauliflower and segment it before boiling and puréeing in a food processor. Try adding a shot of white truffle oil, or a pinch of coriander to this mild-mannered vegetable.

CELERY ROOT: Peeled and cut into even chunks for boiling, this round root is great paired with potatoes in a 50/50 mash with a splash of cream.

JERUSALEM ARTICHOKES (ALSO SOLD AS SUNCHOKES): Peel the thin skins from this delicately flavored vegetable before boiling and then mash with olive oil in place of butter.

PARSNIPS: Peel and boil then mash these with boiled carrots to make a colorful side dish.

SWEET POTATOES OR YAMS: Handled just like russet potatoes, these mash easily. I like to set off their sweet flavors with spices such as cumin, smoked paprika, or garam masala (Note, page 117).

TURNIPS: Browned butter—made by heating melted butter until it turns amber colored and smells nutty—mashed into boiled turnips takes the edge off their mild bitterness.

WINTER SQUASH: Try any one of the heirloom varieties, either boiled or baked, and simply season with salt before smashing with a fork to a chunky texture.

HERBES DE PROVENCE ROAST

with Fig-Red Onion Marmalade

The lean and slender cut called eye round doesn't get the attention of other roasts, and that's a shame. It is mild in flavor, fairly tender, has a uniform shape that slices easily into lovely round servings, and costs far less than others. I lavished this eye round roast with a dry rub of salt and the dried herb blend called Herbes de Provence (a varying combination of basil, rosemary, sage, thyme, savory, marjoram, fennel seeds, and lavender), and let it cure in the refrigerator overnight. Seared on the stovetop before a low-heat roasting, this once humble roast becomes outstanding. It shines here with the accompanying Fig-Red Onion Marmalade (recipe follows). I serve with celery root-potato purée (Mashed Potato Mix Up, page 214).

Makes 6 servings with leftovers

....

2 TABLESPOONS HERBES DE PROVENCE

1 (2½- TO 3-POUND) EYE ROUND ROAST

4 TABLESPOONS EXTRA-VIRGIN OLIVE OIL, DIVIDED

KOSHER SALT

Crush the Herbes de Provence in a mortar and pestle or in a spice grinder. Put the roast onto a piece of aluminum foil to fit, rub it with 1 tablespoon of the olive oil and season it liberally with the kosher salt. Rub the Herbes de Provence all over to coat it evenly. Wrap the roast in the aluminum foil and refrigerate for 12 to 48 hours.

Preheat the oven to 275°F and unwrap the roast. Heat the remaining 3 tablespoons oil in a small roasting pan, with the rack set aside, on the stovetop over medium-high heat. Sear the roast for 2 minutes per side, holding it with tongs to brown it on all sides for a total of 8 minutes. Reduce the heat to medium if the oil begins to smoke too heavily.

Lift the roast, insert the rack, and put the roast on the rack. Pour ½ cup of water into the pan to release the browned bits while it bakes.

Roast until an internal read thermometer registers 115°F, 40 to 45 minutes. Remove the roast if you like it very rare, or check the temperature every 10 minutes and remove it as soon as the center of the roast reaches 120°F for rare or 125°F for medium rare (Timetable for Roasting, page 201). Transfer the roast to a cutting board, tent it with aluminum foil, and let it rest for at least 15 minutes to reach its final serving temperature. Use a sharp knife to slice it ¼ inch thick. Drizzle it with any pan juices and serve it with the Fig-Red Onion Marmalade, if using.

CONTINUES ▶

VARIATION: ROAST BEEF BRUSCHETTA

Top sliced and toasted ciabatta bread or baguettes with a sliver of the roast beef, a spoonful of the fig-onion marmalade, and a few crumbles of blue cheese and warm it in a low (250°F) oven.

MORE CHOICE CUTS:

Sirloin tip roast, aka round tip roast, is another lean and fairly tender roast that's also economical.

Tenderloin, when you're in the mood for a splurge, loves this herbal treatment and slow roasting.

FIG-RED ONION MARMALADE

Based on a recipe I learned to make at the Herbfarm, this quick-cooked condiment is perfect with any sliced roast, hot or cold. Or, use it to make memorable roast beef and Fontina panini or the bruschetta appetizer described in the variation above.

Makes 2 cups

....

1 TABLESPOON EXTRA-VIRGIN OLIVE OIL

2 RED ONIONS, THINLY SLICED

2 OUNCES DRIED FIGS, STEMMED AND COARSELY
    CHOPPED (ABOUT 7)

¼ CUP RED WINE

1 TABLESPOON SUGAR

1 TABLESPOON RED WINE VINEGAR

½ TEASPOON CRUSHED HERBES DE PROVENCE

½ TEASPOON SALT

⅛ TEASPOON BLACK PEPPER

Heat the oil in a large saucepan over medium heat. Add the onions and cook, stirring occasionally, until they turn translucent, about 3 minutes. Reduce the heat to low, add the figs, wine, and sugar, and simmer undisturbed until the onions are very limp and the liquid is syrupy, about 20 minutes. Stir in the vinegar, Herbes de Provence, salt, and pepper. Cover the pan and cook until the onions are very tender, 8 to 10 minutes. Taste for vinegar so that it has a balance of tart and sweet, and serve it warm or at room temperature. (You can make it up to 2 days ahead. Store covered in the refrigerator and bring it to room temperature or warm it over low heat or in the microwave before serving.)

DUTCH OVEN BARBECUE

For anyone without a smoker or the patience to spoon-feed woodchips to a grill, the oven is the answer for barbecued beef. Surrounded by heat, tough roasts slow cook to tenderness in their own juices. I use smoked sea salt and paprika in this dry rub. For a more pronounced smokiness, add one to two teaspoons of liquid smoke (Note, page 254). Serve this meat shredded with Tangy Barbecue Sauce (page 223) or slice it thin and pile it on dark rye with caramelized onions and cheddar cheese for a formidable grilled sandwich.

Makes 6 servings with leftovers

....

2 TEASPOONS SMOKED SEA SALT OR KOSHER SALT

1 TEASPOON SMOKED PAPRIKA, SUCH AS PIMENTÓN DE LA VERA (SOURCES, PAGE 272)

1 TEASPOON GROUND CUMIN

¼ TEASPOON BLACK PEPPER

⅛ TEASPOON CAYENNE

1 (2½- TO 3-POUND) CHUCK ROAST

BARBECUE SAUCE (PAGE 223), FOR SERVING

Combine the salt, paprika, cumin, pepper, and cayenne in a small bowl and mix well. Rub the salt mixture all over the roast, put it in a plastic bag or covered baking dish, and refrigerate for at least 12 hours and up to 3 days.

Preheat the oven to 200°F. Roast covered until you can pry the meat apart easily with a fork and an internal-read thermometer registers at least 180°F, 5½ to 6 hours. When the meat is cool enough to handle, slice it or shred it, discarding any fat or bone, before serving with some of the accumulated broth.

MOJO BEEF

with Black Beans and Rice (*Moros y Cristianos*)

Mojo (*mo-ho*) is a sauce of garlic and bitter orange that hails from Cuba. To mimic those flavors, I mix lime juice and orange juice with loads of garlic and jalapeños to make a great wet rub and marinade for the tough shoulder cuts like arm roast. Slow-roasted in the oven, the jalapeños and garlic mellow into the background while the meat turns fall-apart tender.

For a big meal, I accompany the beef with the stovetop Black Beans and Rice (recipe follows), a side dish Cubans call *moros y cristianos*. Shredded while it's still warm, and folded into warmed flour tortillas with diced avocado and sour cream, this beef also makes excellent burritos.

Makes 6 servings with leftovers

....

8 GARLIC CLOVES, MINCED

3 JALAPEÑOS, SEEDED AND FINELY CHOPPED

2 TABLESPOONS PACKED LIGHT BROWN SUGAR

1½ TEASPOONS GROUND CUMIN

1 TABLESPOON KOSHER SALT

¼ CUP ORANGE JUICE

¼ CUP FRESH LIME JUICE

2 TABLESPOONS EXTRA-VIRGIN OLIVE OIL

1 (3½- TO 4-POUND) CHUCK ROAST, BONE-IN
    OR BONELESS

½ CUP LIGHTLY PACKED CHOPPED FRESH
    CILANTRO

To make the rub, combine the garlic, jalapeños, brown sugar, cumin, and kosher salt in a small bowl and mix well. Add the orange juice, lime juice, and olive oil and stir until blended. Put the beef in a glass or ceramic baking dish that holds it snugly and pour the wet rub over it. Turn the roast over to coat it completely. Cover the baking dish and marinate for 6 to 12 hours in the refrigerator, turning it once.

Preheat the oven to 250°F. Roast uncovered until the meat shreds readily with a fork and an internal read thermometer registers 180°F, 3 to 3½ hours. Separate the meat along the natural seams, trimming off the fat, and slice it thinly or shred. Stir the cilantro into the pan juices and pour them over the meat to keep it moist.

Alternatively, you can use a smoker to hot-smoke this roast at 225°F to 250°F with a drip pan underneath to capture all the juices and recombine them with the sliced or shredded meat for serving.

> ### MORE CHOICE CUTS:
> Cross-rib roast and other roasts from the chuck are usually relegated to the braising pot. With this slow-roasting method, these tough cuts cook in their own juices until tender.
>
> Brisket is another tough cut that needs low heat, either liquid or dry, to break it down. Once it does, its long meat fibers are easy to shred and wonderfully lean.

BLACK BEANS AND RICE (*Moros y Cristianos*)

If using dried beans, you'll need to cook them in advance.

Makes 6 servings

....

1 TABLESPOON VEGETABLE OIL

1 MEDIUM ONION, CHOPPED

1½ CUPS LONG-GRAIN WHITE RICE

3 CUPS LOW-SODIUM CHICKEN STOCK OR WATER

1½ TEASPOONS GROUND CUMIN

1 TEASPOON CRUSHED DRIED OREGANO

½ TEASPOON SALT

1 BAY LEAF

2 CUPS COOKED BLACK BEANS OR 1 (14-OUNCE) CAN BLACK BEANS,
    DRAINED AND RINSED

Heat the oil in a large saucepan over medium heat. Add the onion and cook until it turns translucent, about 3 minutes. Add the rice and stir to coat the grains with the oil. Cook stirring occasionally, until they smell toasted and most of the grains turn golden, about 5 minutes. Add the stock, cumin, oregano, salt, and bay leaf. Cover and reduce the heat to low. Simmer until the rice is tender, 20 to 25 minutes. Add the beans and stir to warm them over low heat. Discard the bay leaf and taste for salt before serving.

COFFEE BEAN-CHILE RUBBED SIRLOIN ROAST

with Cowboy Beans

Coffee and chile are a dynamic duo in a dry rub for a large roast. This recipe offers a marvelous example of using your grill to roast a large piece of meat you then sear—a technique called reverse searing (page 221). As long as you're equipped with a timer and a dependable meat thermometer, this method only looks impressive. Top sirloin roast is an exceptional lean roast with great character for grill-roasting. Slices of this roast served alongside a helping of Cowboy Beans (recipe follows) is like a meal straight off the chuck wagon on the open range.

Makes 6 servings with leftovers

....

¼ CUP FINELY GROUND DARK-ROASTED COFFEE
  BEANS
2 TABLESPOONS ANCHO CHILE POWDER OR OTHER
  PURE CHILE POWDER (SOURCES, PAGE 272)
¼ CUP PACKED LIGHT BROWN SUGAR
2 TABLESPOONS KOSHER SALT
1 TEASPOON BLACK PEPPER
1 (3- TO 3½-POUND) TOP SIRLOIN ROAST
2 TABLESPOONS VEGETABLE OIL

Mix the coffee, chile powder, brown sugar, kosher salt, and pepper in a small bowl. Pat the roast dry, rub it with the oil, and massage the spice mixture all over to coat it thickly. (Store any excess rub in an airtight container for a hamburger or steak.) Let it stand at room temperature for 1 hour or in the refrigerator for up to 24 hours, removing it 1 hour in advance of cooking.

Prepare a charcoal or gas grill for indirect cooking by turning on the flames or building up the coals only on one side of the grill for medium heat (325° to 375°F). Scrape the grate clean and oil it lightly. Put the roast on the rack over the coolest part of the grill, close the cover, and cook until an internal read thermometer registers 115°F for rare or 120°F for medium rare, about 40 minutes. (These temperatures are 5°F lower than usual because the roast will cook further during the searing stage. Alternatively, you can complete cooking at this temperature, skip-

ping the sear, according to the Timetable for Roasting, page 201). Transfer the roast to a platter.

If using a gas grill, turn it up to high and when the heat reaches 425°F to 475°F, or so hot that you can only hold your hand 4 inches above it for less than 5 seconds, place the roast back on the grill. Sear it for 3 to 4 minutes on each side, turning it with tongs when the coffee rub looks charred (it's not) and an internal-read thermometer reaches 125°F for medium rare.

If using a charcoal grill, you can either fire up the coals by replenishing them with hot coals from a chimney lighter (the roast will be fine while it waits for up to 1 hour) or bring it indoors and sear it in a dry, preheated skillet over medium-high heat for 3 to 4 minutes per side. Let the roast rest on a cutting board for at least 20 minutes to finish cooking and slice into ½-inch-thick slices to serve with the Cowboy Beans, if desired.

COWBOY BEANS

When you serve these singular beans with the Coffee Bean-Chile Rubbed Sirloin Roast, the ham hock, which lends another dimension of flavors, is optional. If using dried beans, you'll need to soak, drain, rinse, and cook them in advance.

Makes 6 servings with leftovers

....

1 TABLESPOON VEGETABLE OIL

1 MEDIUM ONION, CHOPPED

4 GARLIC CLOVES, MINCED

2 TEASPOONS GROUND CUMIN

4 CUPS COOKED PINTO BEANS OR 2 (14-OUNCE) CANNED PINTO BEANS, BOTH DRAINED AND RINSED

1 (8-OUNCE) SMOKED HAM HOCK, OPTIONAL

1 CUP LOW-SALT BEEF STOCK (SHORT ORDER STOCK, PAGE 226; ROASTED BEEF STOCK, PAGE 228) OR WATER

½ CUP STRONG BREWED COFFEE

1 CUP BARBECUE SAUCE (PAGE 223)

Heat the oil in a Dutch oven or large heavy-bottomed saucepan over medium-high heat. When it shimmers, add the onion and cook until it turns translucent, about 3 minutes. Add the garlic and cumin and cook, stirring, until fragrant. Add the beans, ham hock, if using, stock, coffee, and barbecue sauce and bring the liquid to a simmer. Cook until the sauce is as thick as gravy, 25 to 30 minutes. Taste for seasoning. The salt from the ham hock, if using, and the barbecue sauce should provide all the salt the beans need.

THE REVERSE SEAR

In this unorthodox method, the beef cooks slowly until it is nearly done, and then gets seared, either on a blazing grill or on scalding-hot pan on the stovetop. It's the reverse order of the typical method of browning first and then cooking meat to doneness. And it really works! (Coffee Bean-Chile Rubbed Sirloin Roast, page 220, is a model to follow for combining grill-roasting with the reverse sear.)

The results are stunning: the meat cooks to a rosy pink medium rare all the way to its crusty edge. For anyone who adores medium rare beef and resents the band of well-done meat along the outer edge, I recommend adopting this technique immediately. Granted, it requires even more attentiveness to catch the roast while it's still below the final desired cooking temperature, but with a reliable thermometer, it's a snap.

The reverse sear adapts to steaks, too: In a preheated 300°F oven, bake the steaks (at least 1 inch thick) to an internal temperature of 95°F. Heat a large skillet over high heat, with or without a tablespoon of vegetable oil, until it smokes. Put the steaks in the skillet and sear for two to three minutes per side until walnut brown and an instant-read thermometer registers 125°F for medium rare.

SMOKED BRISKET

with Tangy Barbecue Sauce

Up the road from my house is a laundromat-car wash where Sherri Currie sells great slow-smoked barbecue sandwiches just like she remembers from her native Texas. I crave her brisket on a regular basis, so it's a lucky thing that she agreed to tutor me in the fine art of barbecue, Texas style.

Sherri massages the meat with a mustard rub then waits for 2 days to let it all soak in. Once the smoker stuffed with cherry wood (applewood and hickory are good and mild, too) reaches 220°F, in goes the beef until it gets that pretty pink smoke ring running one-quarter inch into the meat. She swaddles the beef in aluminum foil to create a moist environment and slow roasts it to a perfect finish.

It all starts with a great piece of brisket, the classic for beef barbecue—on this, there is no argument. The rub, type of smoke, and amount of smoking time are up for debate. The real secret ingredient for all the championship-worthy barbecued briskets is the same: time. You need to plan for about six hours of smoking, plus four or five additional hours for slow-roasting. It's a two-stage method for practical purposes, but you can keep on smoking, if you like. (On the other hand, if you crave barbecue but don't have the smoker or the inclination to improvise one, try the Dutch Oven Barbecue, page 217.) Serve the beef with Tangy Barbecue Sauce (recipe follows), dill pickles, and heaps of your favorite potato salad. Shave the leftovers with a sharp slicing knife for barbecue beef sandwiches on Whole-Wheat Hamburger Buns (page 72).

Makes 8 servings with leftovers

½ CUP PREPARED YELLOW MUSTARD

1 TABLESPOON SWEET OR HOT PAPRIKA

1 TABLESPOON KOSHER SALT

1 TEASPOON BLACK PEPPER

½ TEASPOON CAYENNE

1 (7- TO 10-POUND) WHOLE BEEF BRISKET

Mix the mustard, paprika, kosher salt, pepper, and cayenne in a small bowl until well blended. Put the brisket in a shallow pan. Spread the rub all over the brisket with a rubber spatula to coat it like frosting. Refrigerate the brisket uncovered for 24 to 48 hours.

Prepare a smoker for hot-smoking (200° to 225°F). Alternatively, prepare a charcoal grill for low indirect heat or a gas grill fitted with a smoker box and a drip pan filled with 2 inches of water underneath the grate opposite the heat source. If using wood chips, soak them for about 15 minutes before adding them. Scrape the grate clean and oil it lightly before placing the brisket on the coolest side of the grill with the fat cap side up. Close the lid and smoke for about 6 hours. Monitor the temperatures and smoke levels, and replenish the wood chips as necessary for your type of smoker. When the brisket is smoked to your liking, wrap it securely in aluminum foil, put it on a baking sheet, and bake it in a 250°F oven until you can pry the meat apart readily with a fork and an instant-read thermometer registers 190° to 200°F, an additional 4 to 5 hours more—for a total of roughly 11 hours. Alternatively, you can continue smoking the brisket to doneness in 14 to 16 hours.

To serve, take a peek at the lean underside to see which way the grain is running or start cutting and change direction if need be. Slice it thin against the grain and serve with the barbecue sauce, if desired.

TANGY BARBECUE SAUCE

This is Sherri Currie's recipe for a barbecue sauce that slants toward the vinegary side. It has a low spice level, like burning embers on a dying fire—just the way I like it.

Makes 1½ cups

....

½ CUP KETCHUP (PAGE 73)

½ CUP APPLE CIDER VINEGAR

½ CUP STRONG BREWED COFFEE

¼ CUP WORCESTERSHIRE SAUCE

3 TABLESPOONS PACKED LIGHT BROWN SUGAR

1 TABLESPOON GRATED ONION

4 GARLIC CLOVES, MINCED

1 TABLESPOON CHILE POWDER

1 TEASPOON SMOKED PAPRIKA, SUCH AS PIMENTÓN DE LA VERA (SOURCES, PAGE 272)

¼ TEASPOON CAYENNE

Whisk the ketchup, vinegar, coffee, Worcestershire sauce, brown sugar, onion, garlic, chile powder, paprika, and cayenne in a small saucepan until smooth. Bring it to a boil over medium-high heat then reduce the heat to low. Simmer and cook, stirring occasionally, for 1 hour until it is thick and the flavors are well-balanced. Cool to room temperature before serving.

A FRENCH DIP

A hot sandwich is a worthy second life for any leftover roast beef. Make a jus by simmering 1½ cups of low-sodium, best-quality beef stock in a small saucepan over medium heat with ½ teaspoon prepared horseradish, 1 peeled garlic clove, and 1 bay leaf for 15 minutes. To give it some body, whisk in 2 Frozen Stock Cubes (page 230) or demi-glace, if you like. Pluck out the garlic and bay leaf. For each sandwich, slice, butter, and toast 6-inch long sections of baguettes or submarine rolls. Dip 3 to 4 slices of leftover roast beef into the jus to warm and re-moisten then layer them on the bread. Slice in half and serve with bowls of the warm jus on the side for dipping.

PURE TO THE BONE

By nature, I'm thrifty in the kitchen. The most satisfying meal I cook is one I produce from what I find in the produce bin, plus the odd cup of cooked beans, and herbs about to wither. I hate to see any food go to waste, and I regularly paw through my refrigerator to inspire our supper. Once I witnessed the quantity of good bones that comes from butchering a single carcass—and realized that the vast majority goes to dogs—I could no longer ignore all of those untapped resources. I started making stock again on a regular basis, and now, whenever my stockpiles run low, I call my butcher and ask him to save me a box of bones. He seems bemused that I never seem to have enough.

Good bones are one of the most valuable parts of a cow. Locked within them are the ingredients for some of the most restorative meals conjured from practically nothing. The collagen, marrow, and bits of meat within and around the bones gets freed by heat, water, and time.

So much depends on good stock, from soups and stews to bony braises. All of the recipes in this chapter are based on the best beef stock, which comes from your own stockpot. The chapter begins with a series of recipes for making stock at home. It's a bit of a lobbying campaign, I admit, to win you over to the glories of homemade stock through recipes like Short Order Stock (page 226), 60-Minute Pressure Cooker Beef Stock variation (page 227), and a classic Roasted Beef Stock (page 228). It goes to the extremes with Crystal Clear Consommé (page 231) and homemade Frozen Stock Cubes (page 230) because these are

some of the most important assets a cook can have. (And for those concerned with the source and quality of their beef, consider that canned stock consists largely of processed and artificial ingredients.)

The reward for investing in healthful and flavorful stocks is standout soups, such as Creamy Wild Mushroom-Rice Soup (page 235) and Home-Style French Onion Soup (page 238). Building on the complexity that comes from excellent stock, these soups simmer just long enough to cook the vegetables or the meats, if any.

To highlight the value and versatility of bones, this chapter also includes recipes for meaty bones. Short ribs, shanks, and oxtails are typically included with other braises, like pot roast and brisket (chapter 5, page 100). The muscle meats clinging to those bones do require slow simmering, but I find that they also mandate additional special treatment, especially defatting and sometimes deboning. Ginger-Glazed Short Ribs (page 244) and Short Ribs Rendang (page 241) are two braises that cook the beef on the bone until it is slicked with sauce. For Boneless Oxtail and Buckwheat Crêpe Purses (page 248), the mouthwatering meat is plucked from bones to fill buckwheat crêpes for an elegant appetizer or main dish. In every case, I take pains to remove as much of the fat as possible, but the fats *are* part of the experience of enjoying these meats.

The recipes in this chapter range from peasant-style suppers to dinner party showstoppers, yet they are undemanding, patient, and practical. All of them come from the goodness of bones.

Choice Bone Cuts

While most beef today is sold boneless, these cuts are defined by their bone. Some bones are harder to come by than others, so put in a request to the butcher where you buy your meat to save your favorites. Reserve them in your freezer well-wrapped in plastic, aluminum foil, or resealable plastic bags, as I do, for a day when you have time for bringing out their potential.

BACK RIBS are the section of the rib cage next to the rib-eye muscle. Often this section of ribs is removed to make a rib-eye roast. Some butchers tie the ribs back onto the rib roast so they're easily removed. The meat on back ribs is generally leaner than short ribs.

KNUCKLE BONES are the joints of the leg, what we would consider the knee. These bones are typically devoid of meat, but very useful for making collagen-rich beef stock, especially in combination with marrow bones.

MARROW BONES come from the fore and hind shank but are stripped of the exterior meat. They are often cut into four to five-inch sections and are excellent stock-making bones. The melt-in-your mouth marrow is a delicacy when roasted, and has many uses, including dabbing on a steak, smashing with butter to make marrow butter, or spreading on toast sprinkled with sea salt for an appetizer.

OXTAIL, the upper part of the tail, is a chain of progressively smaller vertebral bones with morsels of meat. Typically, the vertebrae are separated by a butcher or, if purchased intact, can be cut between the bones with a sharp cleaver. The value of oxtail is the collagen released from the bones when cooked slowly in liquid, which makes unbeatably good stock for soups and stews. Oxtails are also served braised, and because prizing off the meat takes a little bit of work, somewhat like picking crab, I prefer to pull the meat off the bone before serving it in soups and stews. A single oxtail weighs approximately two pounds and yields about one cup of lean meat.

SHANK BONES are the fore and hind legs, typically cut into cross-sections, and sometimes called soup bones. The bone is circular and is surrounded by meat that is lean, but tough and sinewy. Like short ribs and oxtail, shank bones become tender with long, slow cooking, making them useful for stock-making as well as for soups and stews.

SHORT RIBS are flat, wide bones connected by layers of meat and fat cut from the chuck, ribs, and plate sections. They may be cut single-bone English-style, thin-cut flanken-style, and are sometimes found boneless. They can be used interchangeably with any cut you'd use for a soup or a stew, and they need long, slow cooking until the meat falls off the bone. You can serve them on the bone, or debone, defat, and cut or shred the meat.

SHORT ORDER STOCK

In my annual beef order, I often get short ribs that aren't quite meaty enough to braise for dinner. I treasure them for making the best stock money can't buy. Meaty bones like these turn water into stock in just ninety minutes—instead of six to eight hours for Roasted Beef Stock (page 228). Make it in a stockpot on the stove, in a slow cooker with at least a six-quart capacity, or use the variation to make it in a pressure cooker in an hour.

You'll get enough stock to make any of the soups in this chapter or the braises and stews in chapter 5. You also get a bit of meat, too, if you choose to use it. Use the stock immediately or refrigerate it for one week, and freeze what you don't need for up to six months.

Makes 10 to 11 cups

....

5 TO 6 POUNDS BEEF SHORT RIBS

½ TEASPOON KOSHER SALT

1 MEDIUM ONION, CHOPPED

3 MEDIUM CARROTS, CHOPPED

2 CELERY STALKS, CHOPPED

1 TABLESPOON TOMATO PASTE

¼ TEASPOON WHOLE PEPPERCORNS

1 TEASPOON FRESH THYME OR ¼ TEASPOON
    DRIED

1 BAY LEAF

Trim any thick layers of exterior fat from the short ribs (page 51) and, if necessary, cut between the ribs to expose more surface area. Rub the ribs with the kosher salt, and put them in a large stockpot. Add the onion, carrots, celery, tomato paste, peppercorns, thyme, and bay leaf. Pour 3 quarts cool water over the bones, enough to cover them by about 3 inches.

Bring the water to a boil over medium-high heat. Use a slotted spoon or ladle to skim the foam and particles that rise to the surface. Reduce the heat to low and adjust it as necessary to maintain a slow, steady stream of small bubbles for 1½ to 2 hours. The longer the stock simmers, the stronger it will be.

Use tongs to transfer the short ribs into a bowl and set them aside to cool if you're reserving them for the meat. Strain the stock through a fine-meshed strainer into a 3-quart container and discard the vegetables. If you intend to use the stock immediately, leave it undisturbed for 10 minutes then defat by ladling off and discarding any yellowish liquid from the surface. If you are saving your stock for the next day or storing it for future use, place the stock uncovered in the refrigerator to chill at least 6 hours until the fat congeals into a thin layer on top. Use a spoon to lift off the fat and discard it. Pour the stock into 1-pint storage containers and store in the refrigerator for 1 week or in the freezer for up to 6 months.

When the short ribs are cool enough to handle, trim the meat from the bones, discarding all the bones and excess fat. Chop or shred the meat while it's still warm, drizzle it with a few tablespoons of stock to keep it moist, and use it within 3 days.

VARIATION: 60-MINUTE PRESSURE COOKER BEEF STOCK

I thank Lorna Sass's excellent guide *Pressure Perfect* for leading me to this method. It produces a smaller quantity because you can't fill the pressure cooker more than two-thirds full. You'll end up with 8 cups, enough for all of the soup recipes in this chapter and plenty for pot roast or stew.

Pressure cooking tends to wash out flavors, so use the same quantity of vegetables, herbs, and spices for half the quantity of short ribs (2½ to 3 pounds) and put them in a 6-quart or larger pressure cooker. Add 2 quarts of cool water just to cover the ribs, secure the lid, and bring it to high pressure over high heat. Adjust the heat to maintain high pressure for exactly 60 minutes. Let the pressure come down naturally or run the whole pot under cool water to quick release the pressure. Open the lid with care and lean away from the steam. Strain, defat, chill, and store the stock as directed in the main recipe above. Pull the meat from the bones while still warm and use it within 3 days.

MORE CHOICE CUTS:

Shank and oxtails with a similar ratio of meat and bone also make excellent stock.

Brisket and any chuck roast also makes exceptionally good beef stock, but will take 3 to 3½ hours of simmering to become tender. Trim these cuts well in advance to reduce the amount of defatting you'll need to do and be sure to shred or chop the meat to use in soups, sandwiches, or for tacos.

ROASTED BEEF STOCK

Homemade stock may take time, but your investment in water and low-cost ingredients will pay you back many times over. With hours of slow simmering and little work on your part, you'll be rewarded with a multi-purpose stock—whether you want a truly spectacular Grassfed Pot Roast with Parsnips, Carrots, and Fingerlings (page 104) or Home-Style French Onion Soup (page 238). This recipe is also the starting point for making Frozen Stock Cubes (page 230) to use in place of bouillon cubes and Crystal Clear Consommé (page 231), a soup all its own or an extra-rich stock for soup making.

Excellent stock comes from roasting the bones and vegetables in a hot oven and then simmering them all in a stockpot long enough to extract every bit of their flavor. The best soup bones are the knuckles from the fore and hind shanks, which are stripped of the meat, but loaded with the collagen that gives the stock its gelatinous body. Use them in combination with meatier options, such as shank, oxtails, or rib bones. I salt the bones lightly, but the stock does not taste salted. I also use the green tops of leeks and parsley stems when I have them on hand, but I don't go out of my way to include them.

It's common to simmer this stock on the stovetop, but occasionally I put the stockpot in a 200°F oven and leave the stock to do its work overnight. If I strain it and let it cool during the workday, I come home to ready-to-use liquid gold. This recipe makes enough to use for soup now (or refrigerate and use within a week) and some to stash in the freezer for up to six months.

Makes 14 to 15 cups

....

6 TO 7 POUNDS BEEF BONES, INCLUDING SOME
    MEATY BONES, SUCH AS SHANK, OXTAIL,
    SHORT RIBS, OR BACK RIBS
2 TABLESPOONS VEGETABLE OIL
1 TEASPOON KOSHER SALT
2 LARGE ONIONS, CHOPPED
3 LARGE CARROTS, CHOPPED
2 CELERY STALKS, CHOPPED
1 HEAPING TABLESPOON TOMATO PASTE
1 HEAD GARLIC, OUTER PAPERY SKIN REMOVED
    AND TOP ⅓ CUT OFF TO EXPOSE THE CLOVES
1 TEASPOON CRACKED BLACK PEPPERCORNS
1 TEASPOON FRESH THYME OR ¼ TEASPOON
    DRIED
2 BAY LEAVES

Preheat the oven to 425°F. Rub the bones all over with the oil and sprinkle them with the kosher salt. Arrange them in a single layer in a large metal roasting pan or on a rimmed baking sheet. (If the pan is smaller than 11 x 17 inches, you may need to use two.) Roast the bones for 30 minutes. You'll hear them sizzle and the kitchen will smell like roasting meat, which you'll taste later in the stock. Turn the bones and add the onions, carrots, celery, and the tomato paste to the pan. Continue roasting for 15 to 20 minutes more. The bones will be as dark brown as coffee grounds on their ends, the vegetables will be browned in spots, and the tomato paste will be brick colored.

Use tongs to transfer the bones into your largest stockpot, at least 8 quarts, and scoop in the vegetables using a slotted spoon. Pour in 4 quarts cool water.

Discard any excess fat from the roasting pan, if necessary, and add 2 cups of water. Use a wooden spoon or heat-proof spatula to scrape up all of the browned bits off the roasting pan and add all of this liquid into the stockpot to cover the bones completely. Add the garlic, peppercorns, thyme, and bay leaves.

Set the stockpot over medium-high heat and bring it to a simmer. Use the slotted spoon to skim any foam from the surface and discard it. Reduce the heat to low and simmer gently for at least 6 hours and up to 18 if you have the time. The liquid should look like it's percolating with small bubbles rising to the surface. The longer it simmers, the more concentrated the flavors will be. (Alternatively, put the stockpot, uncovered, into a preheated 200°F oven for at least 6 and up to 18 hours.)

Strain the stock through a fine-meshed strainer into a 4-quart container. If using the stock immediately, leave the stock undisturbed for about 10 minutes then defat it by ladling off and discarding any yellowish liquid from the surface.

If saving your stock for the next day or storing it for future use, cool the pot of stock in a sinkful of cold water for 30 minutes. Then put it uncovered in the refrigerator to chill for at least 6 hours until the fat congeals into a thin layer on top. Use a spoon to lift off and discard the fat. Once chilled, your stock will be wonderfully gelatinous, and you may want to warm it until it becomes pourable. Distribute the stock into 1- or 2-quart containers for storage in the refrigerator for up to 1 week or freezer for up to 6 months.

FROZEN STOCK CUBES, READY-TO-USE

Bouillon is a convenience that's hard to live without, but the list of ingredients in commercial brands contains items I like to avoid. My alternative is to make a homemade beef concentrate from stock to freeze in ice cube trays and safeguard in the freezer.

The method of radically reducing a beef stock until thick and glossy is the same used for making a meat glaze or demi-glace. It can be painful to watch more than half of your giant pot of stock evaporate away, but what is really happening is a distillation of all its flavors. It saves storage space and you can reconstitute the stock with water at your convenience.

Bring four cups of your homemade, low-salt beef stock, such as Roasted Beef Stock (page 228) or Short Order Beef Stock (page 226) to a boil over high heat in a small saucepan. Lower the heat to medium-low so that bubbles break continuously over most of the surface. Skim the surface whenever any foam appears. Let the stock reduce to one cup, which will take about two hours. It will be glossy and the color of toasted walnuts. You can best gauge the evaporation rate by watching the surface level fall three-quarters below the original fill line that cooks onto the side of the pan.

When this stock chills, it becomes aspic, a Jello-O-like solid thanks to the collagen in the beef bones. Store the stock in the refrigerator for up to two weeks and steal a heaping spoonful whenever you want to make a pan sauce or enrich a soup, a pot of beans, or rice pilaf. For longer storage, pour one tablespoon of the warm concentrate into each slot in an ice cube tray and freeze for two hours. You should have about sixteen. Pop the bouillon cubes out of the trays and into plastic storage bags for easy retrieval from the freezer for up to six months.

CRYSTAL CLEAR CONSOMMÉ

This pure amber-colored soup is a thing of beauty that never should have gone out of style. Free of fat and lush in body, consommé is especially valuable for making soups that depend on exceptional stock, like Pho (page 237) and Tortilla Soup (page 240). You may also flavor the consommé with a handful of wild mushrooms, fresh herbs, shaved truffles, or baby vegetables. For more substance, add a few of the Spelt Dumplings (page 243), Beef Ravioli (page 96), or Scorched Croutons (page 168).

For food science geeks, the clarification process is a wonder. The convection action swirls the stock through a purée of ground beef and egg whites. When they congeal into what's called a raft, they strain out any particles while concentrating and harmonizing its flavors into one perfect broth.

Makes 7 to 8 cups

....

8 OUNCES GROUND BEEF, 85 TO 90 PERCENT LEAN

1 LEEK, WHITE PART ONLY, FINELY CHOPPED

2 BAY LEAVES

¼ CUP LIGHTLY PACKED CHOPPED FRESH PARSLEY

3 EGG WHITES

2 QUARTS LOW-SALT BEEF STOCK (SHORT ORDER STOCK, PAGE 226; ROASTED BEEF STOCK, PAGE 228), CHILLED

1 TEASPOON SALT

Purée the ground beef, leek, bay leaves, and parsley in a food processor until very finely ground. Whisk the egg whites in a stockpot until frothy. Add the ground beef mixture, stock, and salt and stir until well blended, using the spoon to push the ground beef mixture against the sides of the pot to break it up completely.

Place the pot over medium heat and stir continuously as it comes to a simmer. Stop stirring, reduce the heat to low, and maintain a slow, steady simmer. The liquid will look disastrous and cloudy at first, but within 15 minutes, the egg whites will bind the ground beef mixture and it will all clump together into what's called a raft that floats neatly on the surface. Use a spoon to gently push some of the solid mass aside at the edge of the pot to make an opening wide enough to fit a ladle through it. This will serve as an open pool where you can monitor the simmering and skim as needed. Simmer, skimming 2 to 3 times, for 1 to 1½ hours. Taste for salt.

Strain the consommé through a fine-meshed strainer lined with cheesecloth or a damp cloth into a clean saucepan by ladling it out through the hole in the raft. The consommé will be clearest if you can keep the raft intact until you've transferred all the stock. Then, discard the raft. The consommé is ready to use right away or to store in the refrigerator for 1 week or in the freezer for up to 6 months.

NEW ENGLAND SIMMERED SUPPER

with Whole-Grain Mustard

All over the world, cooks make magical soups by combining fresh water with inexpensive meats, humble vegetables, and ample time. In my native Massachusetts, it's called New England Boiled Dinner, but, as a reminder never to let the pot boil, I think of it as "simmered supper." On inclement-weather weekends, I can accomplish all my household projects while making several days' meals in a single pot: one hearty meal of falling-apart beef and tender vegetables to eat out of wide soup bowls with Whole-Grain Mustard (recipe follows and is easier than you think) and a garlicky stock appropriate for a substantial soup like Pho (page 237), plus leftovers.

Bone-in cuts are best, but many beef cuts can bring life to a plain old pot of water. My fall-back is the 7-bone chuck roast. If all you have is bone-less chuck roast, meaty soup bones like short ribs and shanks are a great supplement. The vegetables, too, are versatile, and though I especially love rutabaga and celery root, I'll add whatever root vegetables I have on hand.

I've refined this recipe over time under the influence of Judy Rodger's pot au feu recipe in *The Zuni Café Cookbook*. When I serve this to company—delightfully old-fashioned and unexpected—I boil Brussels sprouts or chunks of cabbage in a separate pot of salted water so they don't sully the broth. I serve the meat and vegetables arranged on my biggest platter and set the table with ample crusty bread for a generous and frugal feast.

Makes 6 servings with leftovers

....

1 (3½- TO 4-POUND) BONE-IN CHUCK ROAST

1 HEAD GARLIC, OUTER PAPERY SKIN REMOVED AND TOP ⅓ CUT OFF TO EXPOSE CLOVES

2 TEASPOONS FRESH THYME OR ½ TEASPOON DRIED

2 BAY LEAVES

4 WHOLE CLOVES

1 MEDIUM ONION, PEELED AND CUT IN HALF

1 TABLESPOON SALT

½ TEASPOON BLACK PEPPER

4 MEDIUM CARROTS, TRIMMED, PEELED, HALVED LENGTHWISE AND CROSSWISE

1 LARGE RUTABAGA OR TURNIP, PEELED AND CUT INTO 1-INCH CHUNKS

1 MEDIUM CELERY ROOT, PEELED AND CUT INTO 1-INCH CHUNKS

2 LEEKS, WHITE PARTS ONLY, SPLIT LENGTHWISE AND THOROUGHLY RINSED

COARSE SEA SALT, FOR SERVING

Fill a large stockpot with 3 quarts of cool water. Add the beef, garlic, thyme, and bay leaves. Bring it to a boil over medium heat.

Meanwhile, heat a dry, small skillet over high heat. Stick the whole cloves into the rounded sides of the onion and put the halves cut side down onto the skillet. Let the onion cook undisturbed, about 5 minutes until blackened to deepen the flavors of the stock. Add it to the pot along with the salt and pepper.

When the water comes to a boil, reduce the heat to low and simmer. With a slotted spoon, skim and discard any foam that rises to the top. Adjust the heat so that the liquid is percolating with small bubbles lazily rising to the surface. Simmer slowly, uncovered, for 2 hours.

Skim again and taste the stock for salt and pepper. It should be as flavorful as a good soup. Add the carrots, rutabaga, celery root, and leeks, using tongs to push them down into any available space in the pot. Bring back to a slow simmer until you can pierce the roast with a skewer, 1 to 1½ hours more for a total of 3 to 3½ hours.

Use tongs to lift out the chuck roast, let it drip into the pot, and then place it in on a cutting board. Collect the vegetables with a slotted spoon and put them in a large serving bowl. Separate the chuck roast along the fat seams, trim the excess fat, and slice against the grain ¾ inch thick. Arrange the meat among the vegetables in the serving bowl and cover to keep it warm.

Discard the bay leaves and onion from the stock. Fish out the head of garlic and set it aside. When it is cool enough to handle, squeeze the softened cloves into a small bowl. Smash the garlic with a spoonful of the stock and stir it back into the pot.

Bathe the meat and vegetables with a few ladles of hot stock to moisten them. Bring the serving platter to the table and serve portions of meat, vegetables, and stock in heated shallow bowls. Pass the coarse sea salt and mustard, if using.

If you'd like a clearer broth, pour the remaining broth through a fine-meshed strainer. Use a ladle to defat it, or chill it for 6 hours or longer and lift off and discard the layer of fat. Store the stock in the refrigerator for 1 week or freeze for up to 6 months.

MORE CHOICE CUTS:

Short ribs, beef shanks, or oxtails are bonier and less meaty than chuck roast, so use 6 to 7 pounds of any of these in the recipe and defat the stock well before serving.

Tongue lends the stock incredible richness and plenty of meat even without adding extra bones, both for this meal and for very thinly sliced tongue sandwiches.

WHOLE-GRAIN MUSTARD

Make this mustard at least eight hours in advance to allow the bite to mellow and the flavors to blend. It keeps refrigerated for up to one month. Use this lively mustard, and the variation sweetened with fruit preserves, for a sandwich spread and to garnish a stew or pot of beans.

Makes 1 cup

....

½ CUP DRY MUSTARD

1 SMALL SHALLOT, PEELED

1 GARLIC CLOVE, PEELED

¼ TEASPOON BLACK PEPPER

1½ TEASPOONS SALT

¼ CUP APPLE CIDER VINEGAR

2 TABLESPOONS BROWN MUSTARD SEEDS

Combine the dry mustard, shallot, garlic, pepper, salt, and ½ cup water (use cold water for more kick and boiling water for less) in a food processor and purée, scraping the bowl a few times, until the mixture is very smooth. Add the vinegar and mustard seeds and purée until blended, but most of the seeds are still whole. Transfer the mustard into a glass or ceramic container and refrigerate until ready to use. If necessary, thin the mustard by stirring in a tablespoon or two of water, since it thickens while standing.

VARIATION: FRUIT MUSTARD

Stir ¼ cup fruit preserves, such as currant, cherry, or apricot into ½ cup of the mustard until well blended.

CREAMY WILD MUSHROOM-RICE SOUP

Wild mushrooms are one of the luxuries that grow naturally in the Pacific Northwest. Just after the snows melt in May, if I'm lucky enough to find morels I use them to make this earthy, caramel-colored soup. When I don't find any, cremini mushrooms stand in, supported with a handful of mixed dried wild mushrooms from the supermarket. To give the stock more body, I thicken it slightly and splash in some cream just before serving.

Makes 6 servings

....

½ OUNCE DRIED WILD MUSHROOM MIX OR DRIED
    PORCINI MUSHROOMS

1 TABLESPOON EXTRA-VIRGIN OLIVE OIL

2 TABLESPOONS UNSALTED BUTTER

8 OUNCES FRESH MOREL OR CREMINI MUSH-
    ROOMS, THINLY SLICED

1½ TEASPOONS SALT

¼ TEASPOON BLACK PEPPER

1 MEDIUM ONION, CHOPPED

3 GARLIC CLOVES, MINCED

3 TABLESPOONS ALL-PURPOSE FLOUR

7 CUPS LOW-SALT BEEF STOCK (SHORT ORDER
    STOCK, PAGE 226; ROASTED BEEF STOCK,
    PAGE 228)

¾ CUP WILD RICE BLEND

1 TEASPOON FRESH THYME LEAVES OR
    ¼ TEASPOON DRIED

½ CUP HEAVY CREAM, OPTIONAL

Put the dried mushrooms into a small bowl and cover them with 2 cups of boiling water. Let them soften for 20 minutes. Drain the mushrooms, and reserve 1 cup of their soaking liquid. Chop the mushrooms coarsely, return them to the reserved soaking liquid, and set them aside.

Heat the oil and butter in a stockpot over medium-high heat. Add the fresh mushrooms, salt, and pepper and cook, stirring occasionally, until they release all of their liquid and begin to brown, about 6 minutes. Add the onion and garlic and cook until the onion is translucent, about 3 minutes. Add the flour and cook, stirring for 1 minute to cook off the starchy taste.

Add the stock and use a wooden spoon to scrape the bottom of the pan clean. Bring the stock to a simmer and add the rice, thyme, and the reserved mushrooms and their soaking liquid. Cover and simmer the soup over low heat until the rice is tender, 50 to 55 minutes. Stir in the cream, if using, and taste the soup for salt and pepper before serving.

WINTER MINESTRONE

This peasant-style soup—materialized from my pantry—restores hope during our long snow season. In place of tomato, this minestrone employs beef stock, fortified with Parmesan rind, as the base for the colorful collection of vegetables, beans, and pasta in every spoonful. (If using dried beans, you'll need to soak and cook them in advance.) Along with Olive Oil Breadsticks (page 178), this meal-in-a-bowl gets my gang running to the supper table.

Heat the olive oil in a stockpot over medium heat. Add the pancetta and cook to render some of the fat. When it is sizzling and starting to crisp, add the onion, carrots, celery, and garlic. Cook, stirring occasionally, until the onion turns translucent, about 6 minutes. Add 2 cups of water, the stock, squash, kale, salt, fennel, pepper, rosemary, and bay leaf. Drop in the Parmesan rind, if using. Bring the liquid to a boil and reduce the heat to low. Simmer the soup partially covered for 30 minutes. Taste for salt and pepper and discard the bay leaf and Parmesan rind, if using.

Add the beans and the pasta and simmer until the pasta is al dente, about 9 minutes more. Serve the soup in wide bowls with Parmesan liberally sprinkled on top.

NOTE: **When making this well in advance of serving time or for freezing, leave out the pasta until you reheat the soup since it will absorb most of the precious soup broth.**

Makes 6 servings

....

2 TABLESPOONS EXTRA-VIRGIN OLIVE OIL

2 OUNCES PANCETTA OR BACON, FINELY CHOPPED (ABOUT ½ CUP)

1 MEDIUM ONION, CHOPPED

3 MEDIUM CARROTS, CHOPPED

2 CELERY STALKS WITH LEAVES, CHOPPED

2 GARLIC CLOVES, MINCED

8 CUPS LOW-SALT BEEF STOCK (SHORT ORDER STOCK, PAGE 226; ROASTED BEEF STOCK, PAGE 228)

1 SMALL DELICATA SQUASH, CUT INTO ½-INCH CHUNKS (ABOUT 1½ CUPS)

2 CUPS (ABOUT 6 OUNCES) PACKED FINELY CHOPPED KALE LEAVES OR CABBAGE

2 TEASPOONS SALT

½ TEASPOON GROUND DRIED FENNEL

¼ TEASPOON BLACK PEPPER

1 SPRIG FRESH ROSEMARY OR ¼ CUP LIGHTLY PACKED CHOPPED FRESH FLAT-LEAF PARSLEY

1 BAY LEAF

1 PARMESAN CHEESE RIND (ABOUT 2 x 4 INCHES), OPTIONAL

1 CUP COOKED WHITE BEANS, SUCH AS CANNELLINI OR NAVY BEANS OR 1 (14-OUNCE) CAN WHITE BEANS, DRAINED AND RINSED

½ CUP ACINI DE PEPE OR OTHER TINY DRIED PASTA

FRESHLY GRATED PARMESAN, FOR SERVING

PHO

This fortifying Vietnamese rice noodle soup is beef's answer to chicken noodle soup. Like French onion soup, it starts with a base of great stock, such as consommé or the leftover broth from New England Simmered Supper, page 232. It then takes a new direction with an infusion of ginger, star anise, and cinnamon. The soup becomes complete with boiled rice noodles and slices of steak that cook in the piping hot stock. With a platter of bean sprouts, fresh herbs, jalapeños, and limes on the table, as well as bottles of hoisin sauce and chile sauce such as Sriracha, everyone can spike the soup to please.

Makes 4 servings

....

8 OUNCES TOP SIRLOIN STEAK

8 CUPS EXCELLENT LOW-SALT BEEF STOCK
    (ROASTED BEEF STOCK, PAGE 228; CRYSTAL
    CLEAR CONSOMMÉ, PAGE 231)

2-INCH PIECE FRESH GINGER, UNPEELED AND
    SLICED INTO ¼-INCH ROUNDS

2 WHOLE STAR ANISE

1 (3-INCH) CINNAMON STICK

3 TABLESPOONS FISH SAUCE

1 TEASPOON SUGAR

PINCH OF SALT

2 CUPS (6 OUNCES) FRESH BEAN SPROUTS

½ CUP LIGHTLY PACKED FRESH BASIL OR MINT
    LEAVES

½ CUP LIGHTLY PACKED FRESH CILANTRO LEAVES

1 JALAPEÑO, THINLY SLICED INTO ROUNDS

1 LIME, QUARTERED

1 (6- TO 8-OUNCE) PACKAGE DRIED RICE VERMI-
    CELLI NOODLES (MAI FUN)

Wrap the steak in plastic wrap and put it in the freezer for about 20 minutes to firm it up, which allows you to slice the meat very thin.

Meanwhile, put the stock, ginger, star anise, and cinnamon stick in a large saucepan and bring it to a boil over medium-high heat. Add the fish sauce, sugar, and salt. Reduce the heat to low and simmer until it is fragrant, about 20 minutes. With a slotted spoon, remove and discard the ginger, star anise, and cinnamon stick. Taste the stock for salt and keep it at a simmer over low heat.

Arrange the bean sprouts, basil, cilantro, jalapeños, and limes on a serving platter. Use your sharpest knife to slice the steak against the grain as thin as you can (aim for ⅛ inch).

Bring a pot of water to a boil over high heat and plunge in the noodles. Depending on the particular type, they will cook quickly, some in as little as 1 minute, so stand by and drain them as soon as they are tender to the bite.

To serve, portion the drained rice noodles into deep, wide soup bowls and top with 3 to 4 beef slices. Ladle the hot stock over it all and serve immediately with the platter of vegetable and herb garnishes.

> **MORE CHOICE CUTS:**
> Top round steak has good flavor for serving in this soup and is tender to the bite when sliced very thin.
>
> Brisket or chuck roast, left over from such recipes as New England Simmered Supper (page 232) is a fantastic addition to this soup, on its own or in combination with the steak.

HOME-STYLE FRENCH ONION SOUP

This magnificent soup depends on excellent beef stock, such as Roasted Beef Stock (page 228) or Crystal Clear Consommé (page 231) and well-caramelized onions. In order to achieve the dark, brown-sugar color that will bring real depth to your soup, plan on an hour to cook the onions. While they don't need your constant attention, be on hand to scrape them from the bottom of the pot in between other tasks you can do distractedly. Once the onions are done, it's an easy stride to serving time. If you only have a tall stockpot that will steam the onions, consider using a large sauté pan for this step and switching to a stockpot once they're caramelized.

As much as I love the elements of French onion soup, I always manage to burn my chin as I wrestle through the blanket of cheese and croutons. So, I serve it the way it was served to *me* by my host mother in France: wide bowls of steaming hot soup and with a plate of croutons and a bowl of grated cheese on the table. Everyone gets to swirl the cheese into their own soup—adding more as they progress—and float or dip a crouton, depending on whether they like it softened or crunchy. Every spoonful delivers onions, melted cheese, and ambrosial stock. Of course, you have all the elements to serve it the classic way too, by passing crouton- and cheese-topped bowls of soup, lined with a baking sheet, beneath the broiler until browned and bubbling.

Makes 4 to 6 servings

....

2 TABLESPOONS UNSALTED BUTTER

5 LARGE ONIONS, HALVED FROM ROOT TO STEM AND THINLY SLICED

2 TEASPOONS SALT

1 BAGUETTE, SLICED

2 TEASPOONS ALL-PURPOSE FLOUR

½ CUP DRY WHITE WINE OR DRY VERMOUTH

7 CUPS EXCELLENT LOW-SALT BEEF STOCK (ROASTED BEEF STOCK, PAGE 228; CRYSTAL CLEAR CONSOMMÉ PAGE 231)

1 TABLESPOON FRESH THYME OR 1 TEASPOON DRIED

1 BAY LEAF

¼ TEASPOON BLACK PEPPER

1 CUP FINELY GRATED EMMENTALER OR OTHER GOOD-QUALITY SWISS CHEESE

Melt the butter over medium-high heat in a medium heavy-bottomed stockpot. Add the onions and the salt and cook undisturbed until the onions turn limp and liquidy, about 7 minutes. Stir, and continue cooking the onions, stirring every 5 minutes or so as they start to sizzle and brown. Once they begin to brown, reduce the heat to medium, and leave them to cook until you fear they might burn. Use a wooden spoon to scrape up all the browned onions from the pot, and repeat this process until all of the onions are the color of dark brown sugar, about 1 hour total.

Meanwhile, preheat the oven to 375°F to make the croutons. Arrange the baguette slices on an ungreased baking sheet and bake them until they are crisp and golden, 9 to 10 minutes. Set them aside.

Add the flour to the onions and cook stirring for 1 minute to cook off the starchy taste. Add the wine and cook until the liquid nearly evaporates, about 4 minutes. Add the stock, thyme, bay leaf, and pepper. Simmer for at least 15 minutes to develop the flavors. Taste for salt and pepper. Remove and discard the bay leaf.

Ladle the soup into shallow soup bowls. Sprinkle on a handful of the cheese and top with a crouton. Pass the remaining cheese and croutons at the table.

TORTILLA SOUP

Fast to make and fun to eat, this soup features a chile- and lime-laced tomato stock with spiced ground beef over crunchy tortilla chips. It's traditional to deep-fry corn tortillas, but with so many good-quality chips on the market (I use the rectangular "tortilla strips"), opening a bag keeps everything simple and stress-free. The quick-simmered stock offers just enough time to prepare the avocado, cilantro, and sour cream embellishments. Then, it's time to load up the bowls with a little of this and that—including a few refills of tortilla strips as you reach the bottom of the bowl.

Chop half of the tomatoes and set them aside. Preheat the broiler. Broil the remaining tomatoes and jalapeño until they are blistered and slightly charred, turning them once, about 6 minutes. Transfer them to a food processor or blender along with the garlic and ½ cup of the stock. Purée until very smooth and set aside near the stove.

Heat the oil in a large saucepan over medium heat. Add the onion and cook, stirring occasionally, until it turns translucent, about 3 minutes. Add the ground beef, tomato paste, chile powder, salt, cumin, and oregano and cook, breaking up the ground beef into crumbles with a wooden spoon, until it is no longer pink. Add the reserved tomato purée and the remaining 3½ cups of stock and bring the liquid to a simmer. Reduce the heat to low and simmer for 15 to 20 minutes. Add the reserved chopped tomatoes and lime juice and taste for salt.

To serve, put a handful the tortilla strips or chips into each bowl. Ladle the soup over them and garnish to taste with the avocado, cilantro, and sour cream.

Makes 4 servings

....

1 POUND PLUM TOMATOES, QUARTERED (ABOUT 4), DIVIDED OR 1 (14-OUNCE CAN) DICED TOMATOES, DRAINED

1 JALAPEÑO, SEEDED IF YOU PREFER MILDER HEAT

2 GARLIC CLOVES, PEELED

4 CUPS LOW-SALT BEEF STOCK (SHORT ORDER STOCK, PAGE 226; ROASTED BEEF STOCK, PAGE 228), DIVIDED

1 TABLESPOON VEGETABLE OIL

1 WHITE ONION, CHOPPED

8 OUNCES GROUND BEEF, 85 TO 90 PERCENT LEAN

1 HEAPING TABLESPOON TOMATO PASTE

2 TEASPOONS ANCHO CHILE POWDER

1 TEASPOON SALT

½ TEASPOON CUMIN

½ TEASPOON DRIED OREGANO

2 TEASPOONS LIME JUICE

FOR SERVING:

STORE-BOUGHT TORTILLA STRIPS OR CHIPS

1 AVOCADO, PITTED AND CHOPPED

½ CUP LIGHTLY PACKED CHOPPED FRESH CILANTRO

¼ CUP SOUR CREAM, THINNED WITH 1 TABLESPOON WATER

SHORT RIBS RENDANG

I'm enthralled with this Malaysian favorite called rendang, which reverses the standard braising method of browning meat before simmering it in a liquid with a technique called dry-braising. Submerged in the spice-infused coconut milk, the beef short ribs first cook to tenderness under cover with gentle heat. Then, the cover comes off and they go into a blazing oven until the liquid is nearly dry and they brown in their own fat.

On the stovetop, where rendangs typically simmer, this takes ages, and most of the browned bits stick to the bottom of the pan. By transferring the whole process to the oven, the short ribs brown quickly and evenly. For the saucier "kaliyo" style, remove them from the oven before the coconut milk has completely evaporated, or go all the way to make true dry-braised "rendang." Whichever way you choose, serve the fragrant short ribs with plenty of steamed rice.

Makes 6 servings

....

4 GARLIC CLOVES, PEELED

2 SHALLOTS, PEELED

1 STALKS FRESH LEMONGRASS, FINELY CHOPPED
OR 2 TABLESPOONS LEMONGRASS PURÉE
(SOLD IN A TUBE)

2-INCH PIECE GINGER, PEELED AND VERY FINELY
CHOPPED (2 TABLESPOONS)

1 CUP COCONUT MILK

1¼ TEASPOONS SALT

1 TEASPOON GROUND TURMERIC

1 TEASPOON LIME ZEST

½ TEASPOON BLACK PEPPER

¾ TEASPOON RED PEPPER FLAKES

⅛ TEASPOON GROUND CLOVES

3½ TO 4 POUNDS MEATY SHORT RIBS

1 (2-INCH) CINNAMON STICK

1 BAY LEAF

LIME WEDGES, FOR SERVING

Preheat the oven to 300°F. Put the garlic, shallots, lemongrass, ginger, coconut milk, salt, turmeric, lime zest, pepper, pepper flakes, and cloves in the bowl of a food processor or in a blender. Purée, scraping down the sides as necessary, until it is very smooth.

Trim any thick exterior fat from the short ribs (page 51) and cut between the bones to separate them, if necessary. Crowd the short ribs in a single layer into a baking dish. Pour the coconut milk mixture over them and turn to coat them well. Tuck in the cinnamon stick and bay leaf. Cover the baking dish securely with aluminum foil. Bake the short ribs in the oven until the beef is fork tender, 2 to 2½ hours.

Increase the oven temperature to 425°F. Bake the short ribs uncovered, turning them once, until they are speckled brown and the sauce is thick and the fat is pooled around the edges of the pan, 18 to 20 minutes. (Or, if you prefer them in the saucier style, bake them for 8 to 10 minutes.) Spoon off the layer of fat, remove and discard the cinnamon stick and bay leaf, then serve the ribs with the lime wedges.

MORE CHOICE CUTS:
Boneless short ribs take some of the work out of eating, and you'll only need 2½ to 3 pounds to serve 6.

Stew beef is the standard when making rendang, and I like it best in hefty 2-inch chunks.

GOULASH

with Spelt Dumplings

When I learned that the word *goulash* means "soup of the cowboy," I had to include a recipe. Who knew there were cattlemen in Central Europe? Cowboys and everyone else will enjoy this delicate but memorable blend of paprika and caraway, rounded out with tomato and bacon. If you thought paprika was just for color, this soup will prove otherwise—as long as you use good-quality Hungarian paprika that is less than six months old (Sources, page 272).

Many of the references I consulted to create this recipe, most notably Mimi Sheraton's *The German Cookbook*, recommend making it one day in advance. There are two good reasons for this. Once chilled, the soup is easily and thoroughly defatted. The resting time also allows the symphony of subtle flavors to come forward. The Spelt Dumplings (recipe follows) are a snap to mix and simmer in the soup while it reheats. In place of the dumplings, substitute one cup of dried egg noodles, boil them in salted water until tender to the bite, and serve right away with the goulash.

Makes 4 to 6 servings

....

1½ TO 2 POUNDS BEEF SHANKS

1½ TEASPOONS HUNGARIAN PAPRIKA

1 TEASPOON KOSHER SALT

3 OUNCES BACON (ABOUT 3 SLICES), CHOPPED

2 MEDIUM ONIONS, CHOPPED

3 MEDIUM CARROTS, CHOPPED

2 TABLESPOONS APPLE CIDER VINEGAR

1 TABLESPOON TOMATO PASTE

2 GARLIC CLOVES, MINCED

1½ TEASPOON CRUSHED CARAWAY SEEDS

1 TEASPOON CRUSHED MARJORAM

½ TEASPOON BLACK PEPPER

7 CUPS LOW-SALT BEEF STOCK (SHORT ORDER STOCK, PAGE 226; ROASTED BEEF STOCK, PAGE 228) OR WATER

Put the beef shanks in a large mixing bowl, rub them with the paprika and kosher salt, and set them aside.

Cook the bacon in a stockpot over medium heat until it renders its fat and lightly browns, about 5 minutes. Use a slotted spoon to remove the bacon to a small bowl and set it aside. Brown the beef shanks in the bacon fat, searing them well on each side. Return them to the mixing bowl and set aside with the bacon.

Add the onions and carrots to the pot and cook until the onions turn translucent, about 6 minutes. Add the vinegar and tomato paste and stir with a wooden spoon, scraping up all the browned bits from the bottom of the pot. Add the garlic, caraway, marjoram, pepper, and stock. Add the beef shanks and bacon. Bring the pot to a simmer then reduce the heat to low and cook partially covered for 1½ hours until the beef is fork tender.

Use tongs to lift the beef shanks from the pot. When they are cool enough to handle, shred the meat, discard the bones, and return the beef to the pot. Use a large spoon to skim off any fat from the surface and taste for salt and pepper. (If making the soup in advance, store it in the refrigerator for up to 2 days. Use a slotted spoon to lift off and discard the layer of fat.) Bring the goulash back to a simmer, and if serving with the dumplings, follow the directions in the following recipe to cook them directly in the pot before serving immediately.

MORE CHOICE CUTS:

Ground beef or stew beef shortens the cooking time considerably, but be sure to use good beef stock for the best soup.

Short ribs and oxtail will take an additional 1 to 1½ hours of simmering time.

SPELT DUMPLINGS

An ancient relative to wheat, spelt is a whole grain with excellent nutritional properties and a nutty taste that's welcome in the goulash. Substitute equal parts all-purpose flour and whole-wheat flour for the spelt, if you like.

Makes about 40 teaspoon-sized dumplings

1 CUP (4½ OUNCES) WHOLE-GRAIN SPELT FLOUR (SOURCES, PAGE 272)

½ TEASPOON SALT

1 EGG, BEATEN

½ CUP MILK, LOW-SALT BEEF STOCK (SHORT ORDER STOCK, PAGE 226; ROASTED BEEF STOCK, PAGE 228), OR WATER

Whisk the flour and salt together in a medium mixing bowl. Add the egg and milk and whisk until smooth. Drop the dumplings by half-teaspoonfuls into the gently simmering goulash or stock. Cover and cook until they float to the surface, 9 to 10 minutes.

GINGER-GLAZED SHORT RIBS

I like my ribs sweet and sour and sticky. These Asian-inspired short ribs deliver on all counts, complete with an invigorating hit of fresh ginger. They're cooked twice: first by simmering to tenderness as in any basic braise, then by roasting or grilling until they sizzle and brown. This technique is useful for any sauce you like on your beef ribs—from Tangy Barbecue Sauce (page 223) to hoisin sauce.

The ginger-laced sweet-and-sour sauce is loosely based on Fuchsia Dunlop's version in *Land of Plenty*. In addition to a glaze, it is wonderful as a dipping sauce for Finger Steaks (page 183) or as a ready-made stir-fry sauce.

Makes 4 servings as an entrée;
8 as an appetizer

....

2½ TO 3 POUNDS MEATY SHORT RIBS

KOSHER SALT

1 MEDIUM ONION, CHOPPED

1 CARROT, CHOPPED

1 CUP LOW-SALT BEEF STOCK (SHORT ORDER STOCK, PAGE 226; ROASTED BEEF STOCK, PAGE 228) OR WATER

GINGER SAUCE:

1 TABLESPOON CORNSTARCH

3 TABLESPOONS SUGAR

¼ TEASPOON SALT

2 TABLESPOONS RICE WINE VINEGAR

1 TABLESPOON SOY SAUCE

1 TABLESPOON PEANUT OIL OR VEGETABLE OIL

2 GARLIC CLOVES, MINCED

1 INCH-PIECE GINGER, VERY FINELY CHOPPED (1 TABLESPOON)

1 TEASPOON TOASTED SESAME OIL

Preheat the oven to 300°F.

Trim the thick band of fat from the exterior of the short ribs (Trimming, page 51), cut between the bones, if necessary, and season the meat liberally with the kosher salt. Put them into a roasting pan or baking dish that fits them snuggly in a single layer. Scatter the onion and carrot over the ribs and pour in the stock. Cover the baking dish tightly with a lid or aluminum foil and bake until the ribs are fork tender, 2 to 2½ hours. Remove the short ribs from the cooking liquid and discard it.

To make the ginger sauce, whisk together the cornstarch, sugar, salt, vinegar, and soy sauce with ¼ cup water in a small bowl until smooth. Set it aside.

Heat the oil in a small saucepan over medium heat. Add the garlic and ginger and stir until fragrant, about 30 seconds. Add the cornstarch mixture and whisk while it comes to a boil. Cook for 1 minute until the sauce becomes very thick. Remove the pan from the heat and stir in the sesame oil. (You can prepare the short ribs and glaze up to this point in advance. I like to trim the meat from the bones while the short ribs are still warm and cut it into cubes to sauce and glaze in the oven the following day.)

Raise the oven temperature to 425°F. Use a pastry brush or spoon to spread the ginger sauce over the short ribs to coat them completely. Roast until they are glossy all over and browning at their edges, turning once, 15 to 20 minutes.

Alternatively, preheat a charcoal or gas grill for high heat (425° to 475°F), scrape the grate clean, and oil it lightly. Cook the glazed short ribs until they brown, turning 1 to 2 times, 4 to 5 minutes total.

MORE CHOICE CUTS:

Back ribs left over from a standing rib roast supper only need to be glazed and roasted or grilled before you dive in, preferably with your fingers.

Korean-style short ribs are cut ¼ inch thick, so you can cook them over a flame without braising first. Just grill or broil them and slather on the ginger sauce during the final minutes of cooking.

BRAZILIAN BEEF SHANKS WITH CHORIZO

There are glories to be had from shank, an odds-and-ends cut often sold as soup or dog bones. With just the right amount of meat, shank makes terrific stew in the grand tradition of osso bucco. In this recipe adapted from *The South American Table* by Maria Baez, the beef takes on a unique accent with flavorings of paprika, cumin, and garlic. If you've ventured to make homemade Chorizo (page 263) and serve it with Black Beans and Rice (page 219), all the better.

Makes 4 servings

....

2 TABLESPOONS VEGETABLE OIL

2 MEDIUM ONIONS, CHOPPED

1¼ TEASPOONS SWEET PAPRIKA

1 TEASPOON GROUND CUMIN

3½ TO 4 POUNDS BEEF SHANKS, CROSS-CUT
    ABOUT 1½ INCHES THICK

5 GARLIC CLOVES, MINCED

2 TEASPOONS SALT

¼ TEASPOON BLACK PEPPER

1½ CUPS LOW-SALT BEEF STOCK (SHORT ORDER
    STOCK, PAGE 226; ROASTED BEEF STOCK,
    PAGE 228) OR WATER

¼ CUP RED WINE VINEGAR

2 BAY LEAVES

1 POUND CHORIZO LINKS (PAGE 263)

¼ CUP LIGHTLY PACKED CHOPPED FRESH
    CILANTRO

Heat the oil in a Dutch oven over medium heat. Add the onions, paprika, and cumin and cook, stirring occasionally, until the onions turn translucent, about 3 minutes. Add the beef shanks, garlic, salt, pepper, stock, vinegar, and bay leaves. Bring the liquid to a simmer, then cover and cook over low heat until the meat is fork tender but not falling off the bone, 1½ to 2 hours.

Spoon off the fat from the surface and discard the bay leaves. (You can prepare it up to this point, chill overnight, and lift off the layer of fat. Bring it back to a simmer before continuing.)

Heat a large skillet over medium-high heat. Add the chorizo and cook, turning it 2 to 3 times. When it is nicely browned, remove it, and cut it into 1-inch-thick slices. Add the chorizo to the beef shank mixture and simmer uncovered until the liquid reduces to a sauce and the meat is nearly falling off the bone, 25 to 30 minutes more. Skim any fat, stir in the cilantro, and serve portions of the beef shank and chorizo with a spoonful or two of the sauce on top.

MORE CHOICE CUTS:

Oxtail and short ribs are natural substitutes for the shanks and will take up to 60 minutes more simmering time to become tender.

Stew beef is a leaner, boneless option for this chunky, sausage-laden stew.

WHITE TRUFFLE RISOTTO WITH ROASTED MARROW BONES

Just a dribble of white truffle oil is all it takes to make a pot of risotto an ethereal eating experience. Enriched with exceptional beef stock, this risotto is finished with hot, roasted marrow that melts into it to lend a beefy flavor as subtle and profound as the truffle oil's. This off-white dish looks particularly posh served in wide pasta bowls as a dinner party first course. Yet, it's also a straight-from-the-cupboards dish that I make without the marrow bones to eat with my husband, Benjamin, once the girls are put to bed, in front of a Friday night video.

Makes 4 to 6 servings

....

5 CUPS LOW-SALT BEEF STOCK (SHORT ORDER
    STOCK, PAGE 226; ROASTED BEEF STOCK,
    PAGE 228)

½ TEASPOON SALT

3 TABLESPOONS EXTRA-VIRGIN OLIVE OIL, PLUS
    ADDITIONAL FOR ROASTING BONES

1 SHALLOT, FINELY CHOPPED

2 CUPS RISOTTO RICE, SUCH AS CARNAROLI OR
    ARBORIO

1 CUP DRY WHITE WINE

1 TO 1½ POUNDS MARROW BONES (ABOUT 4),
    SOAKED FOR 8 TO 12 HOURS IN COLD WATER

2 TABLESPOONS UNSALTED BUTTER

1 TEASPOON WHITE TRUFFLE OIL (SOURCES,
    PAGE 272)

1 CUP FINELY GRATED PARMESAN CHEESE, DIVIDED

FRESHLY GROUND BLACK PEPPER

Heat the stock in a saucepan and keep it warm over low heat. Add the salt and stir until it dissolves to season the risotto as it cooks.

Heat the 3 tablespoons of the olive oil in a large saucepan over medium heat. Add the shallot and cook, stirring, until it turns translucent. Add the rice, stir to coat in the oil, and cook, stirring ocassionally, until the grains of rice become more translucent and smell toasted, about 3 minutes.

Add the wine and let it simmer, stirring occasionally, until it is nearly evaporated. Add the hot stock one ladle at a time and keep the heat at a steady but gentle simmer until the stock is absorbed. Continue adding the stock 1 or 2 ladlefuls at a time, stirring occasionally, until the rice is tender to the bite, 30 to 35 minutes.

Meanwhile, preheat the oven to 400°F. Drain the marrow bones, pat them dry, and rub them with olive oil on a baking sheet. Roast the bones until they are deeply browned, 15 to 20 minutes. You'll hear them sizzling. Set them aside until they are cool enough to handle. Use the end of a spoon or your finger to push the warm tube of buttery-soft beef marrow from the bones and slice it into thin rounds. Cover to keep it warm.

While the risotto is still unctuous and loose, like a nicely thickened stew, stir in the butter, truffle oil, and ½ cup of the Parmesan cheese. Taste for salt. Spoon the risotto into pre-heated pasta bowls, top with slices of marrow, and shower each serving with some of the remaining Parmesan cheese and black pepper to taste.

BONELESS OXTAIL AND BUCKWHEAT CRÊPE PURSES

with Chive-Horseradish Cream

This is a pull-out-all-the-stops party recipe that elevates the boniest beef cut to four-star status. Since I don't like to mess around with bones at the dining table, I braise oxtails in wine ahead of time and collect their nuggets of collagen-rich meat to fold into buckwheat crêpes (recipe follows). The musty, earthy taste from the buckwheat is a great match for the meat. Roasting the bones in the oven instead of on the stovetop results in better overall browning. You can make the braise up to two days in advance (or up to a month if frozen) and the crêpe batter and horseradish cream one day in advance. On the day of the party, assemble and reheat the "purses" and serve as either an elegant appetizer or as an entrée accompanied by oven-roasted beet wedges, which are equally wonderful with the horseradish cream sauce.

Makes 6 servings as an entrée;

12 servings as an appetizer

....

OXTAIL FILLING:

4 POUNDS OXTAIL (ABOUT 2), CUT INTO 2-INCH
   SEGMENTS

2 TABLESPOONS EXTRA-VIRGIN OLIVE OIL, DIVIDED

KOSHER SALT

FRESHLY GROUND BLACK PEPPER

1¼ CUPS DRY RED WINE

2 MEDIUM ONIONS, CHOPPED

2 MEDIUM CARROTS, CHOPPED

2 GARLIC CLOVES, MINCED

1 LARGE SPRIG FRESH THYME OR ½ TEASPOON
   DRIED

1 BAY LEAF

1½ CUPS LOW-SALT BEEF STOCK (SHORT ORDER
   STOCK, PAGE 226; ROASTED BEEF STOCK,
   PAGE 228) OR WATER

12 8-INCH BUCKWHEAT CRÊPES (RECIPE FOLLOWS)
   OR STORE-BOUGHT CRÊPES

12 LONG FRESH CHIVES FOR TIES

HORSERADISH CREAM:

2 TEASPOONS FRESHLY GRATED OR PREPARED
   HORSERADISH

½ CUP HEAVY CREAM

2 TABLESPOONS FINELY CHOPPED FRESH CHIVES

1 TEASPOON LEMON JUICE

¼ TEASPOON SALT

⅛ TEASPOON BLACK PEPPER

To prepare the oxtails, preheat the oven to 450°F. Put the oxtails on a rimmed baking sheet and rub them with 1 tablespoon of the olive oil. Season them liberally with the kosher salt and pepper and roast in the oven until they are deeply browned, about 25 minutes. Use tongs to transfer the oxtails to a large bowl.

Pour the wine onto the hot baking sheet and use a metal spatula to release the browned bits and add this liquid into the bowl with the oxtails. Reduce the oven temperature to 325°F.

Heat the remaining 1 tablespoon of oil in a Dutch oven over medium heat. Add the onions and carrots and cook, stirring occasionally, until the onions turn translucent, about 6 minutes. Add the garlic, thyme, bay leaf, and stock, browned oxtails, and wine and bring to a simmer. Cover the pot and cook in the oven until the beef pulls easily away from the bone, 3 to 3½ hours.

Transfer the oxtails into a bowl, discard the thyme sprigs, if using, and the bay leaf. While the oxtails are still warm but cool enough to handle, pull off and shred all of the meat, discarding all of the bones and fat. Skim the fat from the stock, taste for salt, and add the oxtail meat. You'll have about 3½ cups of filling. (Store the filling in the refrigerator for up to 2 days. Spoon off and discard the solid layer of fat that forms on the surface.)

To assemble the purses, have the crêpes on hand. Put a scant ¼ cup of the beef filling into the center of each crêpe. Fold in two of the sides, then fold the bottom edge up and roll the crêpe over, like you're making a loose burrito. Tie the bundle with one of the chives and put it on a baking sheet. Repeat with the remaining crêpes. (You can assemble the crêpes and chill them for 2 hours.)

To make the horseradish cream, whisk the horseradish with the cream, chives, lemon juice, salt, and pepper in a small bowl. Thin with a tablespoon or two of water, if needed, so that it drizzles off a spoon. Taste for salt and lemon juice and set it aside.

When ready to serve, preheat the oven to 300°F. Bake the purses until they are heated all the way through, 12 to 15 minutes. To serve, dollop each plate with a small puddle of the horseradish cream sauce and place one of the purses on top.

MORE CHOICE CUTS:

Stew meat will cook in about half the time, and eliminating the bones means you'll only need about 2 pounds to make the filling.

Beef shanks and short ribs are meatier than oxtail, so you'll need only 3 pounds. Start checking the beef shanks for doneness after 1½ hours.

BUCKWHEAT CRÊPES

If you can make pancakes, you can make these crêpes to create bundles of hearty braised beef. As in pancake making, the first one or two are practice for adjusting the heat and the thinness of the batter (it needs to be very thin to run around the pan). Once you get rolling, the work goes quickly. Make them in advance to store in the freezer for up to three months.

Makes 12 8-inch crêpes

....

1 CUP (4½ OUNCES) BUCKWHEAT FLOUR (SOURCES, PAGE 272)

½ CUP (2¼ OUNCES) ALL-PURPOSE FLOUR

¾ TEASPOON SALT

1 CUP MILK

4 EGGS, BEATEN

¾ CUP LOW-SALT BEEF STOCK (SHORT ORDER STOCK, PAGE 226; ROASTED BEEF STOCK, PAGE 228) OR WATER

Whisk the buckwheat flour, all-purpose flour, and salt in a medium mixing bowl. Whisk in the milk and the eggs to make a smooth thick batter. Whisk in the stock until smooth and let stand at room temperature for 20 minutes. (You can make this up to 1 day in advance refrigerated.)

Heat an 8-inch non-stick skillet over medium-low heat. Lift the pan and ladle in a small amount of the batter, swirling it around until it coats the bottom of the pan, and set it back on the burner. If the batter does not run easily around the pan in a thin layer, thin the batter with 1 tablespoon of water at a time until it does.

When the edges of the crêpe are crisp and dry, about 1 minute, use a heatproof rubber spatula or table knife (taking care to avoid scratching your non-stick pan) to flip the crêpe over. The bottom will be lightly and evenly browned. Cook for about 1 minute more until speckled brown on the bottom. Stack the crêpes on a plate as you finish them. Use them warm, refrigerate until ready to use, or freeze them in a resealable plastic bag for up to 1 month.

CHAPTER 10

SIMPLE HOMEMADE CHARCUTERIE

The term "charcuterie" doesn't get tossed around much in these parts. But the age-old culinary art is widely practiced in this place where hunting is a rite of passage and so many own cattle. Each fall and winter, people grind meat trim into sausage and dehydrate lean roasts for jerky. Some salt cure and some smoke. When I started asking locals for advice on making my own charcuterie, I determined that seasoning formulas and recipes for preserving meats are protected like family heirlooms.

Berkeley transplant Kit Phelps was different. One January day she breezed into my kitchen with her long braid swinging and her notebook recording years of sausage-making projects wide open. Kit had just sold the herd she'd spent the past 30 years raising with her husband Kim. The sale was recent enough that she talked about her cows with the same affection she spoke of her two grown children. This was the first January that she didn't have to feed cattle every morning, and she was celebrating by spending the gray winter days with me. We conducted delicious experiments with fresh, dried, and cooked sausages, jerkies, and other meaty delights.

Charcuterie, I've learned, is very procedural. As with canning, the best results come from adhering to proven methods, staying organized, and practicing excellent food sanitation. For this reason, Kit's experience was as valuable as her recipes, and she shared tips I'd never have learned in a book. One of the first things she told me about seasoning sausage meat was, "The salt

intensifies and the spices recede." To achieve the best distribution, we puréed all of the seasonings with water in a blender, and Kit mixed each batch of ground meat and fat by hand, adding enough moisture so that the meat became sticky. Kit used a squeeze test: when a fistful of meat could squish through the gaps in her fingers, it was well mixed.

Before storing or stuffing, we always tasted— by frying up a mini-burger—to make sure the flavors were quite pronounced, balanced, and pleasing. Practice, more than any particular skill, was what mattered most. Each day we produced a variety of meats worthy of a deli case to savor in the weeks and months ahead.

This chapter offers a host of easy, do-it-yourself recipes that require only bare-bones equipment. An introduction to the simple and practical methods for playing with meat, these recipes open up another realm of possibilities with beef— from breakfast sausage to lunch meat to trail snacks. It's true that pork is the predominant ingredient in most charcuterie, and some of the recipes, such as Sage Breakfast Sausage (page 255) Garlic-Fennel Sausage (page 256) and Grassfed Beef Terrine (page 260), call for pork butt or pork fat. By and large, however, these recipes focus on beef and several are made with pure beef.

In aiming to make these recipes as accessible as possible, I created small-batch recipes generally requiring less than three pounds of meat apiece. For some, you don't even need a meat grinder. The chapter includes sausages made with ground beef, such as Summer Sausage (page 254) and

Peppered Hamburger Jerky (page 268) that is dried in the oven. Recipes that require curing salt, like Deli-Style Salami (page 258) and Pastrami (page 266), call for a brand sold in supermarkets nationwide.

There's real satisfaction in practicing old-fashioned home economics that relies on the least expensive cuts to create ready-to-cook or ready-to-eat meats. It's a whole new way to enjoy beef, albeit in moderation. It is also a fun project to do with a friend or family member. That extra set of hands is useful—whether it's to turn off the water when you're hand mixing the sausage meat or to stuff casings, should you choose to go that route. If there is a beef cut like bottom round roast languishing in the freezer that you wouldn't cook for dinner—or if you find one on special at the store—it's possible with a single day's work to transform it into a delicacy you'll treasure.

Charcuterie Choice Cuts

Making sausages and jerky is the butcher's way of using up the bounty of trim left from breaking down whole animals. For the rest of us, it's easy to find many tough, lean, and cheap cuts to put to excellent use for charcuterie. You may find that these preparations become your favorite way to use some of the least-appreciated beef cuts. Request pork fat from your butcher or see Sources, page 272.

BRISKET is the large, flat pectoral muscle sold whole or in "flat" or "point" halves. It has a coarse grain of muscle fibers and a cap of fat that makes it the top pick for brining and simmering for corned beef, or continuing the process and smoking to produce homemade pastrami.

BOTTOM ROUND, aka rump roast, is the very lean and boneless muscle from the round, or hindquarter. Because it's fairly tough, bottom round is typically ground or cubed. However, this tasty cut deserves more credit since, provided you add fat, it can become a great sausage or terrine. It is also a good candidate for corned beef and yields larger slices than brisket. Finally, bottom round is a top choice for making beef jerky, since jerky meat should be lean to avoid spoilage.

CHUCK ROAST is the name for any shoulder cut with or without a bone. It naturally has a good amount of fat for grinding. On its own, ground chuck roast is great for homemade hamburgers, but grassfed generally requires some additional fat to make optimum sausage.

EYE ROUND is an extra-lean, boneless, and mild-flavored cut from the round that can be ground for sausage in combination with a sufficient amount of fat.

GROUND BEEF consists of grind from many other cuts. Since it's already ground (twice), it gives you a leg-up on sausage making. A fat content of 25 to 30 percent is ideal, or extra-lean beef (15 percent or less) can be augmented with additional fat. The leanest (below 10 percent) is best for jerky.

SHORT PLATE is from the belly, a flat cut with stripes of meat and fat resembling bacon. It usually goes into the grind, but due to its ratio of fat to lean, it is also a valuable meat for sausage making.

SHORT RIBS are the meaty bones from the chuck, or shoulder, plate, and rib sections. English-style ribs are cut into roughly 4-inch lengths that come in four-bone sections (you can cut through the intercostal meat to make single-bone servings). Flanken or Korean-style are very thinly sliced short ribs (about ¼ inch). They have an ideal meat-to-fat ratio for sausage making, requiring no additional fat.

STEW MEAT is cut from the tougher cuts and can vary in the amount of fat and quality of trimming. Stew meat too fatty for braising can be put to good use when ground and used to make your own ground beef or sausage.

SUMMER SAUSAGE

C. Belle Probert was one of the Wallowa County CowBelles, an association of ranchers' wives that produced three cookbooks throughout the 1970s. Her summer sausage recipe is in every edition for good reason: it's a rewarding illustration of the simplicity of sausage making: mix ground beef with seasonings, roll it in aluminum foil into a log, and bake. That's all there is to making a ready-to-eat meat for a sandwich or a cheese and cracker tray.

Faithful to the original *Chuck Wagon Cookbook*, this recipe makes two sausages. I always make the whole batch because my family goes through it quickly. If you want to give it a try with just one pound of ground beef, divide this recipe in half.

Makes 2 sausages, about 8 inches
long and 2 inches wide

....

2 TABLESPOONS MORTON'S TENDER QUICK
    CURING SALT

1 TEASPOON BLACK PEPPER

1 TEASPOON ONION POWDER

1 TEASPOON GARLIC POWDER

1 TABLESPOON YELLOW MUSTARD SEEDS

2 TEASPOONS LIQUID SMOKE*, OPTIONAL

2 POUNDS GROUND BEEF, 75 TO 85 PERCENT LEAN

Dissolve the curing salt in 1 cup of cold water. Stir in the pepper, onion powder, garlic powder, mustard seeds, and liquid smoke, if using. Put the ground beef into a large mixing bowl and pour the curing salt mixture over it. Knead the ground beef with your hands or with the paddle attachment in a stand mixer until it absorbs all the liquid and feels sticky and soft. Cover the bowl and refrigerate for 6 to 8 hours to develop the flavors. Longer than 12 hours, the meat can become overly salty from the curing salt.

Pull off a tablespoon-sized piece of the ground meat mixture and form it into a small patty ½ inch thick. Heat a small skillet over medium heat and cook the patty for 2½ to 3 minutes per side. Let it cool slightly and taste it. Since it will be served cold you want the seasoning to be very forward and bold. Adjust the seasoning, if necessary.

Preheat the oven to 350°F and line a rimmed baking sheet with a wire rack. Divide the ground beef mixture into 2 pieces and shape each into a log around 2 inches thick and 8 inches long. Wrap each log tightly in aluminum foil and twist the ends to seal. Poke holes in the foil with a skewer so that the meat will drain as it cooks. Put the logs on the rack and bake until they are firm to the touch and an internal read thermometer registers 160°F, 1 to 1¼ hours. Cool and chill thoroughly in the refrigerator. To serve, unwrap it, and slice it into ½-inch-thick rounds and store in the refrigerator for up to 3 weeks.

*NOTE: Liquid smoke is not an artificial flavoring but real smoke collected from water vapors condensed and aged for bottling in a liquid form. Filtered of tar and ash, it's actually less carcinogenic than traditional meat smoking methods. Still, for reasons of good taste and health, liquid smoke is best used judiciously.

SAGE BREAKFAST SAUSAGE

It was a happy accident that I planned a sausage-making extravaganza for January. It turns out this is when the hogs are butchered and ranchers have time on their hands for such endeavors. With a new batch of pork fat from a Carman Ranch heritage Tamworth hog, Kit Phelps and I made this beef and pork breakfast sausage. It's based on a tried-and-true recipe from Bruce Aidells' *Complete Sausage Book*. While you can roll this herbaceous meat into a log like the supermarket brands, I make small patties and freeze them with flattened cupcake liners in between each one. I can pry off the number of patties I need for a series of weekend breakfasts from the dead of winter all the way through the springtime thaw.

Makes about 3½ pounds bulk sausage

....

1¼ POUNDS BOTTOM ROUND ROAST, CUT INTO
    1-INCH CUBES

1½ POUNDS PORK BUTT, CUT INTO 1-INCH CUBES

12 OUNCES PORK FAT, CUT INTO 1-INCH CUBES

1 GARLIC CLOVE, PEELED

1 TABLESPOON KOSHER SALT

2 TEASPOONS GROUND SAGE

1 TEASPOON DRIED THYME

1 TEASPOON DRIED BASIL

1 TEASPOON RED PEPPER FLAKES

1 TEASPOON BLACK PEPPER

1 TEASPOON GROUND GINGER

½ CUP FINELY CHOPPED ONION

½ CUP FINELY CHOPPED FRESH PARSLEY

Freeze the beef, pork, and fat for 20 minutes to get it very cold and make it easier to grind. Put the garlic, kosher salt, sage, thyme, basil, pepper flakes, pepper, and ginger into a blender or food processor with ¼ cup cold water and purée until smooth.

Set up a hand or electric meat grinder with the coarse plate (¼ to ⅜ inch) and grind the beef, pork, and fat together into a large mixing bowl. Sprinkle the garlic-herb mixture over the ground meat, add the onion and parsley, and knead it with your hands or with the paddle attachment in a stand mixer until it is very sticky and velvety soft. If it needs more liquid, add 1 tablespoon of water at a time until the mixture squishes through your closed fist.

Pull off a tablespoon-sized piece of the ground meat mixture and form it into a small patty ½ inch thick. Heat a small skillet over medium heat and cook the patty for 2½ to 3 minutes per side. Let it cool slightly, taste it, and adjust the seasonings, if necessary.

Form into individual sausage patties, about ½ inch thick and 3 inches wide. Alternatively, roll the sausage mix into 3-inch-wide logs for slicing. Refrigerate the sausage and use within 3 days or freeze for up to 3 months.

GARLIC-FENNEL SAUSAGE

Grilled with onions and peppers, sliced and tossed with pasta, or crumbed into minestrone soup, Italian sausage packs a powerhouse of garlic, herbs, and savoriness into some of my favorite meals. I used to buy it, but this fresh sausage is a snap to make and keep in the freezer, at the ready whenever I need a last-minute dinner.

This all-beef sausage is an adaptation of one Kit swears is the very best from Bruce Aidells's *Complete Sausage Book*, and she's tried them all. We upped the garlic and used the fennel seeds two ways—half crushed into the mix and half left whole for a wonderful hit of mild anise that makes this sausage unique. I like to stuff this into casings to make links (natural have the best texture and are easier to work with than collagen casings), but you can use it ground or form it into patties for immediate use or freezer storage.

Makes about 4 pounds bulk sausage or
20 5-inch sausage links

....

3 POUNDS BOTTOM ROUND ROAST, CUT INTO
    1-INCH CUBES
1 POUND PORK FAT, CUT INTO 1-INCH CUBES
½ CUP DRY RED WINE
4 GARLIC CLOVES, PEELED
2 TABLESPOONS FENNEL SEEDS, DIVIDED
1 TABLESPOON RED PEPPER FLAKES
4 TEASPOONS KOSHER SALT
1 TEASPOON CRUSHED OREGANO
⅛ TEASPOON GROUND ALLSPICE
MEDIUM HOG CASINGS, SOAKED IN WARM WATER
    FOR 30 MINUTES, OPTIONAL (SOURCES, PAGE 272)

Freeze the beef and fat for 20 minutes to get it very cold and make it easier to grind. Put the wine, garlic, 1 tablespoon of the fennel seeds, red pepper flakes, salt, oregano, and allspice into a blender or food processor and purée until fairly smooth. Add the remaining 1 tablespoon whole fennel seeds to the wine mixture and set it aside.

Set up a hand or electric meat grinder with the coarse plate (¼ to ⅜ inch) and grind the beef and fat together into a large mixing bowl. Sprinkle the wine mixture over the ground beef and knead it with your hands or with the paddle attachment in a stand mixer until it is sticky and velvety soft. If it needs more liquid, add 1 tablespoon of water at a time until the mixture squishes through your closed fist. Chill the ground beef mixture for 1 to 3 hours to develop the flavors.

Pull off a tablespoon-sized piece of the ground meat mixture and form it into a small patty ½ inch thick. Heat a small skillet over medium heat and cook the patty for 2½ to 3 minutes per side. Let it cool slightly, taste it, and adjust the seasonings, if necessary.

For bulk sausage, divide the mixture and package it into resealable plastic bags or shape it into logs and wrap in plastic wrap. To make links, attach the stuffer spout to the grinder. Rinse the casing and thread it onto the spout, leaving about 6 inches hanging off the end. Keep this end open as you start stuffing and when the sausage comes out the spout expelling all the air, tie it in a knot. Continue stuffing, twisting the links every 5 inches in alternating directions to make about 20, and tie a knot in the end of the last link. (There will be some sausage left in the stuffer, which you can use to make a patty.) Line a rimmed baking sheet with a wire rack and lay the links on the rack so that they are not touching. Dry the sausages in the refrigerator for 8 to 12 hours, then store them in resealable plastic bags. Refrigerate this fresh sausage for 3 days or freeze for up to 3 months.

MORE CHOICE CUTS:

Eye round, if you're not partial to it as a roast, is an extra-lean beef good for sausage in combination with added fat.

DELI-STYLE SALAMI

Dense and meaty, this cooked salami makes a peppery ready-to-eat treat when sliced for hors d'oeuvres or deli-style sandwiches. The recipe originates from Armandino Batali, who is a master of meat curing and father to celebrity chef Mario. I converted it to produce a pure beef version with short ribs that were a bit too fatty for braising. The fat-to-lean balance turned out to be ideal for this style of salami, but if you don't have short ribs on hand (they are spendy to purchase), choose one of the alternative suggested cuts.

Once ground and seasoned, the mix gets stuffed into a fibrous casing, which looks like a translucent sock. Tough enough to be packed tight, it is lined with protein that causes the casing to shrink with the meat as it cooks in simmering water; this is a synthetic casing you peel off before eating. Curing salts help to keep the salami for three weeks refrigerated, a fact I'm thankful for anytime I'm in need of a pre-dinner nibble with a glass of red wine.

Makes 2 6-inch salami

....

2½ POUNDS SHORT RIB MEAT, CUT INTO
    1-INCH CUBES

2 TABLESPOONS MORTON TENDER QUICK
    CURING SALT

2½ TEASPOONS GROUND NUTMEG

2 TEASPOONS NONFAT DRY MILK

1¾ TEASPOONS GROUND WHITE PEPPER

1½ TEASPOONS WHOLE BLACK PEPPERCORNS

1 FIBROUS CASING, ABOUT 3 INCHES IN DIAMETER
    AND 2 FEET LONG, SOAKED IN WARM WATER
    FOR 30 MINUTES (SOURCES, PAGE 272)

Freeze the beef for 20 minutes to get it very cold and make it easier to grind. Dissolve the curing salt in ¼ cup water in a small dish. Add the nutmeg, dry milk, white pepper, and peppercorns and stir to blend it well. Set the mixture aside.

Set up a hand or electric meat grinder with the coarse plate (¼ to ⅜ inch) and grind the beef into a large mixing bowl. Sprinkle the curing salt mixture over the ground beef and knead the mixture with your hands or the paddle attachment in a stand mixer until it is very well blended and tacky to the touch.

To stuff the casing, tie one end securely with butcher's twine and turn the open end inside out like a sock. Use your hands to put a few fistfuls of the ground meat into the casing. Squeeze and twist the casing to compact the filling tightly into the end. To eliminate air pockets, insert a chopstick into any air spaces, then squeeze and twist the casing once more. Continue packing the sausage until it is about 6 inches long. Make sure that two will fit into your largest pot for cooking later. Twist the open end and tie it tightly with butcher's twine. Repeat with the remaining ground meat mixture to make another salami. Prick the casings in 5 or 6 places with a skewer to allow air to escape during cooking. Refrigerate the sausages for 3 to 4 hours to develop the flavors.

Put the salami in a large pot, cover them with water, and bring it to a simmer over medium heat. Adjust the heat to maintain a low simmer and cook until an internal read thermometer registers 175°F, about 45 minutes. Cool and refrigerate until well chilled. Store in the refrigerator for 3 weeks, keeping the cut end well wrapped, or in the freezer for up to 3 months.

MORE CHOICE CUTS:

Short plate, trimmed of the thick band of exterior fat (page 51) still has ample fat and no bones to cut around for grinding.

Chuck roast can be supplemented with pork fat (a 2-pound untrimmed boneless chuck roast plus ½-pound pork fat) to produce a satisfying salami.

GRASSFED BEEF TERRINE

with Crackerbreads

Terrines make me think of France and outdoor lunches with baguettes and tiny pickles. As a result, creating a terrine for this book became a bit of an obsession. Like a pâté de campagne but made with beef, this recipe makes one loaf of finely ground meat and pork fat that's highly seasoned with spirits and spices. The garnishes of currants and pistachios add sweetness and texture, and keep it interesting from the first bite to the last.

Essentially, a terrine is a sausage baked into a loaf. The best sources for those made with extra-lean meats like grassfed come from game books. I modeled this streamlined recipe after many sources, but I credit Michael Ruhlman's recipe for game terrine in *Charcuterie* with helping me comprehend the basic method. It starts like the other sausage recipes in this chapter, a simple mechanical process of grinding and mixing. But, it adds steps of marinating the meat, reducing the marinade, and adding heavy cream before baking in a slow oven and chilling it overnight. For me, having a terrine on hand is occasion enough to host a cocktail party. So sumptuous in taste, it doesn't need a condiment or sauce, only something crunchy like Crackerbreads (recipe follows) to serve with thick slices of your homemade terrine.

Makes 1 (9 x 5-inch) terrine

....

1 POUND BEEF BOTTOM ROUND ROAST, CUT INTO
    1-INCH CUBES

12 OUNCES PORK FAT, CUT INTO 1-INCH CUBES

1 CUP FORTIFIED WINE, SUCH AS MADEIRA,
    MARSALA, OR SHERRY

¾ TEASPOON GROUND ALLSPICE

¾ TEASPOON GROUND CORIANDER

½ TEASPOON GROUND GINGER

¼ TEASPOON GROUND NUTMEG

1 TABLESPOON PLUS 2 TEASPOONS MORTON
    TENDER QUICK CURING SALT

2 TEASPOONS BLACK PEPPER

½ CUP CURRANTS

½ CUP BRANDY

1 TABLESPOON UNSALTED BUTTER

3 GARLIC CLOVES, MINCED

1 SHALLOT, FINELY CHOPPED

½ CUP HEAVY CREAM

½ CUP PISTACHIOS

Combine the beef, fat, fortified wine, allspice, coriander, ginger, nutmeg, curing salt, and pepper in a large mixing bowl and stir to blend well. Cover and marinate in the refrigerator for 4 to 8 hours. Put the currants in a small bowl, cover them with the brandy, and let them plump at room temperature while the meat marinates.

Drain the meat mixture through a large strainer, reserving the spirits. Drain the currants and add the brandy to the reserved spirits. Set the currants aside.

Melt the butter in a medium skillet over medium heat. Add the garlic and shallot and cook until they turn translucent, about 2 minutes. Add the reserved spirits and bring to simmer. Reduce the heat to low and cook, skimming as necessary, until reduced by half, about 15 minutes. Chill in the refrigerator.

Grind the meat mixture through the fine plate (⅛ to ¼ inch) two times to blend the meat and fat and achieve a uniform texture. Add the reduced chilled spirits and the cream and stir until well blended. Fold in the reserved currants and the pistachios. Test the seasoning by cooking a tablespoon of the filling in a dry skillet over medium heat for 2½ to 3 minutes per side. Taste and adjust the seasonings, if necessary.

Preheat the oven to 300°F and bring a teakettle of water to a boil. Line a 9 x 5-inch loaf pan with a dampened length of parchment paper to overhang the sides by about 6 inches. Spoon the meat mixture into the loaf pan, smooth the top, and rap the pan on the counter to remove any air bubbles. Fold the parchment paper over to cover the meat mixture and seal the pan tightly with aluminum foil. Set the loaf pan into a larger roasting pan and put it on the oven rack. Fill the roasting pan with enough boiling water so that it comes about halfway up the sides of the loaf pan. Bake the terrine until an instant-read thermometer registers 150°F when inserted into the center, 1¼ to 1½ hours.

Carefully remove the roasting pan from the oven and lift out the loaf pan. Refrigerate it for 8 hours or overnight to chill it thoroughly. Unwrap the terrine. There will be a veneer of white fat all over the surface. Run a paring knife around the edge of the pan and use the overhanging parchment paper wrap as handles to lift it from the loaf pan. Slice the terrine into ½-inch-thick slices with a serrated knife and serve with the Crackerbreads, if desired.

CONTINUES ▶

CRACKERBREADS

Mixed in a single bowl, rolled, and hand-cut, these homemade crackers are simple to make, very crunchy, and keep for about five days.

Makes about 3½ dozen crackers

....

1½ CUPS (6¾ OUNCES) ALL-PURPOSE FLOUR

½ CUP (2¼ OUNCES) WHOLE-WHEAT FLOUR

1 TEASPOON SALT

3 TABLESPOONS EXTRA-VIRGIN OLIVE OIL

¾ TEASPOON KOSHER SALT, OPTIONAL

Position an oven rack in the lower third of the oven and preheat the oven to 450°F. Fill a small bowl with water and set it aside with a pastry brush.

In a large bowl, whisk together the all-purpose flour, whole-wheat flour, and salt. Add the olive oil and ½ cup of water to the flour and stir with a rubber spatula until it collects into a soft, crumbly ball of dough. Use the spatula or your hands to press the dough against the sides of the bowl to gather all the stray flour.

Set the dough on a lightly floured work surface. Roll the dough into a very thin rectangle about ⅛ inch thick. Whenever you feel resistance, lift up one edge of the dough and sprinkle more flour underneath before you continue rolling it into a thin sheet.

Use a pastry brush to dampen the dough lightly with water and sprinkle on the salt, if using. With a dough scraper, pizza cutter, or sharp knife, cut the dough in half lengthwise and then cut across to make rectangles roughly 2 x 4 inches. Don't bother trimming the edges; rustic edges give the crackerbreads character.

Transfer the crackerbreads to an ungreased baking sheet. Bake until nicely and unevenly browned and bubbled, about 10 minutes. Cool the crackerbreads on a wire rack and store them in a resealable plastic bag.

CHORIZO

Ranchers Kit and Kim Phelps have fine-tuned this saucy Mexican-style sausage over the past twenty years. Scaled down from the two-hundred-pound batches they make with a crew of friends, this recipe blends beef, bacon, and a generous but not excessive amount of chipotle chile powder. For a milder version, substitute ancho chile powder. If you make links, use it in Brazilian Beef Shanks with Chorizo (page 246). Or store it in bulk to try in place of ground beef in Tortilla Soup (page 240) or cooked and scrambled with eggs for killer breakfast burritos.

Makes about 2½ pounds bulk sausage or
16 4-inch links
....

2½ POUNDS BOTTOM ROUND ROAST, CUT INTO
    1-INCH CUBES

4 OUNCES BACON (ABOUT 3 STRIPS), CUT INTO
    1-INCH PIECES

5 GARLIC CLOVES, PEELED

1 TABLESPOON KOSHER SALT

2½ TABLESPOONS RED WINE VINEGAR

2 TABLESPOONS CHIPOTLE OR ANCHO CHILE
    POWDER

1 TEASPOON CRUSHED DRIED OREGANO

1 TEASPOON BLACK PEPPER

1 TEASPOON RED PEPPER FLAKES

½ TEASPOON GROUND CUMIN

MEDIUM HOG CASINGS, SOAKED IN WARM WATER
    FOR 30 MINUTES, OPTIONAL (SOURCES, PAGE 272)

Freeze the beef and bacon for 20 minutes to get them very cold and make them easier to grind. Put the garlic, kosher salt, vinegar, chile powder, oregano, pepper, pepper flakes, and cumin in a blender or food processor with ¼ cup cold water and purée until smooth.

Set up a hand or electric meat grinder with the coarse plate (¼ to ⅜ inch) and grind the beef and bacon together into a large mixing bowl. Sprinkle the spice mixture over the ground beef and knead it with your hands or with the paddle attachment in a stand mixer until it is sticky and velvety soft. If it needs more liquid, add 1 tablespoon of water at a time until it squishes through your closed fist. Chill the ground meat mixture for 1 to 3 hours to develop the flavors.

Pull off a tablespoon-sized piece of the ground meat mixture and form it into a small patty ½ inch thick. Heat a small skillet over medium heat and cook the patty for 2½ to 3 minutes per side. Let it cool slightly, taste it, and adjust the seasonings, if necessary.

For bulk sausage, divide the beef mixture and package it into resealable plastic bags. To make links, attach the stuffer spout to the grinder. Rinse the casing and thread it onto the spout, leaving about 6 inches hanging off the end. Keep this end open as you start stuffing, and when the sausage comes out the spout expelling all the air, tie it in a knot. Continue stuffing, twisting the links in alternating directions every 4 inches to make about 16, and tie a knot in the end of the last link. (There will be some sausage left in the stuffer, which you can use to make a patty.) Line a rimmed baking sheet with a wire rack and lay the links on the rack so that they are not touching. Dry the sausages in the refrigerator for 8 to 12 hours, then store them in resealable plastic bags. Refrigerate this fresh sausage for 5 days or freeze for up to 3 months.

CORNED BEEF

I was intimidated about making my own corned beef until I understood that it was just a matter of soaking meat in salt and then simmering it until tender. What could be easier? Most of the "work" involves waiting four or five days for the beef to cure in the refrigerator, then waiting again while it simmers very slowly. I know the meat is tender when I can plunge a skewer through it without resistance. It's also fine to cut off a slice and taste it to make sure it's as tender as you want it.

This particular corned beef is brown, not pink, because there's no curing salt. There's no point since it'll get eaten up in grilled Reubens for dinner and corned beef hash with poached eggs for brunch. It's also fantastic cold on dark rye with Whole-Grain Mustard (page 234).

Brisket is the classic corned beef cut, and deservedly so, but I've corned several other cuts that are also worth the investment of time. The hard-to-use bottom round roast, aka rump roast, in this recipe, in particular, is remarkably good and lean. For a complete dinner, serve it with sauerkraut and boiled new potatoes.

Makes 6 servings with leftovers

½ CUP KOSHER SALT

¼ CUP SUGAR

3 GARLIC CLOVES, MINCED

2 TABLESPOONS PICKLING SPICES

3 BAY LEAVES, CRUMBLED

1 TABLESPOON CRACKED BLACK PEPPER

1 (3½- TO 4-POUND) BOTTOM ROUND ROAST

2 MEDIUM ONIONS, PEELED AND QUARTERED

4 MEDIUM CARROTS, PEELED AND CUT INTO
    2-INCH-LONG ROUNDS

Bring 2 cups of water to a boil over high heat in a small saucepan. Remove it from the heat, add the kosher salt and sugar, and stir until they dissolve. Pour the salt mixture into a 4-quart or larger glass, ceramic, or plastic container. Add 4 cups ice-cold water along with the garlic, pickling spices, bay leaves, and black pepper. Add 1 cup ice cubes and stir to chill the brine rapidly or put it in the refrigerator for 1 hour.

Pierce the beef all over with a wooden skewer to help the brine penetrate, submerge the beef into the brine, and refrigerate for 4 to 5 days.

Drain the beef along with the garlic and spices in a large strainer and rinse it briefly in cool running water, reserving the garlic and spices. Discard the brine. Put the beef in a pot that fits it snuggly and fill the pot with cool water to cover the beef by 1 inch. Add the reserved garlic and spices.

Bring the water to a boil over medium heat then reduce the heat to low and simmer gently, partially covered. After about 2½ hours, add the onions and carrots, and continue to simmer until a skewer slides in and out of the beef with ease, 3 to 3½ hours total.

Serve the corned beef warm in thick slices moistened with some of the cooking liquid and with the vegetables on the side. To store, transfer the corned beef into a container, add enough cooking liquid to cover it, and refrigerate it for up to 4 days.

VARIATION: MUSTARD-GLAZED CORNED BEEF

Slather the top of the fully cooked corned beef with Whole-Grain Mustard (page 234) or Fruit Mustard (page 234) and bake it in a roasting pan uncovered in a 275°F oven until heated through, about 1 hour.

MORE CHOICE CUTS:

Brisket is the classic corned beef cut and you can't go wrong with this tried-and-true favorite.

Tongue is another very inexpensive and traditional choice, which brines wonderfully. Be sure to simmer it until you can easily slide a wooden skewer in and out of the meat. Peel the skin off while it's still warm, before slicing or chilling. Serve it as a hot corned beef sandwich with Herb Aïoli (page 187) or Whole-Grain Mustard (page 234).

PASTRAMI

Far from the East Coast Jewish delis of my youth, it's hard to come by a hot pastrami sandwich. So, I relished even my first attempt at this salt-cured, smoked, and steamed delight. A homemade pastrami sandwich with melted provolone on a toasted Whole-Wheat Bun (page 72) with Whole-Grain Mustard (page 234) is worth waiting for—even, as in my case, about twenty years. And wait one must, through nearly a week of salt-curing and an eight-hour day of cooking, but oh, that bite of salty, juicy meat brings everything into focus.

Mind you, pastrami made with grassfed beef is firmer and somewhat chewy, with a prominent beefiness. Like its corned beef cousin, pastrami is routinely made from brisket. Choose the squared-off flat end if you prefer it leaner or the point end for more fat. I've streamlined the curing method by applying a dry rub in place of a brine, which is less cumbersome and doesn't need to be rinsed before the smoking begins. (However, if you prefer less salty pastrami, give it a quick rinse under cool running water.)

I purchased an Oregon-made Traeger grill-smoker, fueled with wood pellets, long before I did much curing and smoking. I can hot-smoke at the flick of a switch. Other smokers, like the Little Chief, also take most of the work out of smoking. You can also smoke meat using a standard gas grill fitted with a smoke pan or charcoal grill using low heat, but you'll need to feed it frequently with handfuls of wood chips and briquettes and monitor the temperature closely. No matter which equipment you use, the fact is that pastrami-making takes time and attention—all well spent. Enjoy it on sandwiches and offer it as an appetizer, thinly sliced with pickles and mustard (page 234).

Makes 6 servings with leftovers

....

3 BAY LEAVES, CRUMBLED

1 TABLESPOON WHOLE CORIANDER, TOASTED*

1 TEASPOON WHOLE JUNIPER BERRIES

1 TEASPOON WHOLE PEPPERCORNS

3 TABLESPOONS MORTON'S TENDER QUICK CURING SALT

2 TABLESPOONS PACKED LIGHT BROWN SUGAR

1 (3½- TO 4-POUND) BRISKET, POINT OR FLAT CUT

Crush the bay leaves, coriander, juniper berries, and peppercorns in a mortar and pestle or with a few pulses of a spice grinder until coarsely ground. Put the spice mixture in a small bowl, add the curing salt and brown sugar, and stir until it is well blended. Rub the spice mixture evenly all over the beef. Put the beef in a resealable plastic bag and put the bag in a dish or container to catch any drips. Cure in the refrigerator for 4 to 5 days.

Prepare a smoker for hot-smoking (200° to 225°F). Alternatively, prepare a charcoal grill for low indirect heat or a gas grill fitted with a smoker box and a drip pan filled with 2 inches of water underneath the grate opposite the heat source. If using wood chips, soak them for about 15 minutes. Scrape the grate clean and oil it lightly before placing the brisket on the coolest part of the grill with the fat cap side up. Close the lid and smoke for at least 4 hours and up to 8 hours to achieve a smokier flavor.

Preheat the oven to 275°F. Choose a roasting pan with a rack slightly larger than the meat. (If you don't have a rack that fits, roughly chop 1 onion and scatter it around the pan to rest the meat on it.) Add about 1 inch of water to the bottom of the pan, transfer the meat to the rack, and cover the whole pan tightly with aluminum foil. Steam the meat for 3 to 4 hours more until it pulls apart readily with a fork and the internal temperature reaches 190° to 200°F.

Let the meat rest for at least 20 minutes before unwrapping and slicing against the grain to serve hot. Or, chill it in the refrigerator well-wrapped, and serve it cold.

NOTE: To toast the coriander seeds, heat a dry skillet over medium heat. Add the coriander seeds and keep a watchful eye on them so they don't burn. Cook, swirling the pan over the burner occasionally to turn the seeds, until they smell fragrant and darken in color, about 7 minutes.

MORE CHOICE CUTS:

Short plate is from the belly and looks like bacon, only with a red meat color. It has layers of fat, which will please those who expect it as part of their pastrami experience.

Chuck roasts, such as boneless pot roast and cross-rib roast, are smaller cuts that also make great pastrami. For a 1½- to 2-pound chuck roast, cut the curing mixture in half and cure for just 3 to 4 days before smoking and steaming as directed.

PEPPERED HAMBURGER JERKY

Since ground beef is the most versatile meat cut there is, I should not have been surprised to discover that it can also be dried. Still, it felt like a big a-ha to me when a loyal customer to Carman Ranch shared the concept. Ground beef does the best job of absorbing the flavors of whatever you mix into it, and there is a lifetime of seasoning combinations to try. I decided go the classic route with a riveting pepper-flavored jerky. Remember that you want the seasoning to be prominent because it diminishes once it's dried.

As with all jerky, it's best to start with very lean beef for the best keeping qualities. Many old-timers dry their beef in the open air or in food dehydrators. I've adopted an oven method used by Phil Greif of PD Farms, a family grassfed ranch and organic vegetable farm, who makes forty pounds a month. Once the beef cooks and dries within a few hours, I slice it into strips and store batches in the refrigerator—just to be on the safe side—for up to three months.

Makes about 1½ pounds jerky strips

....

2 POUNDS GROUND BEEF, 90 TO 95 PERCENT LEAN

2 TEASPOONS WORCESTERSHIRE SAUCE

2 TEASPOONS KOSHER SALT

1½ TEASPOONS CHILE POWDER, SUCH AS CHIPO-
TLE OR ALEPPO

1 TEASPOON BLACK PEPPER

½ TEASPOON GARLIC POWDER

2 TEASPOONS LIQUID SMOKE (NOTE, PAGE 254),
OPTIONAL

Mix the ground beef with the Worcestershire sauce, kosher salt, chile powder, pepper, garlic powder, and liquid smoke, if using, in a food processor until well blended and fairly smooth. Make a tablespoon-sized patty, fry it for a taste, and adjust the seasonings if you'd like it very spicy or extra peppery.

Preheat the oven to 200°F with 2 oven racks in the center of the oven. Line 2 rimmed baking sheets with aluminum foil and fit them with 2 lightly oiled wire racks. Set them aside.

Pull out about an 18-inch-long strip of plastic wrap or wax paper and put it on the counter. Put half of the ground beef mixture on it. Oil a rolling pin and roll the ground beef to an even ¼-inch thickness. Flip the ground beef onto one of the racks and peel off the plastic or paper. Repeat with the remaining ground beef on a fresh sheet of plastic wrap or wax paper and flip it onto the second rack.

Bake the jerky for 1 hour. Rotate the baking sheets and lower the heat to 175°F. Continue baking until the beef is darkened to nearly black on the edges, dry to the touch, and pliable, 3 to 3½ hours more. Cut the jerky into strips about 1 inch wide and 4 inches long and cool. Store it in resealable plastic bags in the refrigerator for up to 3 months and in the freezer for up to 6 months.

COCA-COLA JERKY

Coca-Cola has a secret ingredient that is an effective meat tenderizer (phosphoric acid) plus a caramel sweetness that tastes great with beef (think burger and a Coke). Used as the marinade for beef jerky, Coke makes the tough bottom round nicely chewy with a sweetness akin to teriyaki. Jerky making is the one occasion when you want to slice the meat *with* the grain for the best texture once dried.

Makes about 1 pound jerky strips

1 (1½- TO 2-POUND) BOTTOM ROUND ROAST

1½ CUPS COCA-COLA

1 CUP SOY SAUCE

1 TABLESPOON CHINESE FIVE SPICE POWDER

1 TABLESPOON GROUND GINGER

¼ TEASPOON CAYENNE

Freeze the meat until it is very firm, about 30 minutes. Slice the beef with the grain into strips as thin as you can (go for ⅛ inch), 1 inch wide and as long as you like.

Whisk the Coca-Cola, soy sauce, Chinese five-spice powder, ginger, and cayenne together in a large glass or ceramic bowl. Add the beef strips and stir to coat them well. Cover the bowl with plastic wrap and marinate in the refrigerator for 3 to 6 hours. Longer, and the meat starts to get *too* soft.

Preheat the oven to 200°F. Lightly oil 2 wire racks and set them into 2 rimmed baking sheets lined with aluminum foil to ease clean up. Drain the beef in a colander, discarding the marinade, and let it drip dry for a few minutes. Arrange the beef on the racks in a single layer so that they are not touching. Dry the beef in the oven until it is black-brown, dry to the touch, and stiff but pliable, 3½ to 4 hours. Alternately, dry the meat in an electric food dehydrator according to the manufacturer's instructions. Store the jerky in resealable plastic bags in the refrigerator for up to 3 months and in the freezer for up to 6 months.

SOURCES

Beef Directories and Resources

Artisan beef is raised in all fifty states. As more ranchers choose to sell their beef directly to customers, locally raised beef is becoming easier to find in more places. Many of these national online databases list ranchers by state or provide searchable maps to locate beef sources closest to you with links to ranchers' websites. Additionally, use these resources to locate pasture-raised pork, pork fat, and suet. Bear in mind that the information is changing quickly and some of the lists may not be perfectly up to date. When in doubt, try a Google search for the type of beef you're seeking including your county or zip code.

ARTISANBEEFINSTITUTE.COM

The founder of this private company, Carrie Oliver, is committed to promoting high-quality artisan meats and butchery along with animal husbandry and land management practices. She developed the beef tasting guide adapted in part for this book (How to Taste Artisan Beef, page 35). This site features tasting notes of artisan beef from selected farms and ranches and other educational information for consumers.

EATWELLGUIDE.COM

Searchable by geography and food type, this national database can connect you directly to beef producers through websites and e-mail—as well as CSAs, butchers, online sources, restaurants, and co-ops. Advanced search allows you to specify production method, such as grass-fed, organic, or kosher beef suppliers.

EATWILD.COM

An authoritative website devoted to pasture-raised foods, eatwild.com offers an alphabetical listing by state of beef producers. Brief descriptions offer details about third-party certifications, other products for sale, and contact information, including phone numbers so that you speak directly to the rancher.

LOCALHARVEST.COM

Another national database of small farms, this site directs buyers to local and organic food sources in all categories, including beef. The search function allows you to limit the distance from your home, locate farms on a clickable map, and read descriptions and ratings for each producer. You can also place orders for a limited number of beef products directly through this site.

National Advocacy Organizations

AMERICAN GRASSFED ASSOCIATION

4340 E. Kentucky Avenue, Suite 311
Denver, Colorado 80246
877.774.7277
www.americangrassfed.org

A grassfed advocacy organization, AGA is a third-party certifier of grassfed beef producers and is working to enact a strict, legal definition of grassfed through the USDA. This site contains a state-by-state listing of grass-fed beef producers, many of them AGA certified and American Welfare Approved.

AMERICAN LIVESTOCK BREED CONSERVANCY

P.O. Box 477
Pittsboro, North Carolina 27312
919.542.5704
www.albc-usa.org

This conservation organization offers detailed historical information about traditional and rare cattle breeds as part of an effort to promote biodiversity.

FOOD ALLIANCE

1829 NE Alberta, Suite 5
Portland, Oregon 97211
503.493.1066
www.foodalliance.org

This nonprofit organization is committed to sustainable agriculture throughout the food production and distribution system. It operates a voluntary certification program for farms and ranches with comprehensive standards and includes separate verifications for pasture-raised and grassfed beef claims.

FOOD ROUTES

RR#1
Troy, Pennsylvania 16947
570.673.3398
www.foodroutes.org

Working toward a vision of strong local, community-based food systems, this national nonprofit supports grassroots organizations to promote family farms, build local food systems, and educate consumers about the multiple and far-reaching benefits of sustainable agriculture.

SLOW FOOD USA

20 Jay Street, Suite M04
Brooklyn, New York 11201
718.260.8000
www.slowfoodusa.org

Part of an international movement to promote local food traditions and social justice, Slow Food works at the national policy level and through local chapters to enhance local food systems, which has a direct and lasting impact on the economy and environment within communities.

Ingredients

BOB'S RED MILL
13521 S.E. Pheasant Court
Milwaukie, Oregon 97222
800.349.2173
www.bobsredmill.com

Whole grains, spelt, buckwheat and other specialty flours,
beans, and seeds

FOODSHED
P.O. Box 12001
Portland, Oregon 97212
503.445.0022
www.ourfoodshed.com

Saba

KOAMART
905 E. 8th Street
Los Angeles, California 90021
www.koammart.com

Miso, instant dashi stock, ponzu, gochujang (Korean hot
sauce)

THE MEADOW
3713 N. Mississippi Avenue
Portland, Oregon 97227
523 Hudson Street
New York, New York 10014
888.388.4633
www.atthemeadow.com

Specialty salts, inclucding coarse sea salts, such as sel gris,
flake, and finishing salts

OREGON MUSHROOMS
11489 Red Wing Loop
P.O. Box 1025
Keno, Oregon 97627
541.882.3687; 800.682.0036
www.oregonmushrooms.com

Wild fresh and dried mushrooms, porcini powder

OREGON WHITE TRUFFLE OIL
600 Ferry Street
Dayton, Oregon 97114
503.550.5910
www.oregontruffleoil.com

All-natural white truffle oil

THAI SUPERMARKET ONLINE
P.O. Box 2054
Issaquah, Washington 98027
888.618.8424
www.importfood.com

Sticky rice, red curry paste, tamarind paste and
concentrate

WORLD SPICE MERCHANTS
1509 Western Avenue
Seattle, Washington 98101
206.682.7274
www.worldspice.com

Sumac, pimentón de la Vera, dried whole chiles, and
Sichuan peppercorns

Equipment

BUTCHER & PACKER

1780 E. 14 Mile Road

Madison Heights, Wisconsin 48071

248.583.1250

www.butcher-packer.com

Sausage casings, meat grinders, curing supplies, and knives

SUR LA TABLE

P.O. Box 840

Brownsburg, Indiana 46112

800.243.0852

www.surlatable.com

Silicone bands, knife sharpeners, and immersion blenders

TRAEGER WOOD PELLET GRILLS

9445 S.W. Ridder Road

Wilsonville, Oregon 97070

855.872.3437

www.traegergrills.com

smokers

Adler, Karen, and Judith M. Fertig. *The BBQ Queens' Big Book of Barbecue.* Boston, MA: Harvard Common Press, 2005.

Aidells, Bruce, and Denis Kelly. *The Complete Meat Cookbook: A Juicy and Authoritative Guide to Selecting, Seasoning, and Cooking Today's Beef, Pork, Lamb, and Veal.* New York: Houghton Mifflin, 1998.

Aidells, Bruce. *Bruce Aidells' Complete Sausage Book: Recipes from America's Premier Sausage Maker.* Berkeley, CA: Ten Speed Press, 1999.

Algar, Ayla Esen. *Classical Turkish Cooking: Traditional Turkish Food for the American Kitchen.* New York: HarperCollins, 1991.

Bastyra, Judy, and Becky Johnson. *Thai: The Essence of Asian Cooking.* London: Hermes House, 2003.

Batali, Mario. *The Babbo Cookbook.* New York: Clarkson Potter, 2002.

Bayless, Rick. *Rick Bayless's Mexican Kitchen.* New York: Scribner, 1996.

Beard, James, and José Wilson. *Beard on Food.* New York: Knopf, 1974.

Beef & Veal. Alexandria, VA: Time-Life Books, 1978.

Bitterman, Mark, and Jennifer Martiné. *Salted: A Manifesto on the World's Most Essential Mineral, with Recipes.* Berkeley, CA: Ten Speed Press, 2010.

Borg, Shannon, Lora Lea Misterly, and Kären Jurgensen. *Chefs on the Farm: Recipes and Inspiration from the Quillisascut Farm School of the Domestic Arts.* Seattle: Skipstone, 2008.

Bsisu, May S. *The Arab Table: Recipes and Culinary Traditions.* New York: William Morrow, 2005.

Cameron, Angus, and Judith Jones. *The L.L. Bean Game and Fish Cookbook.* New York: Random House, 1983.

Chamberlain, Richard, and Betsy A. Hornick. *The Healthy Beef Cookbook: Steaks, Salads, Stir-Fry, and More: Over 130 Luscious Lean Beef Recipes for Every Occasion.* Hoboken, NJ: John Wiley & Sons, 2006.

Child, Julia, Louisette Bertholle, and Simone Beck. *Mastering the Art of French Cooking, Volume One.* New York: Alfred A. Knopf, 1973.

Clancy, Kate. *Greener Pastures: How Grassfed Beef and Milk Contribute to Healthy Eating.* Cambridge, MA: Union of Concerned Scientists, 2006.

Chuck Wagon Cookbook Compiled by the Wallowa County Cowbelles. Lenaxa, KS: Cookbook Publishers, Inc., 1978.

Czapp, Katherine, "Achieving Culinary Success with Grassfed Beef," Weston A. Price Foundation accessed via http://www.westonaprice.org.

Dagget, Dan, and Tom Bean. *Gardeners of Eden: Rediscovering Our Importance to Nature.* Santa Barbara, CA: Thatcher Charitable Trust, 2005.

Daley et al. "A Review of Fatty Acid Profiles and Antioxidant Content in Grassfed and Grain-Fed Beef." *Nutrition Journal,* 2010, accessed via http://www.nutritionj.com/content/9/1/10.

Davidson, Alan, and Tom Jaine. *The Oxford Companion to Food.* Oxford: Oxford University Press, 2006.

Dornenburg, Andrew, and Karen Page. *Culinary Artistry.* Hoboken, NJ: John Wiley & Sons, Inc., 1996.

Dunlop, Fuchsia. *Land of Plenty: A Treasury of Authentic Sichuan Cooking.* New York: W.W. Norton, 2003.

Ellis, Merle. *Cutting-Up in the Kitchen: The Butcher's Guide to Saving Money on Meat & Poultry.* San Francisco: Chronicle Books, 1975.

Fairlie, Simon. *Meat: A Benign Extravagance.* White River Junction, VT: Chelsea Green, 2010.

Fearnley-Whittingstall, Hugh. *The River Cottage Meat Book.* Berkeley, CA: Ten Speed Press, 2007.

Foer, Jonathan Safran. *Eating Animals.* New York: Little, Brown and Company, 2009.

Fussell, Betty Harper. *Raising Steaks: The Life and Times of American Beef.* Orlando: Harcourt, 2008.

Gisslen, Wayne. *Professional Cooking.* Hoboken, NJ: John Wiley & Sons, Inc., 1999.

Green, Aliza. *Field Guide to Meat: How to Identify and Prepare Virtually Every Meat, Poultry, and Game Cut.* Philadelphia, PA: Quirk Books, 2005.

Grohman, Joann S. *Keeping a Family Cow.* Dixfield, ME: Coburn Press, 2001.

Hayes, Shannon. *The Grassfed Gourmet Cookbook: Healthy Cooking and Good Living with Pasture-Raised Foods.* Hopewell, NJ: Eating Fresh, 2004.

Henderson, Fergus. *The Whole Beast.* New York: Ecco, 2004.

Hesser, Amanda. *The Essential New York Times Cookbook: Classic Recipes for a New Century.* New York: W.W. Norton, 2010.

Hibler, Jane. *Wild About Game: 150 Recipes for Farm-Raised and Wild Game, from Alligator and Antelope to Venison and Wild Turkey.* Portland, OR: WestWinds Press, 2008.

Home Meat Curing Guide. Chicago, IL: Morton Salt, Division of Morton Thiokol, 1988.

Hopkinson, Simon, Lindsey Bareham, and Flo Bayley. *Roast Chicken and Other Stories: A Recipe Book.* New York: Hyperion, 2006.

Jaffrey, Madhur. *Madhur Jaffrey's Far Eastern Cookery.* New York: Perennial Library, 1989.

Jones, Steven et al. Bovine Myology and Muscle Profiling, accessed via http://bovine.unl.edu. University of Nebraska, Lincoln, 2004.

Kasper, Lynne Rossetto. *The Splendid Table: Recipes from Emilia-Romagna, the Heartland of Northern Italian Food.* New York: William Morrow, 1992.

Kobler, Chris. *Making Great Sausage at Home: 30 Savory Links from Around the World Plus Dozens of Delicious Sausage Dishes.* New York: Lark Books, 2002.

Kutas, Rytek. *Great Sausage Recipes and Meat Curing: The Bible of Sausage Making.* Buffalo, NY: Sausage Maker, Inc., 2008.

Labensky, Steven, Gaye G. Ingram, and Sarah R. Labensky. *Webster's New World Dictionary of Culinary Arts.* Upper Saddle River, NJ: Prentice Hall, 2001.

Lang, Jenifer Harvey. *Larousse Gastronomique: The New American Edition of the World's Greatest Culinary Encyclopedia.* New York: Crown Publishers, 1995.

LeFavour, Cree. *The New Steak: Recipes for a Range of Cuts Plus Savory Sides.* Berkeley, CA: Ten Speed Press, 2008.

McGee, Harold. *On Food and Cooking.* New York: Fireside, 1984.

McLagan, Jennifer. *Bones: Recipes, History, and Lore.* New York: William Morrow, 2005.

McLagan, Jennifer. *Fat: An Appreciation of a Misunderstood Ingredient, with Recipes.* Berkeley, CA: Ten Speed Press, 2008.

McWilliams, James E. *Just Food: Where Locavores Get It Wrong and How We Can Truly Eat Responsibly.* New York: Little, Brown and Company, 2009.

Mettler, John J. Jr. *Basic Butchering of Livestock and Game.* North Adams, MA: Storey Publishing, 1986.

Nathan, Joan. *Jewish Cooking in America.* New York: Alfred A. Knopf, 1994.

National Cattleman's Beef Association, Research, Education, and Innovation Department, accessed via http://www.beefresearch.org.

Nestle, Marion. *What to Eat.* New York: North Point Press, 2006.

Niman, Bill, and Janet Kessel Fletcher. *The Niman Ranch Cookbook: From Farm to Table with America's Finest Meat.* Berkeley, CA: Ten Speed Press, 2005.

Niman, Nicolette Hahn. *Righteous Porkchop: Finding a Life and Good Food Beyond Factory Farms.* New York: Collins Living, 2009.

Olney, Richard. *The French Menu Cookbook: The Food and Wine of France—Season By Delicious Season—in Beautifully Composed Menus for American Dining and Entertaining by an American Living in Paris and Provence.* New York: Simon and Schuster, 1970.

Page, Karen, and Andrew Dornenburg. *The Flavor Bible: The Essential Guide to Culinary Creativity, Based on the Wisdom of America's Most Imaginative Chefs.* New York: Little, Brown and Company, 2008.

Parsons, Russ. *How to Read a French Fry: and Other Stories of Intriguing Kitchen Science.* Boston: Houghton Mifflin, 2001.

Peterson, James. *Glorious French Food: A Fresh Approach to the Classics.* Hoboken, NJ: John Wiley & Sons, Inc., 2002.

Peterson, James. *Meat: A Kitchen Education.* Berkeley, CA: Ten Speed Press, 2010.

Pullman, Madeleine, and Zhaohui Wu. *Food Supply Chain.* New York: Routledge, 2011.

Purviance, Jamie, and Tim Turner. *Weber's Way to Grill: The Step-By-Step Guide to Expert Grilling.* Menlo Park, CA: Sunset, 2008.

Rimas, Andrew, and Evan D. G. Fraser. *Beef: The Untold Story of How Milk, Meat, and Muscle Shaped the World.* New York, NY: William Morrow, 2008.

Robinson, Jo. *Pasture Perfect: The Far-Reaching Benefits of Choosing Meat, Eggs, and Dairy Products from Grassfed Animals.* Vashon, WA: Vashon Island Press, 2004.

Roden, Claudia. *The New Book of Middle Eastern Food.* New York: Knopf, 2000.

Rodgers, Judy. *The Zuni Café Cookbook.* New York: W.W. Norton, 2002.

Rombauer, Irma von Starkloff, and Marion Rombauer Becker. *The Joy of Cooking.* Indianapolis: Bobbs-Merrill, 1952.

Rombauer, Irma von Starkloff, Marion Rombauer Becker, Ethan Becker, and Maria Guarnaschelli. *Joy of Cooking.* New York: Scribner, 1997.

Ruechel, Julius. *Grassfed Cattle: How to Produce and Market Natural Beef.* North Adams, MA: Storey, 2006.

Ruhlman, Michael, and Brian Polcyn. *Charcuterie: The Craft of Salting, Smoking, and Curing.* New York: W.W. Norton, 2005.

Ruhlman, Michael. *Ratio: The Simple Codes Behind the Craft of Everyday Cooking.* New York, NY: Scribner, 2009.

Sahni, Julie. *Classic Indian Cooking.* New York: William Morrow, 1980.

Salatin, Joel. *Salad Bar Beef.* Swoope, VA: Polyface, 1995.

Sass, Lorna J. *Whole Grains: Every Day, Every Way.* New York: Clarkson Potter, 2006.

Schatzker, Mark. *Steak: One Man's Search For the World's Tastiest Piece of Beef.* New York: Viking, 2010.

Schlesinger, Chris, and John Willoughby. *How to Cook Meat.* New York: William Morrow, 2000.

Schneller, Thomas. *Meat: Identification, Fabrication, Utilization.* Clifton Park, NJ: Delmar, Cengage Learning, 2009.

Slater, Nigel. *Appetite: So What Do You Want to Eat Today?* New York: Clarkson Potter, 2002.

Stevens, Molly. *All About Braising: The Art of Uncomplicated Cooking.* New York: W.W. Norton, 2004.

Terrines, Pates & Galantines. Alexandria, VA: Time-Life Books, 1981.

The Great Beef Cookbook. Sydney: Australian Consolidated Press, 1997.

The Meat Buyer's Guide: Beef, Lamb, Veal, Pork, and Poultry. Hoboken, NJ: John Wiley & Sons, Inc., 2007.

The Minced Meat Cookbook. Sydney: Australian Consolidated Press, 1992.

The Settlement Cookbook: Treasured Recipes Of Seven Decades; The Famous All-Purpose Cook Book for Beginner and Expert. New York: Simon and Schuster, 1954.

The New Professional Chef, 6th ed. Hoboken, NJ: John Wiley & Sons, Inc., 1996.

The Silver Spoon. New York: Phaidon Press, 2005.

This, Hervé. *Kitchen Mysteries: Revealing the Science of Cooking.* New York: Columbia University Press, 2007.

Thompson, David. *Thai Food.* Berkeley, CA: Ten Speed Press, 2002.

Traunfeld, Jerry. *The Herbal Kitchen: Cooking with Fragrance and Flavor.* New York: William Morrow, 2005.

Walsh, Robb. *Legends of Texas Barbecue Cookbook.* San Francisco: Chronicle Books, 2002.

Webster, Harold W. *The Complete Venison Cookbook.* Brandon, MI: Quail Ridge Press, 1996.

Weinzweig, Ari. *Zingerman's Guide to Good Eating: How to Choose the Best Bread, Cheeses, Olive Oil, Pasta, Chocolate, and Much More.* Boston: Houghton Mifflin, 2003.

Wolcott, Imogene. *The New England Yankee Cookbook: An Anthology of Incomparable Recipes from the Six New England States and a Little Something about the People Whose Tradition for Good Eating Is Herein Permanently Recorded.* Louisville, KY: Cookbook Collectors Library, 1939.

Wolfert, Paula. *Mediterranean Grains and Greens: A Book of Savory, Sun-Drenched Recipes.* New York: HarperCollins, 1998.

Young, Grace. *Stir-Frying to the Sky's Edge: The Ultimate Guide to Mastery, with Authentic Recipes and Stories.* New York: Simon & Schuster, 2010.

ABOUT THE AUTHOR

Lynne Curry grew up in New England, tasted and rejected a fashion journalism career in New York City, and moved to the Pacific Northwest "for the summer" in 1989. She landed on Lummi Island off the Washington coast where the traditions of sustainable fishing, organic gardening, and canning were the way of life, and supported herself as a cook at The Willows Inn. She eventually pursued professional culinary training in Seattle, receiving scholarships from the International Association of Culinary Professionals and Women Chefs & Restaurateurs for advanced study in France and New York. Working alongside Jerry Traunfeld at The Herbfarm restaurant fully rooted her in the principles of seasonal and local cooking.

Lynne is a former vegetarian who grew to love grassfed beef when she relocated inland to northeast Oregon's Wallowa Valley in 2001. Drawing on her professional experience and input from local beef producers and her butcher, she learned how to cook every cut on a cow. In *Pure Beef*, Lynne has applied her research skills and inquisitive nature to share the best ways to handle grassfed beef. In addition to food writing, she founded the local Slow Food chapter and has worked as a private chef, cooking teacher, and product consultant.

A James Beard Journalism Award nominee, Lynne is a contributing writer to Zester Daily and a frequent contributor to *The Oregonian* food section. She has published articles and recipes in many publications, including Culinate.com, *Saveur*, *Los Angeles Times*, *Relish*, and *Fine Cooking*. Her food essays have appeared in *Tin House* and *The Oxford Encyclopedia of American Food & Drink*. Lynne lives in Joseph, an artist-agricultural community in the mountains, with her husband and two young daughters.

INDEX

CPSIA information can be obtained
at www.ICGtesting.com
Printed in the USA
LVOW05*1913241017
553622LV00011B/13/P

9 781635 615043